D0171768

REVERBERATIONS
INTERVIEWS WITH THE WORLD'S
LEADING MUSICIANS

REVERBERATIONS
INTERVIEWS WITH THE WORLD'S LEADING MUSICIANS

by Robert Jacobson

William Morrow & Company, Inc.
New York 1974

The author expresses grateful appreciation for permission to reprint the following interviews which originally appeared in *After Dark: The National Magazine of Entertainment:*

> Martina Arroyo
> Placido Domingo
> Dorothy Kirsten
> Leonie Rysanek
> Thomas Stewart

1 2 3 4 5 78 77 76 75 74

Book Design by Helen Roberts

Library of Congress Cataloging in Publication Data

Jacobson, Robert.
  Reverberations: interviews with the world's leading musicians.

  1. Musicians—Interviews. I. Title.
ML385.J18   780′.92′2 [B]   74-13946
ISBN 0-688-02875-6

TO MY PARENTS

REVERBERATIONS
INTERVIEWS WITH THE WORLD'S LEADING MUSICIANS

★ Martina Arroyo ★

In 1970, Martina Arroyo opened the Metropolitan Opera season as Elvira in Verdi's Ernani, *an honor she again had in 1973 as Leonora in* Il Trovatore. *Since we talked in the summer of 1970, the Verdian soprano has gone on to try Lady Macbeth and Tosca (both of which she mentioned), but the Norma has not yet come to pass. She has also moved to New York's East Side, and when asked where, she grinned and quipped, typically, "Oh, just ask for the only colored girl on the block."*

Hot and humid and grey, the mid-summer Manhattan air hangs heavily over the penitentiary-style layout on the West Side known as Lincoln Towers. Inside the shiny elevator in the far tower across Tenth Avenue, a woman holding a Raggedy Ann doll rides the full 25 floors and we exit together. "Is K this way or that?" "Oh, you're looking for Martina?" she smiles as bravely as the heat will let her. "It's just down there." The day brightens. You can tell—Martina Arroyo is *that* kind of person! She comes to the door with a big, dazzling smile.

Mrs. Arroyo is there too, somewhat meekly holding back in the kitchen. And it's soon obvious that despite everything, despite the worldwide fame, despite the fact that Martina Arroyo is one of today's leading prima donnas, and despite the fact she is the wife of Italian musician Emilio Poggioni, it is her mother who still exercises a potent force in the singer's life and whose opinion *really* counts. It was Mrs. Arroyo who, when her daughter sang Elsa, told Mr. Bing that she thought *Lohengrin* was a long, boring opera. It was Mrs. Arroyo who burst out laughing the night a few years ago when her daughter appeared as a Valkyrie in long blond braids and helmet. And it was Mrs. Arroyo who, from the start, opened the windows to the world beyond West 111th Street. "The mentality of my family was that we should have more than they had: education, exposure to another world—and this was meant with love. We went to the theater, museums, and so on; and my mother educated herself this way. I took it more for granted, but she fared best and really appreciated it."

Despite the day being what it is and the living room air conditioner awaiting the services of the building repairman, Mrs. Arroyo presents a nice hot, steaming cup of coffee. Her daughter is insisting on a scotch-and-water, and is delighted to have a willing accomplice. First a plate of liverwurst and crackers is put before us. "Here, eat this before your scotch," Mrs. Arroyo offers before returning to the kitchen. "Oh, it's all right," the other laughs. "She once told a boy whom she'd never met that he drank too much when he asked for a drink." Pause. "Oh, if people wander in and out, don't mind. It's just the neighbors. Two kids down the hall come in every day for 'malted milk,'" she imitates with giggles.

Noting that the prima donna life style must be in transition, she nods, "I'm sick of all that stuff, all that high and lofty business. You can't play the prima donna today. If I slept until one, my mother would say, 'Get out of here, I gotta make the bed.' You can't live in a vacuum anymore. I was a schoolteacher, Ruggero Raimondi a chemist, Reri Grist a social worker. All of us did something, and you can't live away from this kind of background. Somehow we must get to the young people so they can identify with somebody young to know what can happen and *cannot* happen in life. You've got to be a part of a community. To portray life on stage, you've got to know it . . . . that's why I want to do Papagena," she twinkles.

Martina Arroyo was *not* one of those kids who wanted to

be a singer ever since the womb. "I began as a schoolteacher, and both singing and teaching are related to being and working with people. I went to Hunter High and College, and began opera workshop there. I wasn't a rabid standee, but I cut classes to see Tebaldi and Callas, until one night when I saw my teacher in line. For one year I taught at Manhattan P.S. 45 and in the Bronx, so it wasn't really a career. Then I had two-and-a-half years of social work." Her first major break came in the American premiere of Pizzetti's *Murder in the Cathedral* at Carnegie Hall. Shortly after, in 1959, the Metropolitan Opera offered her the offstage Celestial Voice in Verdi's *Don Carlo*. While she went on to starring roles in Europe, the Met offered nothing more than minor parts.

"Oh, yes, it bothered me to be singing one of the Valkyries —I always forget which one—and the Celestial Voice, but things went well from the beginning. But it was people's attitudes, especially at home when people would say, 'If you're really famous, why aren't you on *Ed Sullivan?*' My mother's a real Jewish mamma—she used to tell me, 'All that money and what do we get: a girl in show business.' I'll be enthusiastic after a performance, and my mom will say, 'I saw your kneepad in *Cavalleria*'—but this keeps me healthy. If I led a prima donna life without this, it wouldn't work. I don't know what kind of personality can sacrifice everything for the voice and the career!"

If the Met didn't snap at the Arroyo bait, almost everyone else did. In Europe she was singing at Vienna, Berlin, Stuttgart, Cologne and her home base in Zurich. With the New York Philharmonic she sang the world premiere of Barber's *Andromache's Farewell* in 1963 and in Europe she sang the premiere of Stockhausen's *Momente*. Then came that night every young singer dreams about. Arroyo and her mother were at home planning an evening at the movies when the phone call from the Met came: could she sing *Aida* for the ailing Birgit Nilsson? Instant success. And since that time she has sung only leading roles in the house, filling in a much-needed place in the domain of the Verdi dramatic soprano. So much so that the combine of Arroyo-Placido Domingo-Sherrill Milnes (all Americans) bodes well for Verdi in the seventies. And Verdi is the gentleman dominating the Arroyo itinerary these days: *Trovatore, Aida, Ernani, Vespri Siciliani, Ballo in Maschera, Macbeth, Forza del Destino* and the *Requiem.*

"Yes, I'm concentrating on Verdi, but I also am doing Haydn's *Lord Nelson Mass* and Barber's *Antony and Cleopatra* arias. It's important to keep the voice from doing the same things, from just belting out opera. It's important to sing Bach and Handel to keep the voice fresh. I've done almost all the big Verdi roles except Abigaille in *Nabucco,* but I'm not ready for her yet. You need a quality of voice that won't 'help' the voice in order to say certain things in the text and music. Yet you need a stamina that's unbelievable in *Vespri,* which I like. At first I thought, 'What a bore!' But now I see it's just plain Verdi at his most demanding."

Of all the heroines she finds Leonora in *Trovatore* the most difficult, "because she doesn't do too much. Everything happens *to* her. She is passive until the Fourth Act . . . but you can sing gloriously," she beams. "With her it's hard to be the good, pure, beautiful, nice character the others talk about —especially when Azucena is eating up the scenery and climbing the walls, and rightfully so. I think di Luna is more sympathetic because he is *forced* to do things—he's not the big black villain (pardon me, mother). And do you really think Aida is all that sympathetic? She's a cunning chick to stay in the court all that time and do what she does. She's the cat of that group. Amneris is really the honest one with all her cards right out on the table!"

At the moment, alongside this spate of Verdi—including a new *Aida* for La Scala which also represented Italy at the Munich Olympics, and the 1971 Aida centennial performance in Verona—she is readying what is considered by most sopranos the graveyard role: Bellini's Norma. "I'll do it if I can find the right pair of shoes. No, I'm not scared, because if it is not going well, then I won't do it—and I will know long enough in advance. It's the characterization that scares me, not the vocal part. If it is not intense, well thought-out, a well-motivated character, then forget it—you must make her live and with reason. Even when Callas wobbled and carried on, she brought so much to it." When the suggestion is made that Sutherland perhaps does *not,* she counters, "My teacher calls Sutherland 'the most glorious circus,' and she means it in a nice way. I hear Sutherland gladly as Norma, and Callas too. I can hear Renata Tebaldi and Miss Price too. The choice is only if they are singing on the same night. But my mother prefers Leontyne—she has all her records. The other night we were listening to Caballé's *Zarzuela* album, and then she went in the room to play some Leontyne. Caballé and I have such a rapport because we both like fattening foods—the difference is that she is fat and I'm not. . . . Oh, sure," she chuckles.

One of her best friends is mezzo-soprano Grace Bumbry. "You know, everyone said she should stay away from Salome, but I saw it in London and it was the most magnificent thing. She sang gloriously in the low tones (which you don't usually hear) and in the big top tones. She had the light high phrases and *pianissimo* for the child-like qualities, as well as the big sound. She uses her voice very well in it. I heard it the last night, and after five or six performances she didn't sound at all tired. Oh, we're very honest with one another and don't flatter. But we usually don't talk about music . . . don't ask what we talk about . . . (pause) . . . You're right," she laughs. "My mother is outraged at the jokes we tell on transatlantic phone."

Strange, how in a few years a whole new operatic tradition has been set and is being carried out. Leontyne Price's Met debut in 1960 paved the way for such followers as Miss Arroyo, Felicia Weathers, Reri Grist, Mattiwilda Dobbs and several others. In Miss Arroyo's case, she is singing the Price repertoire at the Metropolitan as well as abroad—but her admiration for the other endures. "Well," she says hesitantly, "there are some bad feelings and maybe it's only natural; but we had a pleasant meeting at a party not long ago and I would like to know her better. You know, she has a lot to live up to, because so much was thrown her way all at once. It's been a pistol for her. She opened up a lot of doors for all of us, and now we can follow her. The Met's hiring of Marian Anderson was only a token-type representation, but Miss Price represents the one who broke through and played all kinds of parts on stage.

"People always asked me, 'How does it feel to be a Negro

playing Elsa or Donna Anna?' and I say I feel very white.
What else can I say?" she shrugs with typical good nature
and candor. "I have been introduced in Zurich as 'This is
our Aida'—and I want to say, 'I do have a name . . . call
me Sambo, call me anything.' My husband really goes up in
smoke when this happens. Once at a dinner party a lady
asked me to sing. I had had enough of this already and I had
had three scotches *and* she had called me 'our Aida' in her
introduction. So I told her, 'Madame, let me pay for my
dinner and we'll forget the whole thing.' "

Her approach to her singing is as simple, uncomplicated
and filled with good-humored sense. "It's frightening to feel
you always have to sing better than yourself, but I say every
time, 'God, *please* be better than the last time.' No, I'm not
a nervous performer. But once I went to a doctor to begin a
crash diet and he asked if I were nervous, to which I calmly
said, 'Oh, no, everything is just fine.' Then my husband began
to disagree and I ended up screaming, 'I'm *NOT HIGH
STRUNG!*' But I feel singing is fun if the voice is OK. I
don't know what it would be like if I didn't feel this way,
because my vocal estate is fine now."

Like most singers, she is already looking ahead years in
advance in terms of bookings, engagements and new roles. "I'd
love to do Tosca eventually, but you can't do everything at
once. You have to digest things. To do more than two or
three new roles a year is suicidal—it took me ten years to
find that out! I'm a quick learner, but it's bad because I have
a tendency to wait too long to do things. You can memorize,
but then you have to sing the role into the voice. But I work
best under pressure. I'd like to add Fiordiligi and Donna Anna
on stage, and I'd like to do more Wagner, especially Elisabeth
and Senta, and then Sieglinde a little more in the future. Elsa
at the Met was a positive experience for me, but I'd like to
try another production for what I call 'my pure white thing.'

"I also want to buy a house, maybe in New Jersey. This
profession is great for a few years, but then what? I want
to have something for the future. I don't want to be a poor
has-been. But if you don't have much to go home to, you
cling to what you have!" With Martina Arroyo you're sure
that there'll always be plenty to go home to.

★ *Janet Baker* ★

A regular recital and concert visitor to America, Janet Baker has yet to sing opera in this country. In her fields, she has established the kind of worshipful following that only Lehmann, Schwarzkopf, Fischer-Dieskau and a few others have had, and rightfully so, for her singing has a rare kind of communicative humanity. I talked with her in 1971 before a Bach St. Matthew Passion *with the Philadelphia Orchestra.*

Just a few days earlier in The Juilliard Theater, Maria Callas had been saying that nothing comes out of health and wealth —only out of unhappiness and struggling. Several winter-end mornings later, Janet Baker sat business-like and assured in her hotel room, looking back on her slow-but-sure progress to the top and quietly reflected: "I've been spoiled to death all my life. I have been lucky in my parents, my husband, my life and my career. Yes, the career is hard work, but things have panned out. I do what I want to do. I haven't had to batter down doors and fight tooth-and-nail—I couldn't, I'm not that sort of person." There is a crisp confidence, a positiveness, an earnestness in the air she breathes, in her use of such words as "instinct" and "honesty."

"It was an instinctive thing," the English singer notes about her early musical experiences. "I would go to something like *The Gondoliers* and everyone would have a rip-roaring time— but I felt that it wasn't *real* music. It's wonderful of its type, but it was not what I wanted to do. I think it's true that a performer is born with this firm instinct, a musician's instinct—a standard for the best—and it's important." A native of York, she calls her musical background "sketchy. My parents were not well off and I was envious of my schoolgirl friends who had pianos and learned to play all those childish tunes. I wanted one too, but to learn *real* music. I always had this instinctive feeling for what was good and bad. I didn't know exactly what I wanted to play, but I knew it wasn't what they were playing. The wireless was all we had, no gramophone— and the BBC had marvelous programs. My music began here. Eventually we got a piano and I began to play."

There were not many concerts in York which lacked (and still does) a good concert hall, but she heard orchestras from time to time. "But there was marvelous repertory theater, which my mother took me to every week—and the Royal Ballet on tour, which I recall vividly. I developed a theater-going sense as a child—I saw everything and anything. Now I am passionately interested in the stage. I feel at home on it and can act. And the business of mechanics on stage fascinates me wherever I go. It's important for an opera singer to have a stage sense, especially today when the standards are so high for the visual. You can't have a stout soprano acting only with her hands anymore. But I did have parents who did their best and gave me what they could. They now live near me and it's a joy of my life to see them so often—one of the nice things of life is that they can join in. Success is really more important to the members of one's family than to the person. Last year I was decorated C.B.E. by Queen Elizabeth and it was a thrill for them—and I'm pleased they're here to see it."

In school, young Janet Baker sang soprano in the choir and studied the piano. But when the voice broke, she was advised to leave it alone until it settled . . . and when it did, both her singing and speaking voice were considerably lower. She then went to Leeds in Yorkshire to study, working as a bank clerk to pay for lessons. There she joined a large chorus during the Coronation Year, singing in a memorable *Zadok, the Priest* (Handel) under Sir Malcolm Sargent. From there she went to London, working in a bank by day and traveling in her off-hours to Hampstead for singing lessons with Helena Isepp (mother of pianist-harpsichordist Martin Isepp). She was taught from the start that singing must be an easy, natural function, unhampered by any superfluity. Also her Yorkshire accent, she smiles, helped immeasurably in handling foreign languages. "The Continental vowel is similar to the flat Yorkshire vowel, such as 'man' is like 'Mann' in German. In the King's English it would be different."

The foundation of her reputation was built with such firm timbers as Arts Council recitals in small towns, winning of the *Daily Mail* Kathleen Ferrier Prize, singing in the Glyndebourne Festival chorus, masterclasses with Lotte Lehmann, the Queen's Prize from the Royal College of Music in 1959 and a grant from the Arts Council in 1960. This led to an Edinburgh Festival recital, an appearance at the Promenade Concerts in an aria from Michael Tippett's *A Midsummer Marriage* and engagements on the Continent. Operatically, she began to accrue experience at Glyndebourne, Aldeburgh, Sadler's Wells, the Scottish Opera and the English Opera Group in Purcell, Handel, Mozart and Britten.

Among the singers Miss Baker idolized in the beginning were Isobel Baillie, Kathleen Ferrier and Victoria de los Angeles, whom she calls "a breath of fresh air." But for each English mezzo or contralto it is the commanding figure of Ferrier which looms large in the past—and for Miss Baker particularly, since she won the Ferrier Prize in 1956. Yet she protests that, "For my generation it was not difficult growing up with this image. She has an untouchable place in the English memory . . . and quite rightly. But over the decades of time . . . it's curious . . . fashions change and the standard is higher now. Ferrier's quality of sound was unbelievable. But in lieder, for instance, there was not time enough to really go in as deeply as I have. And she was not happy on stage, she was not a born actress. Her voice and personality carried her.

"It's a load of baloney about there being no age like the golden past. The singing standard is fantastic today, especially considering the times in which we live. Those ladies of the past had it easy. And ideas change. For me, Fischer-Dieskau's lieder are the topmost peak. It may remain so, but there is no guarantee. A young baritone may come along with Fischer-Dieskau's standard, but he will have to formulate his own thing for his own time. And that is the way it should be—no one should ever copy. One goes on—my generation wanted to be different from Ferrier, even though we still respect her."

Past, present and probably future, singers are notoriously —even intensely—competitive, but Janet Baker reflects a

healthy sensibility when it comes to her profession: "It's nice
not to be a prima donna. As a prima donna you have to live
up to the image people have of you—it's distracting from the
job you have to do." As for competition among her colleagues,
she reasons, "There's one thing in life—the fact that in everything there is always someone coming up from behind as good
or better than you. I worry, but then I hear a colleague and
get so wrapped up in the performance that I end up thinking
it was marvelous. It's egotistical to think you can offer *everything* to the public. When the question of jealousy comes up,
it's important never to forget that as unique individuals we
can each give the public something no other performer can
give. I don't want to be somebody else, with what somebody
else has. I want to be me and as good as I can be. And if we're
honest, we realize that no one fulfills his own potential . . .
really. I know I must not get blasé about my job and myself—
I know I have a personal goal that will never be fulfilled or
self-satisfied. I have genuine admiration and affection for
people in my own voice category—Horne, Ludwig, Forrester.
How can you be jealous when someone like Ludwig comes
back after a Philharmonic concert beaming at you? It's a whole
different thing with sopranos—they have a thing about being
'diva' and that is a lot of baloney."

When she first came to America in 1966, Janet Baker was
known as a concert singer and recitalist. It is only more recently that Baker the opera singer has emerged internationally.
Asked if her voice has changed during the past decade, she
shakes her head, "Not at all—but the public's idea of it has.
I began as a contralto in the repertory works, then as a mezzo
in *Dido and Aeneas* and the Handel works. At this point I
began to feel the real part of my voice—before that I had
a living to earn. Mezzos in England, you know, are a strange
category. You are either a contralto or a soprano. With the
low notes, you sing *Messiahs* and Bach on the concert circuit.
But as a mezzo I began using the best part of my voice and a
wide range. It was here all the time, it had been trained, but
I had had no opportunity to use it. My voice now is the same
as when I finished with my teacher. I had the core of my instrument and have gone on to learn how to balance things so
that my instrument is used to its best advantage. I didn't realize

for a long time I was a mezzo, but the voice could do it from the start because I was trained to use all of my instrument."

At this point in her career, technical problems are a thing of the past. "I look at the music and if it is OK I sing it. I was taught to use my voice as an instrument of interpretation, not to let it master me. When I talk to students, they speak of technical problems only—not the end product. But we are interpreters, not to be bogged down by technical demands. Any instrumentalist does this. Part of the training is to put technique under one's thumb and concentrate on the job. Every voice has its weaknesses and strong points, and you know how to deal with both." [Shades of Callas, who told Juilliard students that a singer must do perfectly well what instrumentalists do and master the technical equipment before anything else—and *then* forget the technique and become a great interpreter.]

"The real difficulties," Miss Baker admits, "are interpreting music, not the sheer technical problems. The interpretive problems come from the limitations of one's self as a person —that's the most terrifying thing. This bothers me the most. One is inadequate as a human being to deal with a great Schubert song. We are on a different creative level from the creative process. Composers need us, yes, it's true. But we are on a different plane of existence. Their mission is a higher one. They inspire us—but who inspired them? The greatest thing for us is to make a phrase sound like you never heard it before." To achieve this, she works alone, but will listen to advice and admits to being a good compromiser. "But I believe I'm employed to deliver my own thing. I'm Janet Baker and no one else. What I believe is one aspect, one view of a work—mine—and it must be valid. You can admire what someone else does, but . . . you cannot imitate. It's a very personal thing. I can't be someone else, only an individual spirit. So, as I said before, the problem of jealousy is a complete waste of time. We are each unique. We have our own being . . . and that's enough."

She is equally candid about what she can and cannot do, particularly when it comes to the less-explored field of opera. "I take a long, hard look at my equipment—and ask what kind of person I am. I'm honest with myself. It's a hard pro-

fession to be at the fringe of, to be halfway up the tree with.
I want to be definite about things and not kid myself about
what I can do. You can't alter your equipment—it is what it
is, and you do the best you can with it. Now I'm recognized
as a singer who's also an opera singer. I've not been compart-
mentalized, except perhaps in America, where I'm known
mainly as a concert and recital singer. But I am a singer who
sings lieder and oratorio and opera. I'm invited all over, but
which way should I go?—to opera only? (which I could do).
Yet I want time in my own country and I want what I do in
America—so I don't want to be tied to one place."

One of the scandals of the opera world had been Janet
Baker's absence on the stage of Covent Garden, her country's
leading opera house. Asked whether she felt any gloating
satisfaction when the management pleaded with her to replace the ailing Josephine Veasey in Berlioz' *Les Troyens* in
the fall of 1969, she smiles, "Well, we did have a triumph
with it in Scotland. I know all the management at Covent
Garden and there are no hard feelings. People try to make
a 'thing' out of it, but we do have good relations. It is ironic,
though, that I stepped in." As for her role on the roster of
any opera house, she explains, "I'm a specialist person. I
can't get into heavy operatic roles of the repertory. Veasey has
a heavier voice and can sing Verdi, Wagner and so on. I
sing Handel, Mozart, *et cetera*. But I'm also a singer of stature,
and it's ludicrous to ignore me. Yet I also understand why they
had never asked me. Now I've been invited for three things,
two of which I turned down—I can pick and choose, so I will
do *Troyens* again, alternating with Veasey." Her repertoire
has included Cavalli's *Calisto,* Monteverdi's *Incoronazione di
Poppea* and *Ritorno d'Ulisse,* Strauss' *Rosenkavalier,* Mozart's
Clemenza di Tito and Britten's *Owen Wingrave* and *Rape of
Lucretia,* which she has sung at Glyndebourne, Covent Garden, Sadler's Wells and Scottish Opera.

When she turns from opera back to concerts is there a
different Janet Baker at work? "Whatever one does," she reasons, "it is the same process basically. Outside things are
different, the exteriors of the stage, of lights and costumes and
sets and so on. When I act a role on stage . . . I do as Dido
exactly as I do in a great Schubert song. There is a whole

opera in *Nuits d'été,* all compressed into twenty minutes. It's the time factor which alters, not the personal process. I use the same technique, the same acting, the same concentration —for each demands being something else in the same moment. I'm just as concentrated as Gretchen in 'Gretchen am Spinnrade' as I am as Dido—I am both and I must be just as real at the moment I do them."

Her teachers, she gratefully acknowledges, are the great conductors with whom she has worked, Barbirolli, Klemperer, Giulini and Szell being the most influential. "My own teacher of 17 years died two years ago and now I look after my own voice. The great conductors are the best sort of coaches a singer can get, because there is an exchange of ideas among musicians." As for sound extra-musical advice, Miss Baker seems to have plenty of that too: "Over-singing is the only thing that affects me. Last-minute things crop up—planes are late, requests come to replace other singers. Then things get out of gear and the voice gets overloaded. But we're all overworked. There's always that fear that we'll wake up one morning and not have a voice. It's a hard and insecure life, and that's the reason why people find it hard to say no. But there are the days when you never forget the loneliness and hardships you had as a student and beginning a career—and this makes me view prosperity level-headedly. My diary is planned years ahead, then the phone rings and a conductor tells me 'You must do this—it would be marvelous.' How does one say no to this? I'm getting better at it. They get cross, but . . . I can't afford to overload my calendar. One thing happens as you grow older: you care less what other people think. No one else will save your voice—they'll just try to exploit you."

Besides being a world-traveled performer, Janet Baker has already left a healthy recorded testament via E.M.I. (Angel in America). She likes recording: "I did a lot of broadcasting and I'm used to the microphone. And the absence of an audience helps one to concentrate more. Yes, I like an audience response, but I can function without it too—even though it is sometimes difficult. It is a matter of producing under different circumstances and a matter of concentration." One of the most satisfying recordings was her "live" collaboration with baritone Dietrich Fischer-Dieskau and pianist Daniel Barenboim in a program of 19th-century duets, a program repeated in Carnegie Hall. "Barenboim had the idea—I was the first singer he ever accompanied before Fischer-Dieskau. We did the program for his summer festival in London. Fischer-Dieskau's mind and mine are attuned in a remarkable way. We hadn't done this program for over a year before New York, and when we began rehearsing we really didn't think it was necessary—our minds and approach to lieder are so alike. Of course, we needed it for purely technical things. I've never had this to such a degree in a colleague before. We 'talk' to one another on stage in indescribable phrases—it's a close musical affinity. Instinctively we do the exact same thing in a phrase, like chamber music. The duets are pure joy, music-making at its most enjoyable. As a rule the pleasure one has as a singer is bound up in his life and work—and the joy is more for the audience."

Intermittently it's hard to believe the lady is a singer . . . and an opera singer at that—so simple, so unegotistical (almost cool) is her attitude toward it all. As she says, "The career for me is merely my life going on. It's exciting for everyone else. I work with people I like. What more could I ask?"

★ Daniel Barenboim ★

In the spring of 1968, Daniel Barenboim had just begun to gain notice as a conductor, although he was well established as a pianist. We spoke just before he brought the English Chamber Orchestra (with Jacqueline Du Pré) for its New York debut during Lincoln Center's Festival '68 and during his dramatic substitution for the ailing Istvan Kertesz with the London Symphony. The Barenboims had been married just a year before in Israel.

In a darkened, midday Carnegie Hall, he is up on stage seated on a stool rehearsing the shirtsleeved London Symphony . . . she is slouched down in one of the sea of red velvet empty seats, listening attentively. Detail by detail, with sharp jabbing gestures, he is working over Schoenberg's *Verklärte Nacht* until the bell rings and the day's rehearsal abruptly ends. Backstage, the black-turtle-necked Daniel Barenboim gasps, "I'm exhausted! Where can I find a sauna? I ache all over!" and he dashes off to change. Jacqueline Du Pré is in another corner, quietly catching up with an old family friend—a hematologist—from the island of Jersey who, by coincidence, is visiting in New York. She is cool and calm in a blue and white suit, the famed Alice-in-Wonderland hair falling over both shoulders. But, of course, she has not been rehearsing, having made the trip just to be with her husband.

At lunch Italian style, the enthusiastic, prodigal 25-year-old Barenboim begins to unravel the tale of the beginnings of his second worldwide career as conductor. "When I was nine, I was studying at Salzburg and playing at the Mozarteum. They had summer classes there in conducting, and I began going to these classes—I was fascinated! I studied conducting there for two years. The problem for any aspiring conductor is where to practice. The great thing about Salzburg was that we had a full symphony available six days a week each day for two months. Then I went to the Accademia Chigiana at Siena—they had a fruitful year there in 1956 with Mehta, Abbado and Barenboim. Since then I actually have conducted very little. I realized I could not do both, having to learn repertory as both a pianist and conductor.

"I took up conducting again at nineteen in Australia in 1962 with the Sydney and Melbourne symphonies. Two years later I led the English Chamber Orchestra for the first time, and now I spend a great deal of time and energy there." But, he is eager to define, he has no official position with the orchestra. He makes tours and recordings with the ensemble, but the rest of the year the work is divided among the Aldeburgh Festival, Baroque concerts with Raymond Leppard and other activities like world tours, visits to America and recordings.

"Now, my time is divided up this way: I do thirty-five

percent playing, thirty-five percent conducting and thirty percent with the English Chamber Orchestra each year. Does one career help or detract from the other? It depends on how you look at it. For me, it is not a question of two separate professions—but, rather, two complementary professions. I have played a program of Beethoven sonatas one night and then conducted the *Eroica* Symphony a day or so later—and one helps the other. As a conductor you need a certain objectivity to hear what is going on outside your own ears; and playing the piano, in turn, helps my conducting. Today, conducting is a question of ego: a lot of people believe they are actually playing the music. It is true that a great conductor inspires an orchestra—they cannot play a *great* performance alone—and the central thing of playing the keys of a keyboard helps in conducting, in 'playing' the orchestra, so to speak."

As a young maestro accustoming himself to the ways and byways of a second (and often hazardous) profession, Barenboim stresses that "the main thing for a conductor is to make his musicians feel he is there to get the best possible results from them and from himself as well. Seriousness and dedication are important. If they play games with a conductor, it is because he plays games with them. No, age is not important in handling an orchestra; but the psychology of orchestral musicians is important to understand. As children, they were told what to do by their parents; in school and in their music lessons they took direction. For some period in their lives, they wanted a solo career, but at some point they realized (for whatever reason) they could not. And now, in an orchestral ensemble, they are still being told what to do every day—still, at middle age!"

Daniel Barenboim's own musical history began in Buenos Aires where he studied piano with his father, a former lecturer at the Vienna Academy of Music—"He taught me a hell of a lot!" He played his first public performance at the age of seven. Three years later, when he was invited by Igor Markevitch to play at Salzburg, the family left Argentina, eventually resettling in Israel. In Salzburg, he worked with Edwin Fischer on the performance of Bach, Mozart and Beethoven; studied chamber music with Enrico Mainardi; and conducting with

Markevitch. His parents restricted his concert-giving to two or three months a year (despite offers from all over the world), insisting on as normal an upbringing as possible. At 13 he became the youngest pupil ever to earn a Master's degree at Rome's Academy of Santa Cecilia. By 1956, when he won the Alfredo Casella competition and made his London debut playing a Mozart concerto at Festival Hall, he had a repertory of some 200 solo pieces and fifteen concertos.

Despite his youth in terms of years, his attitude is one of depth and maturity, incorporating the "dedication and seriousness" he demands of himself as a conductor. "It is essential to keep the freshness, particularly after you have performed a work concert after concert. Rubinstein is 82—but each time he plays something, it is always a new piece. The arch enemy is a routine musical performance, 'routine' in the bad sense of the word. After several performances of a work, the fingers can begin to control the mind, instead of the mind the heart."

The logic and conviction of his musical thinking make him aware that "You cannot divide technique and making music. It doesn't work like that, because you should not know where one ends and the other begins. If I play a passage loudly or softly, it is both a technical *and* a musical problem. When you have musical demands made in the music, then your technique comes into use to carry it out. For most people, a great technique means fast fingers—but a good technique means to do what you must do musically in terms of dynamics, touch and so on—musicianship, in a word. If you try to separate these, you go wrong.

"Young people forget another important thing: to have the knowledge of style and everything else is basic—the instinct is the beginning. You must have the initial impulse—intellectually, you then control the music. Fidelity to the text, for instance, is elemental, but you cannot stop there. If a *piano* is indicated, there are twenty different kinds—warm and full, thin, liquid, etc. This is where you read between the lines, not change the lines. Purity and technical correctness alone make music dead, a museum piece. Music is knowledge and intellectual capacity together. As a result of striving for stylistic correctness a lot of music today is what I call sterilized. We know how to crescendo in Beethoven and so on—but

unless you feel the emotional significance of a crescendo and
its form within the piece, it means nothing. For me, the best
kind of interpreter is the one who combines both the sense
of style and a deep personal playing. Wilhelm Furtwängler
—whom I heard as a child in Salzburg—did this. From the
music of Haydn and Mozart on he had a great personal involvement. I take my hat off to the musician who has the
inevitable sense of music—that when you hear him play, you
think that it could not be any other way."

This kind of intellectual capacity, very much part and parcel
of his own pianism and conducting, finds him putting stress
on the importance of the architectural form of the music he
plays. "In a passage, you may feel you want to do a *rubato*
—but you often must sacrifice it for the overall sense of shape
of the work. For instance, I hate working with a conductor
who goes through a concerto through the development only
and then stops, saying that the recapitulation is merely a
repeat. In every concerto or symphony, the *fortissimo* and
climax of the exposition as compared to the recapitulation
are completely different because of their relation to the end
effect of the whole piece. Look at the enormous sense of relief
that the recapitulation brings in the *Eroica!* Musicians at the
turn of the century had no sense of individual musical styles,
basing their personal style more on personal whim. Both
these extremes of stylistic correctness or the lack of it miss
the form of the music—how much crescendo or accelerando
there is in relation to the whole work."

This same resoluteness he brings to the question of correct
tempos, a question raised when a critic recently discussed
Barenboim's tempos in comparison to those of Schnabel:
"There are no right tempos—for whom and for where? Tempo
depends on the sound of the instrument and the hall. When
people compare Furtwängler with Toscanini and accuse Furtwängler of being slow, they must realize that his harmonic
tensions required this slowness. Tempo is like a drawer—it
depends what you put into it, in relation to rhythmic and
harmonic tensions. If there is less intensity, it must go quickly
—with intensity there must be time to separate and clarify
the details."

As for his own career, he is proud that he has done what

he has wanted, travelled where he has wanted, played the repertory he has wanted, despite his head-shaking over the fact that "we live in a society which works against what we are trying to do. It exploits everything—life is aggressive. And the worst thing you can do in music is to be aggressive. I want to have time to relearn and study. The great master-pieces of the repertory are still new after ten or twenty per-formances—a whole lifetime is not enough. People questioned me when I played the *Hammerklavier* Sonata at 14—'too young,' they said. Of course, I couldn't probe it all, but neither can some sixty-year-olds! There are those who say some music is only for maturity, but it only matures when you play and study and repeat it. Maturity is to realize that it is never finished. I'll never forget how the score of the *Hammer-klavier* shocked me the first time I looked at it. Every time I play it now, I have that same shock. I can never forget the impact of the first time I heard a work—that first reaction is as important as one twenty years later."

While non-stop musical conversation continued over veal scallopini and gnocchi, the radiant Jacqueline Du Pré quietly continued her retreat into the nearest corner, chatting with two friends who had joined us and who addressed her alter-nately as "Smiley" and "Jackie." Almost reticent to put her own oar into her husband's intense musical conversation, she related that she had just completed a film in London called *Jacqueline* (pronounced *à la Française*)—"and everyone will think it's about a French prostitute or something. Actually, it was done around a performance of the Elgar Concerto with Danny conducting, and some of it is biographical." Not French in origin, the Du Pré name comes from Jersey, one of the Channel Islands. William the Conqueror and his Normans came there on the way to England. "That's where my father was born. His family has been there since 1066. But my generation was the first to be born outside the island—I was born in Oxford and brought up in England."

Her discovery of the cello stems from her mother, a pro-fessional pianist who had conducted, composed and taught at the Royal Academy of Music. "When I was four, I heard my first cello over the radio. I loved the sound and said I'd like one of those." Her mother bought her a three-quarter-

length cello for her fifth birthday. Being too big, it meant a
long stretch down for the high notes—but she managed. To
make the hard work of learning less trying, her mother composed little cello tunes with words about witches and sea lions
and elves to fit, as well as drawings to go with them. "I used
to wake up and find a new drawing and tune under my bed
each morning."

Jacqueline Du Pré made her first public appearance at
seven, playing a transcription of a Schubert "Moment Musi-
cale" at a school concert. At 11, in competition with students
up to 21 years old, she carried off the first Suggia International
Award, bringing with it five years of free lessons in London
and abroad. Then, at sixteen, came her debut recital at London's Wigmore Hall. In the spring of 1966, she made her
highly acclaimed New York debut with the BBC Symphony
and Antal Dorati, playing the Elgar Concerto.

"There is one man in London who was my 'cello daddy'—
William Pleeth, once a cellist with the Allegri Quartet. I
studied with him for seven years, and I learned everything
from him." The product of the Suggia Award was the chance
to study for six months at the Paris Conservatoire with Paul
Tortellier, who called her the "Ginette Neveu of the cello."

From January to May of 1966 she traveled to Moscow to
study with Mstislav Rostropovich at the Conservatory. "He
taught me as and when he could. We fitted lessons into his
concert schedule. That meant crazy hours—we might start
at 10:30 P.M. and go on into the small hours. We reviewed
my whole repertory and studied new things, myself at the cello,
Rostropovich at the piano. Technique doesn't interest him
much. He's concerned with the realities: how music should be
felt, phrased and shaped. I love him very much. My last day
was the last of the conservatory year. Those who were graduated gave a public concert starting at 6:30 and ending at 11.
Mine was the last, and my friends at the Conservatory got
together as a student orchestra. I did Haydn's C-major Concerto with them, and Rostropovich conducted—a great occasion for me."

Afterwards, he had told her he felt he had found somebody to carry on his work. She admits she would like to—
"but, after all, I am a woman. A woman cannot play as a

man plays. She hasn't the physique and energy. A woman's hand is a limitation in itself. Rostropovich's hand is phenomenal. He can do anything with it. Of course, carrying the 'thing' was always a problem—but now I have Danny and I don't have to anymore." Does she note any severe lack in the cello repertory? "I find it frustrating to see his," pointing to her husband, "in comparison to my repertory. But the lack of it gives me time to be a wife. I don't have to be feverishly learning every day."

The instrument that is most always at her side now is a reddish 1712 Stradivarius, which an anonymous donor enabled her to buy three years ago. A second anonymous donor, who admired her playing, presented her with a 1673 Stradivarius shortly after her London recital debut. Previous cellos had been a seven-eighths Guarnerius and a 1696 Tachler.

And what do the Barenboims do between a succession of concerts and recording dates? Probably what they were doing toward mid-afternoon near the end of lunch, relaxing with close friends, breaking into a few unison bars of the Third *Brandenburg* Concerto when so moved, or joking about how so many Jewish people in America are named Fergussen—"because when they arrived at Immigration, they couldn't speak English and kept repeating, '. . . vergessen, vergessen. . . .' "

★ *Pierre Boulez* ★

In the spring of 1969 the still relatively unknown Pierre Boulez was scheduled to make his first guest appearances with the New York Philharmonic. I traveled to Boston for an interview while he was fulfilling similar duties with the Boston Symphony. Not long after New York experienced the unique Boulez impact, he was named Music Director of the Philharmonic, a post he took up in 1971 and is contracted to hold through 1977.

Coming face to face with Pierre Boulez today, it seems impossible to reconcile him to the image we came to know from his reputation in Paris over twenty years ago. Then, as an *enfant terrible par excellence,* he flew in the face of the Establishment, exiting from the Paris Conservatoire in disgust, proclaiming that it was a void and its teachers were "nothings." Plagued by financial woes, he found a roof in an unheated sixth-floor maid's room, alone and penniless, decrying academicism, crusading for twelve-tone music and authentic modernity. A revolutionary, he was disdainful, incorruptible and authoritarian, pronouncing that "Any musician who has not felt—I do not say understand, but felt—the necessity of the twelve-tone language is *superfluous.* For everything he writes will fall short of the imperatives of our time." What he chose to combat was the backward state of French music and the hostility to anything new, even at the risk of banishment from government-run radio.

Today, however, celebrated composer-conductor Pierre Boulez relaxes comfortably with his scores and correspondence in the elegance of Boston's Ritz Hotel, conservative in a dark suit and tie, white shirt. His worldwide stature bears all the "right" labels—S. Hurok Presents, Columbia Records, BBC Symphony, Cleveland Orchestra, Blossom Festival and guest weeks with the Boston Symphony, New York Philharmonic, Los Angeles Philharmonic and so on.

How do these two seemingly unrelated pieces of Pierre Boulez puzzle interlock? Like everything he touches—his own music, prose, conducting—there is an air of logic and well-plotted analysis to his method, for he has chosen to make his revolution of the 1960s from the inside, instead of taking swipes from the outside. "As a revolutionary," he confesses, "I'm very Leninistic. I'm all for the efficiency of the revolution, by going to the important organizations to change the sense of them and to convince them by my existence. When you do this, people are finally aware of change. If everyone ignores one another by staying in his separate ghetto, things stay the same way for centuries. In all departments, there are clusters of ghettos, all ignoring the other—in arts, in social things. They all go their own ways and pay no attention to the other."

Although Boulez first made his impact on the European musical scene as a rebel and forward-looking composer, extending the twelve-tone system to its fullest implications (beginning with his Sonatine for flute and piano and his First Piano Sonata in 1946), Boulez today has become an international conductor, eloquently speaking on behalf of the works of the Viennese Trinity (Schoenberg, Berg and Webern), as well as Stravinsky, Bartók and others of the twentieth century —and even Wagner's *Parsifal* at the shrine itself, Bayreuth. "I felt it necessary to change fields," he says. "You cannot always complain about the lack of performances in contemporary music and not do anything about it. I don't believe in passive complaining, though most people do just this. I felt I must change the situation myself. This is the reason for my guest conducting and for taking my BBC position.

"I know the *métier* now and how to manage aspects of the musical life—and also how to change them." It wasn't too long ago that he was referring to the world's orchestras as "dinosaur-like" because they lack the proficiency to play today's new music. "My function as a conductor is to make a new situation in contemporary music. The classics of contemporary music must become classical—a piece such as Debussy's *Jeux,* which everyone talks about and praises, is rarely heard in concert. Then, after this is accomplished, we can go further with the creative aspects—after the orchestra has accepted the language of this music. The orchestras must go the same way as the new composers did. In 1945 and '46 I studied all the scores of the Viennese school, and without them I could not have invented my own music."

By 1945, when the twenty-year-old Boulez had begun championing the music of Schoenberg, Berg and Webern, the music of the Viennese seemed almost a dead issue in Europe, so long had it been silenced under the Nazis. With the liberation of Paris came the liberation of music. That year, the Théâtre des Champs-Elysées gave a special series of Stravinsky concerts, and one night the young (led by young claquer Boulez) in the balcony began to hoot and catcall, creating a musical riot not unlike the one in 1913 when Stravinsky's *Sacre du printemps* outraged its premiere audience. Stravinsky this time, however, was being booed because he was old-fashioned and neo-classical—praised for his rhythmic innovations, damned for his unwillingness to surrender diatonic melody in favor of serialism.

Today, his attitude toward Stravinsky is transformed from ardent detractor to fervent exponent. "I was anti-Stravinsky in the post-War years because there was no judgment in Paris. He had no criticism and his name was used *against* the progress of the Vienna School. It was a myth that in time had to be destroyed. His own admirers were dismayed at the evolution of Stravinsky, but he proved to be more intelligent than they. He was really honest in his eventually turning to serial music. He had had no contact with the Viennese music before the War. When he discovered it, finally, he recognized it as something that went by him years before. I think, too, his problem was a problem of a certain category of creative people: a conflict of aesthetics. I see now that he could not really cope with or like or admit to the technical aspects of the Vienna School. The aesthetics were too far away from his own at that time. Stravinsky was anti-Romantic and could not suffer music still plunged in deep Romanticism. This conflict of aesthetics took him from further inquiry into that music—that he realized that Romanticism was not such a hot point with him."

Boulez, who had studied mathematics and engineering in his home town of Montbrison in the Loire country, had come to Paris to study at the Conservatoire (where he flunked his piano examination!). In 1944 he entered the harmony class of Olivier Messiaen (who systematized and enlarged the use of the Gregorian and Oriental modes and Eastern rhythms), a figure now recognized as the father figure of modern French music after years of abuse by his more conservative colleagues. Boulez was outraged that a man of his musical stature did not have a full professorship in composition and he drafted a petition to that effect, signed by himself and other more liberal students. When no action was taken, Boulez left the Conservatoire in disgust, though he had won a first prize in harmony in 1945. It was from Messiaen that Boulez received the decisive shock of his *"inquiétude rhythmique,"* a shock provoked by the revelation of using rhythmic structures independent of sonorous structures—and this became the source of the "totally" serial music of the frontal French music since that time.

Boulez describes his own musical life up to this crucial point this way: "The most advanced music of the War years in France was by Honegger, a major figure of the period. We had not heard one note of Bartók (in the provinces, it is still a desert like this today). At sixteen or seventeen I had no judgment, of course. I had heard *Meistersinger,* classical music and some French contemporary music—Debussy and Ravel were the most modern I had yet heard. After the War, after 1944, then I discovered everything. I heard *Sacre* for the first time live in 1945. (Actually, there was good music in Paris during the War because people were concentrated and going to concerts. But it was conservative, as were the politics of the time.) And there was a lack of communication. Bartók and the three Viennese composers were published by Universal Edition in Vienna and were not printed under the Nazis. So France had no scores of their music until after the War. The important thing was that we finally had them, because then we could progress, knowing the language of these composers and hearing the music."

André Hodeir in his *Since Debussy: A View of Contemporary Music* writes:

> Boulez felt that his most urgent task was an uncompromising reappraisal of music. It was not enough to write off tonal music in even more drastic terms than Schoenberg had used; Boulez had to make a rigorous diagnosis of the present state of music as a whole. If there were positive elements to be found in the works written between the two World Wars—uneven, incomplete and confused as they were—it was up to him to define and classify these elements. In other words, the construction of a new language presupposed an inventory of salvageable goods. All the elements that might conceivably be fitted together, all the trends that might possibly converge had to be compared with an eye toward an ultimate symbiosis. The guiding principle of this association already existed in the twelve-tone row, but it had to be revised, enlarged and enriched.

When Boulez came to America in 1963 as an Horatio Appleton Lamb lecturer at Harvard, he told one New York journalist:

> After the war, we felt that music, like the world around us,

was in a state of chaos. Our problem was to make a new musical language, seeking out what was good from the past, and rejecting what was bad. Around 1950, and for the following three years, we went through a period of seeking our total control over music. The serial process, which originated with Schoenberg and was refined in Webern, pointed out the way. What we were doing, by total serialization, was to annihilate the will of the composer in favor of a predetermining system. . . . But total control, like the total lack of control, can lead to chaos. Gaining this control was a necessary step in our development, because of our need to transubstantiate our musical heritage. But once there, we were at the zero point as composers. Now we could begin. Our process since about 1955 has been to enlarge and generalize what we had acquired through the period of atomization. In that way, we could gain a freedom through conquest, not merely through *laissez-faire*.

In this period of experimentation, his financial cares were soothed by his association with Jean-Louis Barrault, who had left the Comédie-Française to found his own theatrical company at the Théâtre Marigny, where Boulez orchestrated and perfected his conducting technique.

This was also a period of a series of celebrated pronouncements in stinging articles. Atonal music, he said, was not a break with the past, but the continuation of an abstract tradition going back to Debussy and Webern. A small group of "Boulezists" threw their weight behind this aggressive musician, who proclaimed Schoenberg's doctrines a failure and was not afraid to reverse the order of importance generally used in assessing the three Viennese (placing Webern at the top)— Schoenberg was taken to task for failing to apply serial principles of melodic organization to other aspects of music: mass, color, density and intensity of sound. By lashing out against and antagonizing a large percentage of French musicians, Boulez' music was banned from government-controlled French radio for fifteen years. Every new work stirred controversy, while, with some exceptions, critical response to his music ranged from anger to puzzlement. Even the French section of the jury for the Twenty-ninth Festival of the International Society of Contemporary Music at Baden-Baden in 1955 vetoed a performance of his *Le Marteau sans maître* (a 1954 cycle of nine pieces for six instruments and alto, based on poems of René Char). Only the threat of withdrawal of support by Heinrich Strobel, director of the Südwestfunk (the West German regional radio station, which was sponsoring the Festival) forced a change of mind on the part of the French.

The success of *Le Marteau* speeded his recognition as a composer, and earlier works, previously considered impossible to play, received performances—particularly in Germany, where the Cologne Radio played *Le Visage nuptial,* the Institute for Contemporary Music in Darmstadt performed *Le Soleil des eaux,* Boulez played his Third Piano Sonata at its world premiere in Darmstadt in 1957, and *Poèsie pour pouvoir* (the first work in which he mingled traditional instruments and taped sounds) was first played in 1958. During this period he also wrote his first two *Improvisations sur Mallarmé* for voice and instruments. In a sense, for the first time Boulez the intellectualizing theoretician and polemicist was matched, if not overshadowed, by Boulez the composer. Even in Paris, the habitually conservative Association des Concerts Lamoureux went so far as to commission a score for full orchestra, *Doubles,* premiered in March of 1958.

Boycotted by the musical establishment until this time, Boulez had managed to find private support for the performance of twelve-tone music. In 1954 he had launched a new series, "Domaine Musical," in the small, run-down Marigny Theater, lent by Barrault. The success of these concerts was phenomenal. *"Tout Paris,"* students and the intelligentsia flocked to hear the new music, and the Domaine soon became a leading European platform for the seldom-played works of the Vienna school and the young atonal composers, Stockhausen, Pousseur, Nono, Brown and many others. "I played only what I felt was good," he has said.

At the same time, he saw himself becoming the leader of a counter-establishment, which he viewed as another form of entrapment, and he left France in 1959 to live in Baden-Baden as composer-in-residence with the Südwestfunk Radio Orchestra—but not before he took a parting shot: "The organization of musical life in Paris is more stupid than anywhere else. France has completely lost her importance. Nothing advances."

Ironically, it was only after leaving home that he began receiving offers to conduct government-supported orchestras there: first, from his alma mater, the Paris Conservatoire (which he turned down), then from the Paris Opéra for its premiere of *Wozzeck,* which he accepted in 1963.

"This was not the easiest thing for the first time. I chose it because no one in Paris knew it—the Opéra had never staged it, so the musicians had never played it. So all would have to work hard, all were beginners including me." The widely hailed *Wozzeck* premiere marked Boulez's temporary but triumphant return to the musical world of France. The Minister of Cultural Affairs, André Malraux, told him, "I will not make any decisions concerning music without consulting you." But Malraux fell ill and some of his musical advisers took advantage of the situation to block Boulez' growing influence by asking Malraux to name to the newly created post of Musical Director a neo-Romantic composer, Marcel Landowski, noted for his movie scores and hostility to atonal music. Boulez felt betrayed and sent Malraux a letter in which he said that "By appointing an amateur who will be governed by personal preference . . . you are sending music and musicians back to the ghetto." In an open letter to the French press, he added: "Music is too important to be placed in senile and incompetent hands—I am going on strike against all the official organizers in France."

Since that day of self-appointed exile, Boulez has gained international recognition on the international podium. He has travelled to those places where his demands and standards can be met. "I demand quality of the musicians and goodwill, and this must be in the organization, too. One of the reasons I left Paris—where there were good musicians, even if they were not prepared properly—is that the organization was impossible! Paris is a disaster! It is important for me (and for anyone with artistic responsibility) to have a well-prepared organization and a well prepared and executed concert. The situation is like the iceberg with the vast part underneath—you do not see it, but it is crucial."

How does he face his audiences, in which more than a few pair of ears lag nearly fifty years behind musical development? "I find them responsive, despite the fact that the music of the

Viennese school still sounds foreign to many. But there has been no opportunity before to hear it. I have programmed what I consider the classical contemporary music, the standards—but these orchestras do not ordinarily play these classics, so it is really not like repertoire for them. Last year in Cleveland, for instance, I gave the first performance there of the Berg Opus 6 Pieces, and more recently for the first time in Boston and Los Angeles. I compare the period of Schoenberg to the period of Kandinsky in 1912, with his first abstract paintings. They are not so organized as his next paintings of the Bauhaus period, but it is 'lyric abstraction,' a liberation of motive and figure. And this is related to the music of the time." Boulez has also repeatedly told the average listener to "just listen with the vastness of the world in mind. You can't fail to get the message." New music, he insists, can be understood only with the broadest understanding both of the arts and of such non-artistic fields as physics and psychology. "For modern music, I prefer an audience that has vertical interests —that is, people who are interested in modern movies, modern art, modern literature." The hardest people to reach are "those who are interested in Beethoven as they would be in a cup of tea."

In communicating this music to the uninitiated, Boulez likens the whole process to building a telescope. "The listener is only a reflection of the orchestra and a work in performance is built like a telescope. The focus is the work, and a conjunction of mirrors is used to magnify—first the conductor is mirrored by the orchestra, then the orchestra is mirrored by the audience. The conductor transmits the quality of the work to the orchestra so that they will play it convincingly, and then it goes to the audience. If this is done, the main part of the audience (it is never all of them!) is convinced. For this, the conductor must have a solid technical base and an idealistic conviction to begin."

The attraction for the musical public to return again and again to the concert hall to hear the tried-and-true Boulez relates to the whole life pattern of growing up. "People discover the world intellectually between 18 and 22, maybe at 17 when they first go to the University. Then they begin to have a less tied life, less schedules, more freedom. They begin to discover and they have a freshness and interest. Many, when they finish at 22 or 23, discover no more because social functions and work play more and more a part in their lives. There are family problems, many problems. The culture—'culture' really is not a good word, but rather 'the creative aspects of life'—is acquired in this period of 'No man's land' (I say this because they are no more children, not yet in society) and many people don't survive beyond this. They do not keep the freshness of approach later on, after they've gotten all the cultural baggage for life.

"Then in symphony halls and theaters later they want the same impressions of that period, to rediscover their young life. It's really a narcissistic thing. It's also tied to sexual experiences —all these first experiences are related. I find people my own age whom I haven't seen for a long time and I see how they are drawn into everyday life. These 'creative aspects of life' are treated as a luxury or decoration, like cake after a meal. In all periods of history, there are some people mainly concerned with continuing this adventure they began in their twenties and some who are not—it is as simple as this: some people go out for a walk and some stay closed up in a room. These creative things are only for those who want to respond—they're not for all and not meant for all.

"In this, we confuse entertainment and things to think about. Some people say they have so many problems in life that they don't want them in art—but I think they must be sadder after a happy entertainment, because they think how really sad their lives are." This is not to say Boulez is against popular music or entertainment. "Life would be awful if we were trapped in genius all the time. But pop music is the hamburger of every day. It is everyday-life music—you can't brush your teeth to *Erwartung*. If you go for a quick lunch, you don't have pheasant and a wine of 1935. But I see no way of bringing the two together, as has been suggested— they're not the same activity: one is creative, the other a mass-media entertainment."

As a creator of music for the past two decades, Boulez decries any labeling. "As a composer, I put myself nowhere in music, not in the 'avant-garde' or anything. I am what I am! My music is written for me first—everyone composes for himself. There is no more establishment. The main part of society and all the minorities have rights to express themselves. Even crazy things are accepted in our free society. All are a part of the establishment now. In New York or London or Paris, you can always find 200 or 300 people who follow crazy things—anyone can find followers, this is not difficult. The attitude of categories of the establishment and the avant-garde makes no sense anymore. People who despise one or the other don't realize they're all in one bag now. There is no more heroism in the struggle of one against the other. We are living in a blotter society which absorbs everything."

In this abundance of artistic viewpoints, he cites many which only seem new the first time and then degenerate into experimental facility. Avant-garde movements, he has said, remind him of a bunch of couturiers who must present a new collection each season—"Its function is, like fashion, self-destructive so that it can be replaced by a new collection. To do this in art is to seek a very low common denominator." This self-destructiveness he finds particularly true in music. Experimentation, he says, "starts as healthy scepticism, it questions tacitly accepted rules and exposes their absurdity, but finally it is like a wasp's sting, and as quickly forgotten."

This same abhorrence for fashion for its own sake he finds in the sudden revivals of music out of the past. About the current Mahler-Bruckner upsurge, he comments: "I have the impression the world is an enlargement of Holland, where Mengelberg gave these programs before World War II. As with discovering things later, after their time, there is enthusiasm without much discernment. Besides the truly genuine things, there are the less genuine ones, like the lengthy rhetoric. For the audience, they want unfamiliar things but with the same kind of sound to replace the nine symphonies of Beethoven, the four of Brahms, the two or three of Tchaikovsky. The audience might be fed up with Beethoven and Brahms —but they must have food, yet not the *same* food. It is true with the revival of Baroque music, too, which is really an ersatz form of the *Brandenburg* Concertos—people could not hear the same six pieces over and over."

Of the American school, Boulez finds Elliott Carter the most impressive, "because he is the most articulate. Someone like John Cage is also necessary in the musical life—he kills the germs of academicism with the freshness of his thinking. His main aspect is that he is provoking in the best sense of the word, not just the scandal and outrage." As for the current interest in Charles Ives, Boulez confesses to having played only his *Three Places in New England,* and "I do not consider him a top musician because of the great weaknesses in *métier,* the lack of mastering the material, the lack of homogeneity and evolution. He is an erratic phenomenon—every piece has something bizarre along with certain achievements. The works are incomplete because of a lack of contact with professional people, both by will and by circumstance. In the orchestral works, there is an obsession with bringing in tunes, but it is only good for a while. The New England aesthetics are not interesting in themselves—it is only beyond this, in the original language of the *Concord* Sonata and Fourth Symphony (which has both the great and the dreadful) that we see the astonishing size of his language and his remarkable rhythms."

The one department in which Pierre Boulez has not tactfully moved in to reform from the inside is opera—and his views on this very subject caused tremors throughout the European operatic firmament. In the September 25, 1967, issue of *Der Spiegel,* he sounded off about modern opera and opera production, with fuel added to the fire in a debate with the Hamburg Opera's Rolf Liebermann in January of 1968. Not since *Wozzeck* has one modern opera been written, he stated, and he then proceeded to dismiss Hans Werner Henze (one of the most prolific present-day opera composers), Gunther Schuller and almost everyone else that comes to mind. He also took on the pioneering Hamburg Opera, a kind of opera house, to Boulez's mind, that will soon be going to heaven—the conventional opera houses are outmoded, relics of centuries past.

A few years later he has not changed his mind on the subject. "I'm not interested in an opera career—only some things, such as the new *Pelléas et Mélisande* at Covent Garden. If you see how the opera houses function, it is impossible for someone with responsibility to operate there. If concerts were given under these same conditions, people would be shouting about the bad performances. In a normal opera house—with constant changes of orchestra and cast and no rehearsals—who wants to conduct? Anyone who bears this is dishonest. And who conducts opera today? There is only one great opera conductor—Solti, and he has his own opera house, discipline and *stagione* system; Böhm and Karajan conduct only under special circumstances in Vienna and Salzburg.

"As for new opera, the connection of music and theater is not dead—it needs only to find a new connection in a new form. Some aspects of the young musical theater are nearer to the formula than new operas, they are more genuine and more inventive—though the music itself is often banal. Peter Brook's *U.S.* is a music-and-theater experience, and nearer my heart than any modern opera. Genet is the only one who seems closest to this concept of Brecht—a playwright with a real visual sense." Any chance of a Genet-Boulez collaboration that will give the key to the operatic future? Well . . . "No, I've found no way to escape the conventional frame."

★ *Aaron Copland* ★

When I drove up to Peekskill, New York, in July of 1970, it was a few months before Aaron Copland would celebrate his 70th birthday with four concerts of his own music with the New York Philharmonic, as well as engagements with many other major American orchestras. It was a celebration that rightfully went on all through the 1970-71 season with guest appearances and tributes all over the world.

All was well with Aaron Copland's world as the late summer crept closer to his 70th birthday in November to be celebrated by many of the world's great orchestras. The brilliant July sun glinted on the sweeping Hudson (which you can see through the trees from the housetop) . . . the roses were in

full bloom . . . Copland himself was occupied with various
conducting dates on the summer festival circuit . . . and he
seemed not unduly concerned over two not-yet-finished commissions. Oh, yes, there was that patch of grass below the
sweeping terrazzo patio which was turning brown in spots
("It's perfect in May and June, and then a mess every July and
August," he shakes his head) . . . and there was a wasp
who had found his way through the screen door into the
spacious, windowed studio. Yet there was definitely an air
of peace and contentment and well-being. As the car edges
through the long, densely wooded drive and pulls up to the
high-perched, stone-wood-glass house, a frisky collie sounds
the alarm, and momentarily Copland appears, flashing that
familiar smile. "Oh, he's Sultan or Sultane as he's called in
French—he's just three months old and belongs to the Belgian
cook and gardener." The house, dramatically dominating the
middle of his four acres from a time-worn rock, is encircled
by another fifty acres of woods and hills (not his). Copland
has lived here for the past ten years and is very much at home
strolling across the terraced gardens and lawn—"You should
have seen this in the spring," he exclaims passing by the
rhododendrons and azaleas. "They were covered with flowers."
Picking off a few drooping daylily blossoms, he beams, "That's
the extent of my gardening." The air, the sun, the quiet, the
seclusion, he agrees, make it the perfect place for a composer.
"A friend says that I'm still close enough to swoop down on
New York and take a look," he chortles.

Inside, the tree-framed studio, with its wide working desk
and piano, is oddly uncluttered. The bookshelves are lined
with recordings of his music, his scores bound in deep blue
and gold and a sizable music library. There are translations
of his *What To Listen For In Music* in everything from German and Italian to Swedish, Norwegian, Dutch, Persian,
Egyptian and Japanese. "When I conducted the orchestra in
Japan there was a press conference with about twenty journal-
ists, and one asked me how many books I had written. After
I told him four, one man got up and announced, 'I have translated one and here it is'—then I began wondering if he had
the right to do this, so I found the local McGraw Hill office
(they had published it in the U.S.). I asked them about the

author's copyright protection and they told me there was none in Japan for ten years," he shrugs.

There are also photos of such disparate figures as Liszt and Ruggles (seated in his backyard), and a shining copper plaque from the Phi Alpha Sinfonia Fraternity, naming him "Man of Music 1970"—"These things just *happen* to you! I got it at Interlochen where Phi Mu Alpha was having its triannual convention, and where I was conducting my *Tender Land* Suite, *Danson Cubano, Our Town* and Shostakovich's Ninth Symphony with the student orchestra." There are copies of *The Nation* and *Partisan Review,* the latter because Harold Clurman was his roommate in Paris. On the black grand is a photostat facsimile of Beethoven's Opus 111 Sonata given to Copland in 1926 "on a summer's afternoon" (probably on one as idyllic as this) and another of Debussy's *L'Après-midi d'un faune.* Near the phonograph are recordings of his own works in European editions and some French discs of Dutilleux and Roussel. "You know, my music is *never* played in France—it's an unrequited love that goes back to my student days there."

As he nears the age of seventy, Aaron Copland has travelled far from that "drab" street in Brooklyn which he has described as his birthplace. "That word 'drab' has been quoted more than any other word," he muses. "Two years ago I drove past that place on the way to a lecture in Brooklyn, and I told my driver, 'Let's stop.' When I stood there, the whole street seemed to have shrunk in size—the foyer of the building seemed half the size of what I remembered, and the three stories seemed dwarflike after twenty years." Of the five children, three remain—the composer is the youngest in a family where his first contact with music was a brother who played the violin to his sister's accompaniment. "Of course, there are nephews and nieces and cousins—it goes on and on. One branch of the family on my mother's side is in Texas. She lived in Dallas and Peoria after coming from Russia as a child. My father came here as a young man from Lithuania, bringing his mother, father, brothers and sisters. He talked with an accent, so I considered my mother's family more American."

When time had been set aside for an afternoon with Copland, he warned over the telephone, "You'd better get up

here as soon as possible . . . before I'm all talked out!" And
as he begins to relate early experiences, he interrupts (as he
will do many times during the interview), "You know, I wrote
all this down"—and indeed Copland has been not only one
of America's most important composers but also one of the
most articulate musical spokesmen in his books, articles, interviews, radio programs, symposia and the like since the Thirties.

"Music as an art was a discovery I made all by myself," he
once wrote in *The New Music*. There had been piano lessons,
but at the age of fifteen, "the idea of becoming a composer
seems gradually to have dawned upon me." In the fall of 1917
he began harmony lessons with the late Rubin Goldmark, who
"had an excellent grasp of the fundamentals of music and
knew very well how to impart his ideas." In the natural course
of things, his curious young mind happened upon new music
—Goldmark discouraged this leaning, thinking the young
composer's early efforts were already too advanced. Soon it
was evident that he would have to go abroad to finish his
studies, and the name of Copland, Aaron, headed the list
of enrollments for the first summer of a new music school
for Americans in the Palace at Fontainebleau. Studying with
Paul Vidal of the Paris Conservatoire, he quite by accident
happened upon Nadia Boulanger's harmony classes, and as
he relates, "I had never before witnessed such enthusiasm and
such clarity in teaching. I immediately suspected that I had
found my teacher." That fall he asked her to accept him as
a pupil, becoming her first full-fledged American composition
student—the beginning of a long line still going on.

Looking back over seventy years rich with experiences and
personalities. Copland instantly settles on his Paris years as
the most important. "As I've said often before, to have been
twenty in the Twenties was picking it carefully. No one could
have known that it would be the liveliest, most stimulating
spot of the time. The meeting with Boulanger was crucial. I
had never heard of her, and before that I couldn't imagine
that I'd ever study composition with a woman—but I spent
three years. And, of course, my eventual meeting with Serge
Koussevitzky there was crucial. Without him I would not have
had a consistent interest in my music. He was the ideal composer's patron—he was interested in the work . . . and the

performance . . . and the next work . . . and how you'd live until you composed it. He was a frustrated composer and took it out by helping young composers.

"It was a lively time in Paris as Koussevitzky pushed to establish performances of new music. Four years of the First World War had stopped artistic communication, followed by a spurt of suppressed activity in the 1920s. So I heard Schoenberg, Stravinsky, Bartók, Falla, Milhaud, Honegger, Auric, Les Six, Hindemith, Prokofiev and many others for the first time. Koussevitzky did what he liked. He hired an orchestra for five concerts in the fall and five in the spring at the Opéra. Later he premiered my *Music for the Theatre* with the League of Composers, then the Boston Symphony, then in Brooklyn and then in Paris. In Brooklyn he had put it on the first half with Strauss' *Alpine Symphony* on the second half. *Music for the Theatre* was written for chamber orchestra, for what the League could afford. At the intermission the Board of the Academy came backstage and was disturbed—'We paid for the Boston Symphony and we only have a small group.' Koussevitzky told them, 'Don't worry. We'll play the *Alpine Symphony* next—it uses a monster orchestra, so you'll get more than your money's worth!' "

It was Boulanger's commissioning of a Symphony for Organ and Orchestra and Koussevitzky's suggestion to the League of Composers that it commission Copland to write a new work (*Music for the Theatre*) that launched the composer in the Twenties, providing the foundation upon which he built the long line of some sixty works, from the Piano Concerto and *Symphonic Ode* to the *Dance Symphony*. Short Symphony, *Statements, El Salón México, Billy the Kid* and *Appalachian Spring* ballets, *Our Town* and *Of Mice and Men* film scores, the *Twelve Poems of Emily Dickinson,* the Piano Sonata and Variations, *Quiet City,* Third Symphony, Piano Quartet, Piano Fantasy, *Connotations* for Orchestra and *Inscape*—to name but the highpoints. His musical styles have run the gamut from strict serial writing to the very popular ballets, radio and film scores. "These personal musical styles were not so much a conscious effort—not a cold-blooded decision to do something different in music—as much as the general atmosphere and changes happening and the opportunities to do something," he clarifies. "In other words, they were outside things such as having a film score offered you and then doing it. My serial writing goes back to a song in 1927—you know, I heard the atonal *Pierrot Lunaire* in 1922 conducted by Milhaud. With my more recent works, I didn't feel a return to serial writing, because I never felt I had left anything. It's a question of what you're asked to do and the materials given, the musical ideas. An idea may suggest 12-tone treatment perhaps, and then maybe it won't."

Copland has observed: "As I see it, music that is born complex is not inherently better or worse than music that is born simple"—and his language has served both for nearly fifty years. Does he feel that a composer—not unlike a novelist or playwright or poet—faces a crisis after he has poured forth what comes naturally in the initial spurt? "One's attack changes and there are new problems," he agrees, "as when you begin to write a symphony after you have written songs. For me there was the challenge of a simpler style for a wider audience, a change of attack . . . or vice versa, to do 12-tone pieces that I knew would have a hard time audience-wise. Stravinsky is the archetype of renewing himself by change of approach— and he has been often chastized for this very thing." Copland has frequently stated: "You don't want to repeat yourself. On the other hand, you don't want to jump on any band wagons just because it's the thing to do."

He himself believes there has been a consistent line of development, rather than what has been often designated as "two styles" or "two Coplands." He then quickly thrusts at an interested party an analysis he feels best sums up his *oeuvre* and his own feelings on the subject: Peter Garvie's article from a 1962 *Canadian Music Journal.* Garvie notes that "it is not a large output; a substantial work about every two years. His course as a composer has been one of continual development and exploration, but it would be naïve to think of it as a progress or improvement, or as a decline. He was a fully mature composer at thirty, and it is simply inadequate to categorize the rest of his output as an Abstract Period, a Popular Period and a Return to Absolute Forms. A glance at the chronology ought to be enough to show that his development is not explained by attractions to, and reactions from, certain styles and forms. And by this time we should also have given up the concept of the two Coplands, the accessible and the remote. His development is the resolution of problems, musical and cultural, that were presented to his imagination; and the resolution is in individual musical works."

Garvie traces Copland's experience with American academicism, the impact of the new music, the French musical tradition, music related to his own personal environment (particularly jazz), music of concentration and severity of style in the Thirties, functional music by way of commissions ("In the mid-1930's to reach an audience, to communicate, may have been as much a matter of conscience as had been the problem of integrity of style a few years earlier. The abstract works brought his style to the point of greatest potency. The next problem was to communicate, to move outwards again, without sacrificing the quality of style attained.") and further explorations with serial technique in the Piano, Quartet and Fantasy, *Connotations* and *Inscape*. "*Reculer pour mieux sauter* has turned out to be one of the maxims of Copland's imagination," Garvie concludes.

Which brings us up to date with his music. "I'm now supposed to be writing a flute piece with piano, commissioned by the students of William Kincaid in his honor [completed shortly thereafter and premiered by Elaine Schaeffer]. There also is a String Quartet for the Juilliard—a commission, but I already missed the deadline and they said 'whenever.' I also did a fanfare for the Metropolitan Museum Centennial with several other American composers, which is on a souvenir record—and another fanfare to inaugurate a new Calder sculpture in Grand Rapids. I've also orchestrated eight of the Emily Dickinson Songs." Noting that these songs seem to crop up more and more, he reasons: "It often takes a while, you know, for a piece to gain any sort of foothold in the repertory. For instance, the Clarinet Concerto—which was composed over 20 years ago—just now seems to be coming into its own." Does he have any preferences among his works? "Some you like because everyone does and some you like because you're the only one who does—that's sort of like a neglected child. Some you've sweated over, like the Piano Fantasy, which took two years to write and lasts half an hour in one movement—

it hasn't turned into a hit number exactly, but the effort was enormous. Incidentally, William Masselos's performances of it are a composer's dream."

Every composer, he believes, turns out " 'those works' that are not performed. He often senses in advance that some are more acceptable than others to the big public. There is the tendency, too, of conductors to settle for the more familiar part of one's output. *Appalachian Spring* is, if anything, over-played, while the Short Symphony—one of my best works—is almost never performed. At the time it was new, it wasn't published, I had written pieces of more public appeal. The *Symphonic Ode,* too. Every composer can point to similar examples. Some come around eventually, such as the Clarinet Concerto . . . but that was never difficult to listen to. Do you know what is the *most* played of all my works in the past year, according to my accounts? *Lincoln Portrait,* which is 25 years old! It had about fifty performances by different orchestras and has gained gradual currency. The words seem to be appropriate no matter what year and what world situation. I picked them and they still have relevance 25 years later. You know, I wasn't going to do a Lincoln portrait at the beginning. When Kostelanetz asked me, I thought of a Whitman portrait, but he said Kern was doing one on Twain and Thomson was doing the *Mayor LaGuardia Waltzes*—and he wanted a statesman or politician. The only one I could think of was Lincoln—it's hard to think of Washington for a musical portrait!" he laughs. "I found quotes in Lord Charnwood's paperback biography. I'm not exactly a Lincoln scholar but. . . ."

It is as Aaron Copland the conductor as much as Aaron Copland the composer who keeps his name before the public eye today. And as conductor he is producing for Columbia a series of what can be termed "definitive" recordings of his own works. "Oh, yes, there is a definitive satisfaction in this, especially to have left a 'document' for other performers. It's not that I want to be imitated, but such a thing can be illuminating for tempos and the like. Of course, other conductors can reveal something I had not thought of. There is the fun of having your works open to interpretation. Someone may choose a slower tempo to squeeze more juice out of a piece of music or another possibility you may not have ever thought of yourself."

He has related his decision to begin conducting in various ways, writing in *The New York Times* in 1968 that during a visit with Igor Stravinsky, the venerable maestro turned to the other and said: "My dear, you should conduct your own music. All composers should conduct their own music!" Or as he relates in *The New Music,* that after having to refuse to conduct his *Appalachian Spring* with the Cincinnati Symphony because he didn't know it from a conductor's standpoint, he was determined "to learn how to conduct at least my own works. After all, every composer secretly thinks he knows best how his own music should sound. Moreover, I had reason to believe I was something of a performer by nature. I knew that I liked audiences and they seemed to respond to me." The question of how to practice conducting came with an invitation from Carlos Chávez to conduct his Third Symphony with the Orquesta Sinfónica de México in Mexico. He pursued it further in Montevideo and Buenos Aires—everywhere except in the United States, "anywhere I could corner an orchestra . . . just as long as it was far enough away that no one here could know what happened." Finally by 1956 he felt ready to face an American audience when the Chicago Symphony asked him to come to Ravinia. Someone he calls an "elderly and wise woman" gave him some advice too: "Aaron, it is very important, as you get older, to engage in an activity that you didn't engage in when you were young, so that you are not continually in competition with yourself as a young man." The baton was his answer: "Conducting, as everyone knows, is a bug—once you are bitten it is the very devil to get rid of. What makes it worse is the fact that you get better at it all the time—more expert in rehearsing, more economical in gesture, more relaxed in actual performance."

"It's hard to believe," he says with amazement in his voice, "but I've conducted over 100 works with over 100 orchestras in this country, Europe, Japan and South America. It's fun —you're making music and working with musicians—and you have to be a performer in some part of your personality. And

you can do pretty much what you want if you don't have a
regular post." He maintains wide tastes for a composer—most
are notoriously narrow in what they like and wide in their
dislikes. Confessing to be more open than most creators in
their tastes, he smiles, "I guess it's a matter of temperament."
And so his programs include works of Ives, Sessions, Britten,
Busoni, Tippett, Carter, Roussel, Walton, Hindemith, Bennett
and Bernstein.

The current 19th-century Romantic revival, however, holds
little interest for Copland. "In the 1920's that was the enemy,
that was what we were trying to get away from. Schoenberg's
development never appealed to me as much as the Stravinsky-
French development, because emotionally Schoenberg was still
a part of the 19th century, no matter what his technical innovations were. Only later on when the younger men came
along did they show that techniques could be used without the
Romantic apparatus—it's a matter of system versus expression.
While the generation of the Thirties and Forties wrote Ro-
mantic-type music, the separation came in the post-war revolution of Boulez and Stockhausen, who took the technical
revolution without the other."

As to the state of contemporary music today, he comments:
"By and large, you can say there is a dichotomy of what is
being written and what is played in concerts. The concert
repertory for the large public is never very contemporary—its
aspect is special in that one piece is played surrounded by
older things. Through the efforts of societies there was probably a greater proportion of new music in concerts during
the Twenties than there is now. It's narrower and narrower
now, so that the entire new movement is in the universities.
Even in New York it's the outside groups that bring in the
new music. There are more composers now working in the
advanced idiom, but the impingement on the general music
public's conscience is less and less—and it's not a happy picture. Of course, we complained in the Thirties too. Just look
back in old issues of *Modern Music*. The same themes come
back time and again . . . especially how composers grumble
that nobody plays their works. The main gripe of all composers
is that there are not enough performances. If a piece is performed, you get it out of your system—but it's very frustrating

if you have put down all those notes and you cannot hear
them. So composers get performances at schools and with
small groups, abandoning the larger symphonic field. The
trouble with symphonic writing today is that so few works do
get played when they are written. The symphonic idiom has
developed for over 100 years, and the tendency now is to get
bogged down because it is so much associated with the 19th
century."

He is equally disheartened about that other 19th-century
creature known as opera, which Copland has dubbed *la forme
fatale*. In 1933 he had written: "No country's musical life
appears to be entirely mature until its composers succeed in
creating an indigenous operatic theater. I am not quite sure
why this should be so, but I do know that all the history books
give it as a special triumph that the English, the French and
the Germans—after the 'invention' of opera in Italy—should
each in turn have developed their own kind of opera. This
attitude is no doubt partly to be explained by the fact that you
can't very well create a truly national opera without combining the words with a melodic line that really fits—and to
have done so properly inevitably means that you have written
a kind of music suited to the particular language. In short,
there is a close connection between language and tone that
makes their successful marriage in dramatic form, with stage
incidentals, seem like one of the necessities—and when accomplished, one of the triumphs—of any native musical art."

Thirty-seven years later, he shakes his head: "No, American
opera hasn't flowered, and it's hard to analyze. For one thing,
the possibilities of performance are few and far between.
There are not enough houses willing to do enough flops, which
is needed for young composers to profit by experience. The
strength of the musical comedy stage, too, is a deterrent. The
success of *West Side Story* is far beyond anything that's happened in opera, and this takes away from the opera effort.
You need a librettist too, and good ones are rare animals—a
playwright doesn't need a composer. Lenny Bernstein moans
that he can't find a suitable text. But the whole operatic field
is filled with built-in headaches. A composer is responsible
for only a part of it. He works for two years—and then in a
couple of hours its fate is determined. And there are few

second chances in opera, as opposed to a symphonic work which maybe will be played by another conductor, another orchestra, and given a further chance to be appraised. Anyone smart will stay away from it . . . except if he's really only an opera composer, as was Wagner." As for Copland, who has written only *The Tender Land* and *The Second Hurricane* and whose interests have leaned more in the direction of the orchestral-instrumental than vocal, he shrugs, "Well, if you showed me a libretto, then maybe. . . ."

The next day Copland was leaving for a week at the Blossom Music Center and Kent State in Ohio, where he would be conducting, coaching his own music and lecturing. But—and he seems almost relieved in saying it—"but I am doing no more teaching. Actually, I never did it regularly, despite my twenty summers at Tanglewood. People now call themselves my pupils who were with me for two months one summer!" he says incredulously. But despite works in every medium, his long association with the Berkshire Music Center and general widespread influence, Copland has not spawned a school or even a coterie of followers—he has remained very much unto himself. "People are quicker than I to detect my influence in another's music. If I didn't write it, I can't tell. But often it sounds very comfortable—it goes just where I thought it would," he smiles. "As for teaching, I never took anyone from the beginning to the end. I have been more of a specialist to whom young composers brought their troubles to be analyzed. Composers, when they finish a piece, are dying for a reaction. It's hard to stand back and take a calm view of it yourself, so it helps to find someone to take a more dispassionate view and comment on it. My value at Tanglewood was that I had a few students who already had the technical background but who still needed knowledgeable criticism and the reaction of a practicing composer. This was also Boulanger's value to we who were already composing. But she could do both—either at the end, or from the very beginning of a piece, because she had the sensitivity *and* the technique."

Recently, when Copland paid a visit to the Eastman School in Rochester, the *Democrat and Chronicle*'s George Murphy called him the "Dean of American Composers," a title which most would agree is highly and rightfully fitting. "I want you to see this," chuckled Copland as he pulled out a newspaper clipping from *The Times-Union*, dated June 1—a rather irate response from Director Emeritus of Eastman Howard Hanson, entitled "If Age Makes a Man 'Dean.' " Taking exception, Hanson wrote: "My first inclination was to write a 'letter to the editor' saying: 'Dear Editor: Aaron Copland can't be the Dean of American Composers, I am!' On second thought, however, this did not seem to be a wise decision. First, it might not seem modest." But, more important, Hanson felt that "he is much too young! He is a mere youth." At 75 he felt himself too young also, as is Thomson, Sessions and Still and Harris. Walter Piston, at 76, he felt, holds a more valid claim—or 80-year-old Philip James of New York University —or nonagenarian Charles Ruggles. "All of us youngsters would, I am sure, be proud to hail this gallant pioneer as our Dean of American Composers and wish him many more years in office. I am sure that Aaron Copland would agree." Was the young 70-year-old Aaron Copland agreeing? . . . he wasn't saying, but that smile told all.

★ Alicia de Larrocha ★

A 1971 vacation in Spain and Portugal occasioned a stopover in Barcelona to visit the great Spanish virtuosa Alicia de Larrocha on location in the city where she has spent most of her life and at the famous Frank Marshall Academy. Making it even more enticing was the promise the following autumn of the first joint recital of Mme de Larrocha and her compatriot and longtime friend Victoria de los Angeles at Hunter College.

High above the port of nighttime Barcelona, amid colored umbrellas and glowing lanterns, the dark-haired lady throws back her head and aims the spout of the green sherry bottle from high above her broad mouth. Alicia de Larrocha is a *campeón* at what the Catalans call *porron,* as confident with the bottle as she is at the piano, which she has been playing since the age of three. After a savory meal of gazpacho, paella, and crema Catalana on the summit of Montjuich, Alicia and her husband, Juan Torra, set out on a midnight tour of their native city, where they've spent nearly all their lives. Almost at every turn, the pianist is reminded of some moment in her life and career, which had been spent in and around Barcelona until a half-dozen years ago when a persistent American agent literally forced her into international prominence.

Halfway down Montjuich, the Fuente Monumental is still exploding with water and colored lights, mesmerizing the pianist with its changing patterns and tones. "It's just like the piano sonorities of Albéniz," she notes with wide-eyed enthusiasm. Pointing off into the distance, she adds, "I played my first public concert over there at the Missions Palace." The fountain and handsome buildings were built for the 1929 World's Fair, when the five-year-old Alicia de Larrocha bowed in her native city.

Driving past the old university, she relates that her fellow Catalan Victoria de los Angeles was born here (Victoria Gomez Cima), the daughter of a caretaker at the school. They've known one another since their teens but have never appeared together in public. During her student days at the Liceo Conservatory and University, Mme. de los Angeles won a prize in a radio competition while Alicia was then studying and teaching at the Frank Marshall Academy. After the war, the young singer had a chance to make a test recording for His Master's Voice and needed someone to play the piano for her. Urged by a mutual friend, the pianist accompanied the singer in two arias from *La Bohème* and *Madame Butterfly.* That recording and winning the Geneva Competition catapulted the soprano into the world spotlight, while Alicia de Larrocha's career took a different direction.

The figure of the Catalonian Enrique Granados recurs like a *leitmotif* in this Barcelona tour. At the corner of Córcega and Enrique Granados street, the petite pianist almost casually announces that here was her own birthplace. In the quietly deserted Barrio Gotico with its Romanesque Palacio Real

Mayor (where Ferdinand and Isabella received Columbus) and Town Hall, she points out a heavy iron-grilled window: "It's just like Granados, you know, in his 'El coloquio en la reja,' with the girl inside and the boy, declaring his love outside through the grill."

We drive through the Ramblas, Barcelona's perennially bustling thoroughfare, to the Manila Hotel, a favorite stopping place for musicians. Its owner, an art and music lover, heads the Friends of Enrique Granados and has created a museum on the lower level. On the lobby level a small bar in nineteenth-century, red-plush Parisian style pays tribute to the famed Catalan singers—Gay, Capsir, Hidalgo, Viñez, Barrientos, Supervia, Badia, Caballé, Aragall, and, of course, de los Angeles. Down a staircase is the Camarote Granados, a reproduction of a stateroom on the *SS Sussex,* the ship torpedoed by the Germans in the English Channel in 1916, killing the 48-year-old composer, who was returning from the premiere of his *Goyescas* at the Metropolitan Opera. The walls are covered with signed photos of all the leading Spanish musicians, a portrait, letters, and handwritten scores of Granados, manuscripts of other Spanish composers, and printed title pages of works by Turina, Falla, Rodrigo, Albéniz and Granados himself.

While the Camarote celebrates the glorious past, at No. 10 Callé del Savatierra the past and the present uniquely join hands. Here at the Frank Marshall Academy an extraordinary piano tradition lives on through the efforts of Alicia de Larrocha and Juan Torra, directors of the privately run and self-sustaining academy—which was founded by the composer in 1909 and carried on after his death by his English pupil and de Larrocha's longtime teacher ("He was like my father") Frank Marshall. The great Spanish musical past is everywhere in the faded red-velvet, brocade-wallpaper charm of the studios and offices. There is the harpsichord where Falla wrote his Concerto, the book of *Los Caprichos* by Goya which inspired *Goyescas,* original manuscripts of Granados's works and valuable finger exercises, Lorca's "Epitafio a Isaac Albéniz" which he improvised at the grave of Albéniz in 1935 in the presence of Falla and Marshall, and the letter from Felipe Pedrell, the father of Spanish nationalism in music, telling the alien Marshall that it is his obligation to continue the work of Granados. And there is the dining room much as Marshall left it at his death in 1959—where Falla, Artur Rubinstein, Sauer and Cortot were feted among wood and silver.

Picking up one of Marshall's carved canes still standing in one corner, Mme. de Larrocha notes, "He was a real English gentleman, elegant, but Spanish in temperament. I still can see him," and she struts down the hallway in fine Chaplinesque style. As she energetically darts into every nook and cranny of the fascinating but well-worn rooms, she laughs girlishly, "Tradition is one thing—dirty is another."

Alicia de Larrocha has known this atmosphere encompassing the piano classrooms, noted performers, and composers all her life. The first Marshall Academy at Rambla de Cataluña was not far from her house, and she went there at age three. "It was my home. I spent all my time there at the piano and playing games. I was never forced to play, so it was never work. My toy was my piano." Her aunt, who to this day at age seventy-eight still teaches at the academy, had pupils at home. One day after they had left, two and a half-year-old Alicia climbed up on the piano bench and began to play what she had heard the others do. Her aunt took her to Marshall, but he cautioned that it was too early to begin teaching her. Still, the piano became her plaything, as she insisted on putting crayons and pencils inside it and playing with the keys. "Once my aunt locked it and I was so unhappy I cried. I put my head on the floor and banged it. I was in a real temper, and I did it so hard that blood began to flow out—and at this moment my aunt said, 'Well, we'll start.' So we went to Marshall, and I screamed at him, 'I want to play the piano!' and he told me to come the next day." At age five she made her recital debut, and at nine she was playing Mozart with the orchestra in Madrid, with Arbos conducting. At an early age, she took her place among Marshall's assistants, eventually combining teaching with a limited career.

Granados, Mme. de Larrocha asserts, taught his own style of piano at this school. "In fact, he was the first in Europe to create a school especially for the study of the pedal. He also concentrated heavily on the sonority of the piano—something fantastically new for his era. No one before him had paid attention to sonorities with such intelligence. Granados loved the music and style of Scarlatti, and he brought the technique of the harpsichord to the romantic, virtuoso piano repertory of the day. He also felt a great affinity for Schumann and was considered a leading interpreter of his music. In the second part of Granados's life, Schumann cast a spell over his music." Mme. de Larrocha stresses that Marshall did not let her study Spanish music until she was seventeen. "First it was Bach and Mozart and the wide range of the European piano repertoire. This is a necessary base for a pianist. You cannot begin playing Spanish music without it." Today at the academy (with 100 pupils and seven instructors), the teaching is based on the Marshall plan, slightly renovated every few years.

"To the pianist, Granados, Albéniz and Falla are the cream of Spanish music. It was Felipe Pedrell, a Catalonian, who first collected all the popular Spanish songs and eventually became the teacher of Albéniz, Granados and Falla. He instilled a national-historical sense in his students and he guided them to this vast source of Spanish folk music, encouraging them to use it in their works.

"Of course, the colorful region of Andalusia became the most influential region of Spain in the piano music during the late 19th and early 20th centuries. It was the music from this section of the country which had been the most popular and most commercial on the international market. This 'flamenco sound' was an export, like bullfights and mantillas—it was thought to be 'typical' of Spain. Many lesser composers took this colorful music and capitalized on it; but the few great ones —like Falla and Albéniz—took the essential values in this music, adapted them to the classical style and created masterpieces. The popularity of Andalusia has made it difficult for the music of other regions—Castile, Galicia and others—to emerge and to make an impression, though their music is equally beautiful and exciting. A few, like Nin and Rodrigo, have written fine works based on the folk melodies of these other regions."

In comparing the three masters of Spanish music—Granados, Albéniz, and Falla—Mme. de Larrocha calls the first the real romantic poet. "Everything he did was spontaneous, yet restrained—a reflection of his temperament," she said. "His music is patrician and elegant, reflecting the Spain of the aristocracy. He is like a picture that is part typically Spain and part the decoration of nineteenth-century romanticism." Albéniz she calls more colorful, full of spirit and power, brilliant in his palette. Falla was more under the spell of gypsies, "and his music speaks of the tremendous strength of the Spanish gypsy, of *cante hondo,* the deep tragic sound, the ageless sorrow of Spain that is generally heard more in vocal writing than in piano music. Falla—who composed very little for the piano, concentrating more on the orchestra—is also the most cosmopolitan and universal, mirroring the influences of France and the impressionism of Debussy, Dukas and Ravel. Falla once said that his music has its origins in all that is greatest in the musical heritage of our race—it must be sincere and natural, however universal in aspiration; and it was to remain profoundly Spanish in essence.

"For the pianist, the peaks of Spanish music are *Iberia* and Granados' *Goyescas.* This music is completely separate from all the other piano repertory. Technically, it is very different and difficult. It is not that you have to be Spanish-born to play this music, but it is impossible if you don't acquire the special technique that is needed. This has to do with the sound and rhythm of the music, as well as the colors. One of the clues to this style lies in the fact that both Albéniz and Falla took the guitar as their instrumental model. And this style has something to do with the same qualities that our great flamenco dancers have—it is the sense of excitement held tightly under control; there is no hysteria or flamboyance. It is crucial to keep the emotional excitement in the context of complete control. With this comes the quality of seduction, a certain arrogance, or haughtiness, or Spanish pride."

"I never thought about a career," Mme. de Larrocha says, shrugging her shoulders. "Music has been the one thing of my life, nothing else. I never thought of it as a profession. My teacher said to experience music in public, and so I did it— but not to show myself off. It was the best way to begin, and then I found myself with concert tours and was surprised, because I never did anything to get concerts." This began after the Civil War and then again after World War II, when she ventured out to the Canary Islands, Spanish Morocco and

Europe. She recalls the hardships of the Civil War: "We had no food in the last six months; it was a tragedy. My father went to the mountains to get greens to eat because we had no wood, no bread, no oil. On the other hand, many people who were ill when they had too much became healthy now that they couldn't eat."

In the early 1950s Alfred Wallenstein heard her in Europe and asked her to come to California for concerts with the Los Angeles Philharmonic (1954), after which she played a successful Town Hall debut under the sponsorship of some Barcelona friends (1955). For ten more years she continued to play in Europe, while teaching at home and making some recordings for American Decca. Then publicity agent Herbert Breslin began to write her in an effort to coax her back, eventually promising four New York Philharmonic concerts and a Hunter College recital. "I didn't think this was possible, we couldn't believe it. Records, you know, are dangerous, and that's all he knew of me." So she came back to America in 1965 and quickly obliterated the stigma of being just another "lady" pianist by becoming *the* woman pianist of the day (following the death of Dame Myra Hess in 1965) for the majority of the critics and public, loved and admired by her fellow musicians. Her lengthy annual seasons in the United States include dozens of orchestral concerts and recitals. "I am too much in America," she says half-jokingly. "I want to make music, not the machine."

Ironically, while Alicia de Larrocha has played all over the world, she hadn't appeared in her hometown for the past seven years. "It is natural, because always the attraction is the foreigner," she says matter-of-factly, without rancor. When she returned for two concerts last April she was met by full houses and ecstatic receptions—one critic dubbed her *"una personalidad excepcional."* Playing the Chopin Second Concerto, she received an ovation even before the performance, a rare occurrence in Spain. "It is goose flesh for me to talk about it," is her only comment.

Although her recording career has produced some extraordinary documents (via Decca, Columbia and Hispavox, Epic, and now London), she is rarely happy with the results. "It's my problem, my nightmare. Recordings are the results of one moment, and, of course, I am always changing my mind and mood. When I listen, it is a different time from when I made it. I want to repeat and redo always, because every day I am different. Sometimes what I thought bad later sounds good, and vice versa. I know what I want and what I am doing, but there are things like the acoustics of the hall and the piano tone which surprise me when I listen back!" Her choice of piano, one to suit her small body and arms, is another problem, although she prefers the Steinway 55 in New York and the Hamburg Steinway for recordings. "The ones I like for a big tone are hard in action. So sometimes for big pieces with difficult technique I sacrifice tone to get an easier action."

As for the few master classes she has held in this country, she declares, "I *hate* them! In one class it is impossible to learn how to play. The first thing is to know the student and all his possibilities—and he must know his teacher too. If not, it is *inutile*. A two-week course, that is another thing. Otherwise call it a lecture of anecdotes, questions and answers, examples on the piano. But I cannot explain what I do." Whenever in London or New York for a few days the pianist generally turns up at a recital or concert. "I go because I like to hear all points of view," she states, summing up succinctly her attitude toward the keyboard and her profession.

Alicia de Larrocha's calm and lack of artistic "theatrics" are legendary. She admits that the only thing that really makes her nervous is being home with Juan and the children (Alicia, twelve, and Juan, fourteen) "when I have to practice and do *everything*. On tour I relax with my job and enjoy life with friends . . . eating, sleeping, and playing. It is a job: I am a woman going to do my thing. And, thank God, I'm a pianist, because I can eat and stay out late before a concert—I couldn't do this if I were a singer." On the night before she was to play in New York's "Mostly Mozart Festival" last August she was with friends until late, drinking wine and devouring a dish redolent with garlic. Backstage after the concert she flashed that childlike smile and winked. "You see, Mozart *likes* garlic."

★ *Placido Domingo* ★

I interviewed tenor Placido Domingo in the fall of 1972 after a spate of debuts at Covent Garden, Barcelona, Holland and the Teatro Colon in Buenos Aires, which gave him prominence in almost every opera capital of the world. In 1971 he had opened the Metropolitan season as Don Carlo for Rudolf Bing's final season as general manager, and in 1973 he again did the honors, this time in Il Trovatore. *He was already on his way to becoming the most recorded tenor, with full-length operas on RCA, Angel, Philips and Columbia.*

Backstage at the Met one cold winter morning, with the Bumbrys and Merrills and Tozzis whisking in and out, Placido Domingo resembled nothing less than an overfed teddy bear. His long, brown broadtail coat is capped by a full beaver collar which blends into his curly brown hair and swarthy complexion. And he smiles his big teddy bear smile. There is hardly an opera house, continent or country today that is without the voice and presence of the Spanish-born, Mexican-reared tenor. The world's opera houses are hungry for tenors. Of all the voice categories, the tenor is in shortest supply. In the 1960's, once beyond Corelli, Bergonzi, Tucker and Pavarotti in their various repertoires, that was it for first-rate tenor sounds. Enter Domingo, willing and able—his healthy instrument in readiness and a willingness to sing every other night of the week if need be . . . and bingo! A career was born. The more he sang, the more he was asked. And any time someone dares to look askew at his timetable, he generally retorts, "Well, when the voice goes, I'll conduct." So far, the voice has held out, and his itinerary reads like the who's who and what's what of operadom at the Met, Covent Garden, Hamburg, La Scala, Barcelona, San Francisco and the Teatro Colon.

It's a schedule to make a traveling salesman's head swim, let alone a tenor's. "Oh, yes, I hear people say that I sing too much, but I am healthy and singing well—so what else can I do? I suppose others sing as much as I do . . . but you don't hear so much about them. Even in Mexico City, where I began amid much enthusiasm, they said, 'He won't be singing next year.' And the same thing happened in Israel and at the New York City Opera. For me it's important to make it easier than it sounds. And the more I am on stage, the better I feel. If I am away for a month making records or on vacation, I feel terrible. I *have* to be among the public. I may slow down a little . . . next year," he adds, but not very convincingly. "I think it's a duty for a singer while he is at his best to let everyone around the world hear him." Spoken like a true tenor.

The thirty-one-year-old teddy bear was born in Madrid—his parents were stars of the Zarzuela Theater there, his mother a soprano and his father a baritone (and now a stage director) —but he was brought up in Mexico, where he began singing in the traditional Spanish operettas. He made his operatic debut there in 1961 as Alfredo in *La Traviata,* and that same year (he was twenty) he sang opposite Joan Sutherland in *Lucia* with the Dallas Civic Opera. He then joined the Hebrew National Opera in Tel Aviv and returned to America in 1966 to sing the title role in Ginastera's *Don Rodrigo,* a world premiere which opened the New York City Opera's first season at the New York State Theater. A year and many performances later, he joined the Hamburg State Opera, and in 1968 he made his Metropolitan Opera debut four days earlier than planned because Franco Corelli conked out of *Adriana Lecouvreur* one Saturday night at the eleventh hour. Since then it has been Verona, Milan, Vienna, Berlin, Rome and so on. By December 5, 1970, Domingo was already celebrating his 700th operatic performance!

He relates that since his parents sang, he had the bug early. He took informal lessons from his mother, but learned every day by hearing singers in person and on recordings. He then went to Carlo Morelli (a former Met baritone living in Mexico) to study interpretation. Then, in Tel Aviv, he and a colleague, Franco Iglesias, "went every day to the theater to rehearse on stage and go over each performance to find what was right and wrong. So it was a practical training." In Israel he sang mainly in Italian and French, but both *The Pearl Fishers* and *Eugen Onegin* had to be learned in Hebrew. Two and a half years there was sufficient preparation, and he wrote for auditions in New York. Julius Rudel heard him and that was it. He also recalls that in Mexico he sang one of the drunkards in *My Fair Lady* for 165 performances. "Only once was I a drunkard," he winks.

His idols have been Caruso, Gigli, Fleta, Bjoerling and Di Stefano—the latter he calls "in real life the one I feel closest to and admire. Only a few recordings do him justice, but I saw him on stage in Mexico, where he was a big idol. I did small parts in those operas." Thirty-one last January, Domingo feels that the best years for a tenor are from thirty to thirty-eight. His own voice has changed a good deal in the last year. According to him, it is "more secure, larger, darker and fuller in volume." His dream is to one day do Otello, but not for a while—at least five years, "if I get there." From there it would be Tristan in ten years, but never Tannhäuser. He's already sung Samson seven times and loves it—but now puts it in the "after Otello" category.

Domingo's repertory is mainly Italian, with some French and some German, too. Uniquely, it encompasses both lyric and dramatic roles. "I find it comfortable to combine them. If it is constantly dramatic or lyric, my throat gets tired. But even in dramatic parts you have lyric spots. The whole thing is not dramatic, and then you color what is written, too. Manrico in *Trovatore* is more lyric than dramatic—Radames in *Aida,* too. And so you have to be able to portray lyricism in these heavier parts." Asked for favorite roles, he says he has ten but will name only five: Des Grieux in *Manon Lescaut,* Andrea Chénier, Alvaro in *La Forza del Destino,* Rodolfo in *Luisa Miller* and Canio in *Pagliacci.* Rodolfo is a recent acquisition, but he finds it fantastic for acting and singing. "It is a preparation for Otello. The recitatives are not light; the substance of the role is in these big recitatives—and you need a big, dark sound with dramatic intention. The aria is lyric, but the *cabaletta* dramatic. So it is a slow preparation for Otello. But even in that role, it is not all one thing: the first act is lyric, the second dramatic, and the third and fourth both—the death is lyric with a dramatic interpretation. Pinkerton in *Butterfly* is a lyric part, but the first act is dramatic—and Rudolfo in *Bohème* gets dramatic in the third act. Don José in *Carmen* is considered a dramatic role, but two acts of it are lyric. I judge two things in choosing a role—first, if it doesn't hurt the throat, and second, if the public likes it. And at the Met you have to be selective because the public is strange. I would never do Don Ottavio in *Don Giovanni* here because it would not be appreciated. But in Vienna and Hamburg, yes, and I would have as much success with it as I do in *Forza*.

"One thing I want you to put in big eight columns across the page," he goes on non-stop. "The one thing I hate at the Met is the note in the program that the public is requested not to interrupt the music with applause. That should be destroyed. What we need is to be encouraged to applaud," he says in true tenor tradition. Another thing that bugs Domingo is too much rehearsal: "It is ridiculous to have five or six weeks of rehearsal—it is the fault of the director. Then you have just a few performances and the artist has to go. Two weeks rehearsing and ten performances is a better solution. I turn down productions because they demand six weeks of rehearsal. You get tired and at the performances you are dead! No opera, except a new one, needs more than two weeks preparation. There's too much emphasis on the director today. Sometimes you see 'the Zeffirelli *Carmen*' or 'the Visconti *Traviata*' and you can't find the name of Bizet or Verdi or the mezzo-soprano or the soprano because their names are so small!"

With the present interest in early Verdi, plus the fact that most of the middle and late works have become regular commodities in the repertoire, it is natural that the bulk of his singing is given over to Verdi. The voice of Montserrat Caballé, he finds, is the ideal Verdi sound, "with phrases sung *pianissimo* the way Verdi asked for. If the voice is too dramatic, this cannot be done. Verdi definitely wrote better for the voice than most other composers," he has decided. "He had great knowledge. I feel safer in Verdi than in any other composer. Wagner was a contemporary of Verdi's, but he makes so much of the middle voice and this is bad. Then you arrive on an A-natural with fatigue. In Verdi you use all the range, up and down—and the high notes you anticipate with pleasure. But in Wagner they are like a whole building coming down on top of you—in Verdi they are like taking off in a plane. So he is healthiest for the voice. Puccini had less knowledge of vocal technique, but a marvelous, flowing, melodic imagination. It is easier at the beginning of a career because he demands less technique—but it can ruin the voice."

Not only is Placido Domingo ubiquitous in the opera house, but in the recording studio as well. "Now I am starting to get happy about my recordings. Before I wasn't always satisfied because I lack the contact with the public." He admits he is pleased with the sound of his own voice, but not with the meaning of words and phrases: "I compare a 'live' performance with recordings and find the 'live' is much more exciting." Generally he hasn't demanded much altering of the sound levels and confesses that perhaps that's one reason why the sound of his album of duets with Sherrill Milnes is so disappointing. Now the tenor and the baritone are about to partake in this stunt of conducting for one another in an RCA album of arias. "So the first time I'll conduct will be on record, and then we'll try to do a concert. We've had offers from the Hollywood Bowl and Ravinia. I always had the idea of conducting, even before I sang—and I studied piano and conducting at the Conservatory."

While living in Mexico he met his wife Marta, who is his constant companion. "We separate weeks at the most. I could be away five months, but we break it up with three days or so here and there, somewhere along the way." Now they and their three boys live in New Jersey, but Domingo is making plans to move to Spain. "I want the boys to be educated there. There's lot of trouble here with drugs and many bad influences. I want to do the best for them and show them. We have a lot of family feeling and life together. I, too, grew up this way. We have a house in Barcelona, where I may sing three or four performances a year. But you see what it's like when I'm here in the U.S. with rehearsals, performances, interviews, photos. In Barcelona I can go home between cities for three days and just be there to take a vacation." A holiday in Domingoese is a weekend spent lying at the seaside in Spain. "I don't like long vacations . . . even if I had the time." Commenting that he and Martina Arroyo are constantly paired at the Met, at La Scala, in Buenos Aires, in Munich, in Miami, etc., he smiles, relating that the soprano told him that the best thing to do would be to share a room. "But Marta said, 'As long as we have three beds . . . and one for Emilio [Martina's husband] when he comes.' "

★ Eileen Farrell ★

Since we talked in the fall of 1970, to coincide with the soprano's appearance with Leonard Bernstein and the New York Philharmonic in scenes from Wagner's Götterdämmerung, Eileen Farrell has gone on to a teaching career at the University of Indiana at Bloomington, where she is enjoying the kind of success she still has on stage in concert and recital.

"Come on up, dear," rang out the hearty voice on the other end of the hotel house phone, and so I made my way across the coolly quiet lobby of the Regency, into the equally sedate elevator and down the chichi hallway. As the door swung open, the familiar Irish ear-to-ear grin was as dazzling as it always has been on stage and television—the manner as open and friendly as the lady-next-door. Eileen Farrell was just back from singing a program for the annual New York Philharmonic luncheon at the Waldorf—"just some Schubert and Poulenc and three arias. Twenty years ago—*more* than twenty years ago—I sang for the luncheon for the first time," she recalls. "Mrs. Lytle Hull—what a wonderful woman!—told me that was the first time she had heard me. 'I saw this girl,' she told me today, 'and I wondered if she could sing. Now I know,' " as she shrugs her shoulders with a hearty laugh. Miss Farrell's long attachment to the New York Philharmonic goes back over two decades.

In her blue-green dress, short blonde hair combed simply back, Eileen Farrell made herself comfortable in her elegantly impersonal Regency room—yet you long to see her really at home on her three acres in New Hampshire or at her "camp" in Maine, preferably over a cup of steaming coffee at the kitchen table. Nearly three decades before the public—in every conceivable medium: radio (*Eileen Farrell Presents . . .*), television (*Garry Moore Show*), concerts (Isolde to Bach), opera, film (*Interrupted Melody*)—have merely transformed a simple New England girl into a warm, simple New England lady who relishes chatting about vegetables more than about Verdi, family more than Fauré.

"Thank God I have a family!—they're all grown up now—for me this is an important part of a career . . . to maintain the balance. There's a lot more to life than just singing. You get out of balance when that is the only thing in your life. I never was like this," she shakes her head, "though I have a lot of colleagues who are. Actually, I never in this world thought I'd be a singer—it was the farthest thing from my mind. My mother and father were professionals and I had music all my life. My mother was a teacher and organist, and I just fell into it with none of those driving ambitions."

Miss Farrell was born in Willimantic, Connecticut, where she had her first lessons from her mother. Her career had its beginnings in New York in radio with a job in the CBS chorus. Her solo professional debut came, oddly enough, as "the voice of Rosa Ponselle" in a *March of Time* program. "Someone thought I sounded like her and I sang four bars of 'Home, Sweet Home.' Now we're good friends. I have a recording we made in her home in Baltimore—we were horsing around at the piano, singing and playing and forgetting all the words to everything. She's a great gal, just marvelous."

Opera she first remembers from the Saturday afternoon broadcasts—"that was the greatest thing for us and we all listened. Of course, in those days, when you're young, you don't realize who you're hearing and you don't appreciate it.

But I remember Martinelli in *Aida,* the day he collapsed on stage—we heard this and my sister began to cry because she didn't know what was happening."

In the big days of radio, the soprano began to sing as soloist on the *Songs of the Century* program, which led to her own *Eileen Farrell Presents* . . . , a half-hour program that ran for five years and became a standard on radio. In 1947 she turned to concerts and hasn't stopped since. Her long association with the New York Philharmonic goes back to Mitropoulos' tenure with the orchestra. When asked about this, she sounded genuinely surprised: "You mean you've never heard about this? Well, when Mitropoulos was conductor, the Philharmonic was hired as the stage show at the Roxy Theater and I was asked to be the singer. We did four shows a day for two weeks—I think it was the most money they ever made at the Roxy. They played music with lots of life, nothing too serious. The first week I sang 'Un bel dì' and 'The Last Rose of Summer,' which I did with a harp. I'm not kidding you—the harp was on 50th Street and I stood on 51st Street—that was one long piece of stage! I did 'The Last Rose' because the movie was *Black Rose.* The second week I did only 'Pace, pace, mio Dio,' and believe it or not, even after four shows a day, I didn't hate Verdi. Later at the Philharmonic I did the *Choëphores* of Milhaud with Mitropoulos. I think I'm the only singer who has ever done so much with the orchestra—*Messiahs, Missa solemnis,* Beethoven Ninths and what else? . . . ," the voice trailed off.

Since her Roxy days, she has been an almost annual guest with the Philharmonic, including opening night at Lincoln Center in September of 1962. For the Orchestra's 125th anniversary concert in December of 1967 she sang "Ozean, du Ungeheuer" from Weber's *Oberon,* and for two seasons she has sung Wagner excerpts under Bernstein's baton—Act I of *Die Walküre* in 1968 and scenes from *Tristan und Isolde* in 1969. [In 1970 she added scenes from *Götterdämmerung.*] "You know, I've never sung a complete Wagner opera on stage *or* in concert. For a long time I felt I wasn't ready to do it because I am not a Wagnerian soprano—you really need stamina for these roles. I was not a Wagnerian voice, I felt, and I did not want to ruin my voice. Now I can't imagine doing Wagner without Lenny—he makes it so beautiful. Every time I've heard Wagner I thought it sounded so cut-and-dried, but he stresses the emotions and the words. Today, I'm not worried about the stamina, but as for singing Wagner on stage, I haven't thought about it."

Though the Farrell career goes back to the early Forties and concert appearances began in 1947, it wasn't until 1955 that she ventured into the world of opera and made her operatic debut in Tampa, Florida, as Santuzza in *Cavalleria Rusticana*. In 1958 she opened the San Francisco season as Cherubini's *Medea*, which she also sang for the American Opera Society. Finally, in December of 1960 came her long-awaited, and long-overdue, Metropolitan Opera debut as Gluck's Alceste. Her Met career lasted a mere five seasons in such roles as Santuzza, Maddalena in *Andrea Chénier*, La Gioconda and Leonora in *La Forza del Destino*—rather shocking considering the current dearth of true dramatic sopranos.

"Frankly," she shrugged, "I don't know what happened. When Bing finally asked me to come to do *Alceste*, he told me he had read in all my publicity that I had never been asked —'So now I'm asking,' he said. The strange thing is that before that I had refused to do Marie in *Wozzeck*, and he *hates* people who refuse. I suppose my biggest fault is that I'm an American singer. At one point after my debut he said he would see if a foreign singer would relinquish some performances to me, and I told him, 'Don't bother!' When the Met moved to the new house, Bing wrote my manager and said he had nothing for me. I asked only that my name be removed from the roster, and that was that.

"Of course, many singers *do* play ball with him, they go along with whatever the management wants. Then what happens? After a few seasons they're in vocal trouble, because they'll do anything they're asked to do, right or wrong, just to stay with the company. He uses people with no regard for human dignity. This is terribly important—after all, the house is going because you're singing there. You must stoop very low if your dignity is taken away. I'm just not constituted that way."

Yes, certainly, she misses the operatic stage, but what time she gives to music is filled with orchestral concerts and recitals.

"I don't tour, really. I generally go out for a few dates and come home. And I try not to do that much each season and would like to cut down even more. You know, I'm now in my thirtieth year in this business. It's not that I haven't enjoyed it, but I would like to let down and enjoy life for my RE-MAINING YEARS," she proclaimed with mock heroics. "I don't sing at all in the summer. As soon as school closes, we pack up and spend three months at Lake Moosehead in Maine, where we have a big house on a huge lake with a boat house and five boats—I think it's the largest lake within one state in the country. We even spent one Christmas there and it was marvelous with the snow and dry cold.

"I like to fish, but I don't have to catch any to enjoy it—not like some people who are f-u-r-i-o-u-s if they don't get any. I also golf a lot—no, I'm not in the least good, but I have a marvelous time. Just to get out on the course and swat the ball —I love that sound. When I go to the driving range at the beginning of the season, my husband is smacking the balls with all his might, really working himself up. I tell him just to relax and enjoy it and not to try so hard. But he puts so much energy into everything he does." The husband in question is ex-policeman Robert Reagan.

"Next year," she sighed, "my daughter goes off to college and I tell my husband we'll have the rest of our life alone—to fight! Robby is 22 and a lieutenant in the Air Force. He's a big six-foot-three, and he finished school at the University of New Hampshire after three years at Fordham. Kathy is 16 and a senior in high school. Right now she's picking out a college—she wants medicine and Georgetown and nothing else. Oh, she's active and smart, and into everything. In the Manchester newspaper the other day was published a list of the five highest honors in her high school and she was one of two girls. She's also assistant manager for the senior play— they're doing *Connecticut Yankee*," she smiled. "She's also a basketball manager and in the French Club and National Honor Society and, let's see, what else. . . . We lived on Staten Island for a long time and then on 62nd Street for three years—my husband told me he was going to build me a tunnel right into Bloomingdale's. What a f-a-n-t-a-s-t-i-c place. But the city's not fun any more—it's all aggravation.

My husband is retired and now we don't have to live here, so we have what you call 'residential country living' in a ranch house on three acres in New Hamphire. The air is marvelous up where we are—now I can't breathe when I come into the city. Tomorrow I'm spending *all* day at Bloomingdale's. . . ."

When she was told that she is one of the few opera-concert singers with real naturalness and good spontaneous fun on her frequent TV exposures—one particular delight was the night she sang "The Big Spender" with Carol Burnett and Marilyn Horne—she winked, "Either you got it or you don't! But I grew up in radio with my own program, and I would fill in for a guest on the Sinatra show or in any spot for the network. I never did the blues in public, though, before Spoleto in 1959 —only at parties, where my resistance was very low. I was there for a Verdi *Requiem* and a recital, and Ed Sullivan came to tape Louis Armstrong for his show. Armstrong got pneumonia from staying in Gian Carlo's unheated palace and they asked me to fill in. It took two days just to get up enough courage. I sang 'On the Sunny Side of the Street' and three records followed.

"I'd love to do a Broadway show, too, but then I think of those eight shows a week—we're not schooled that way. I'd love to do the mother in *Gypsy*—isn't that a great show? I was called for a new show based on the early life of the Marx Brothers. I thought it wasn't for me now . . . but you never know. I just read that Shelley Winters is doing it," she offered. "The other day when I got here, someone said, 'So, you're having a new TV series,' and I said 'Marvelous'—they even knew the name of it, *At Home with Eileen Farrell,* because it was somewhere in the columns. I told them to just keep saying it and maybe it would happen.

"You know, the columns also reported I had broken my leg. Well, I *did* have an accident and this is actually the first day I haven't had a pill or any pain. I was in California to open the Los Angeles Symphony season in the Beethoven Ninth and I was visiting someone. On a step this high," she motioned, "I lost my balance and fell the wrong way. I picked myself up and sang the two performances and then flew to Denver for a concert. But suddenly the pain came and I was in the hospital in a brace. In the fall I had torn muscles in my back

—it was absolute agony. Usually you cancel because of laryngitis or voice problems, but my voice was in top shape and I had to cancel Denver, Calgary, Edmonton and some other dates. It was a real doozey. When I flew home, I stood all the way to Boston, because sitting was too painful. I couldn't pick up anything off the floor and don't you think I dropped e-v-e-r-y-t-h-i-n-g!"

Barely pausing for the next breath, she asked, "Do you like to cook?" Having found a comrade, her eyes sparkled and she charged on: "I love to experiment, don't you? I just found a dish that is marvelous: stuffed cabbage cooked in one big pot. First you line the pot with sauerkraut, then with browned spare ribs, see. Then the cabbage is stuffed with chopped meat and rice and spices and is put on top. Then more sauerkraut and *then* tomatoes—then you cook the whole mess for three hours. And t-h-e-n you pour sour cream over it all. Couldn't you die?

"My husband is a marvelous cook—he had Irish *and* Italian parents. So we make our own pasta and bread. You see—we never should have started this. We're a cooking family. Both my son and daughter cook—I think it's important to be able to do all these things. It's a real outlet—people should be ashamed to say that they can't cook."

An hour with Eileen Farrell convinces the visitor of one thing: life for her is good, and it radiates from every pore. "Yes, it really is. In this crazy, mixed-up world I am thankful for so many things. Why complain, it could be a lot worse, too. Around Thanksgiving time I heard people being interviewed on the radio—ah, some are so stupid. One man, however, was asked what he was thankful for and he said, 'I'm thankful just to be able to say I'm thankful.' That's me."

★ Carlo Maria Giulini ★

I recall sitting huddled with Carlo Maria Giulini in the coffee shop of the Barbizon-Plaza Hotel one warm Saturday morning during the 1968 visit of the Rome Opera to the Metropolitan, during which the Italian maestro led a memorable Le Nozze di Figaro. *The next December he returned to make his New York Philharmonic debut, and he has since been an annual New York visitor with the Philadelphia Orchestra, as well as Chicago's principal guest conductor.*

Carlo Maria Giulini is that kind of *rara avis*—a man completely devoted to his art, the art of music. With modesty bordering on self-effacement ("A conductor is a servant of the servants of music," he seems to say on the podium), with remarkable and scrupulous dedication, with total and genuine involvement, Giulini has toweringly stood apart from the new breed of young maestros who have doggedly sought the public eye, the glamorous milieu, the "career at any cost."

"I am a man," he offers with disarming simplicity. "I love very much the human being. Playing music is the love approach. I suffer very much in music, but I try to do as best I can. All my life I have been completely in the music, I have dedicated to the music all my spirit, all my human experience. And I give all my love to it."

The tall, aristocratic Giulini points to the past for the seeds of his musical involvement and philosophy. Born in Basletta on the Adriatic in 1914, he studied composition and viola at the Accademia di Santa Cecilia in Rome. From the start, music meant hard labor. While still a Conservatorio student during the mid-1930s, he joined the old Augusteo Orchestra in Rome as a violist. During the Augusteo season, he would

get up at six and do counterpoint exercises as prelude to five
and a half hours of orchestral rehearsal, his schedule being
rounded off by hours of solo practice and string-quartet sessions with student friends.

"I had the great luck," he recalls, "to play in Rome under
the great conductors of a great generation—all except Toscanini, who was in America at that time. I played under Walter,
Furtwängler, Klemperer, Strauss, Mengelberg, Kleiber, as well
as with all the great soloists, too. I still have the sound of
Horowitz in my head, the notes with life and blood in them—
how they came out physically and plastically *degli spiriti,* full
of vitality. And Huberman—one of the great experiences of
my life. That is to say that my generation had the great chance
and happiness to live *in* an orchestra, to sit in the chairs and
do it physically, not just to listen to rehearsals of an orchestra
—but physically to play and feel oneself involved. It was fascinating, for instance, to play Brahms under all these different
men, to see how the same problems were handled by Walter
or Sabata." Bruno Walter and Klemperer are those he remembers best; they taught him much he would never otherwise
have learned as quickly, if at all, about that element in music
on which all the rest depends: form—through which a great
freedom and warmth of expression can then shine.

Later, he finally did meet Maestro Toscanini, when he returned to Italy after the war and settled in Milan. Giulini,
then director of the Milan Radio Orchestra, was literally on
the elder's doorstep. As did many other cultivated Italians,
Giulini looked upon Toscanini as a sort of god—and he never
worked up the courage to approach him. But in March of
1951, Giulini conducted a broadcast of Haydn's long-fallow
Il mondo della luna. Two days later, he received a call from
Wally Toscanini, the Countess Castelbarco, who told him her
father had heard the broadcast and was very pleased, and
that he wanted to meet the young maestro. He was greeted by
wide-flung arms and a smile under the bristling moustache.
He said, among other things, that before the broadcast he
had not known a note of *Il mondo,* but he was sure Giulini's
handling of the score had been right in all ways—tempo,
dynamics, style, characterization, the lot. The friendship, or
disciple-guru relationship, which began that day ended only

with Toscanini's death in 1957. "It was an unforgettable experience, because I knew the man Arturo Toscanini, and I tried to drink in all his experience in all kinds of music. He was a marvelous speaker and talker with an unbelievable memory of the past. I didn't lose one minute to put questions and get answers."

What Maestro Giulini evolved out of all this early experience was a truly international perspective of music. Today, he emphasizes, "I don't believe in iron curtains between Italy or Austria or Germany or Russia. Regionalism in art is lost. A few years ago in Venice, at a modern art exhibit, I saw works that resembled one another from Mexico, Europe and so on. Styles were interchanged, not bound by nations. Before, yes, we had very different customs, architecture, characteristics in each country. But now, when you fly into an airport, you don't know where you are—Tokyo or Rome or New York. When I drive from Rome to Milan, I pass through Umbria, Assisi, Tuscany, Siena, Emilia, Bologna, Parma—each town and each region not so long ago had its very different clothes, habits, customs, food, language, as well as landscape. Now, in Japan the girls are wearing mini-skirts.

"Great art," he firmly believes, "is universal, for everyone. In each person's interpretation, his human and cultural and practical experience comes out. But there is no reason that an American can't conduct Verdi and Schubert as he does Copland and Bernstein, though he will give a different spirit in interpretation. I think the great art, music, is for all humanity and forever. True, society and humanity are always changing. It is not the same today as during the 16th and 17th centuries —we eat and think differently now. As for musical performance, we don't know how they did it, except by theory. Generally, they performed very badly, I'm sure. If we heard their performances, we would be shocked—and if composers like Beethoven and Rossini could hear ours today, they would be very happy.

"Yes, I think there exist styles—you definitely cannot play Bach as you do Brahms. But I don't think it is right to try to make a museum of the music. Of course, if you have a medieval or Gothic statue, it is *there*—but music lives out of performance: performance is life. I deeply believe that the first element in performance is life and love. And, then, I think it is important to have much experience and knowledge about the history of the time of the music to go with this. A letter of Mozart's, for instance, tells how he would be happy to have an orchestra of 100 violins, or that although Bach's possibilities were small for the orchestra in the B-minor Mass, the music itself is big like the world."

The conductor has carefully weighed these problems of style over the years, but he relishes two tales that prove his point. Wilhelm Furtwänger was in Paris with the Berlin Philharmonic on tour, and at the first concert he played a Bach suite. "The next day there was a great scandal—everyone said that this was not Bach but Romantic playing. At a press conference, he was asked about this polemic of style and replied: 'I think when an audience doesn't go to sleep, they think the style is wrong.' If a performance is not boring, they say the style is wrong.

"Hindemith (an unbelievable man and talent, a beautiful mind and music) used to perform concerts in Germany. Once he started rehearsing Bach with a famous orchestra and the strings played all *staccato,* with no vibrato, and no dynamics, only between *mezzo piano* and *mezzo forte.* After five minutes, he stopped and asked them for a more beautiful sound and sonority. The leader said he was very sorry but 'we come from the direct Bach tradition and this is the style, this is the right way.' Hindemith paused, then commented that this was very interesting. 'But I don't know how, with no vibrato, Bach could have so many sons,' " and a broad smile sweeps across Giulini's face.

"Man," he continues, "always loved, laughed, suffered, enjoyed, was desperate and so on all through history. And this is so today—it is the problem of generations and was true three thousand years ago. You can see this is the same with the birds in Central Park. The expression is different in the Mozart G-minor or *Tristan and Isolde* or the B-minor 'Agnus Dei' and the Beethoven *Missa solemnis* 'Crucifixus'—but the sentiment that dictated them came from the same need to express a great emotion. The human problems are always there in the heart. And I think it is terribly dangerous if style and tradition are put into an iron vest. They must be allowed to breathe, to move, with no rigid rules."

To amplify his point further, he dramatizes a black period in his career when he began to conduct after the war. He led the first concert in Rome after the liberation, in the Teatro Adriana, his very first concert after years of study. "Right after, they asked me for more concerts at Santa Cecilia, and they asked me to perform the six *Brandenburg* Concertos. I said I was not yet ready, that this music had great problems and I was too young and with too little experience to play this great music. I resisted, they insisted. They sent a musician, Giulio Augusti—a fine and intelligent man whom I respected and admired—and he said to me, 'Look, after all the terrible unrest and unsettling in Italy, after all this, it is not allowed for you to think this. The people need music and to start to believe again. You are a musician—you must do it and take the risk. You must do it for the man who needs music." Giulini himself had spent months in hiding as a political dissentient during the Nazi occupation of Italy.

"I said I would do it, and then I said to myself that Bach is in the sky," and he reaches high above his head with a firm, but graceful, movement. "I am nothing, just a small stone. I am on the knee of Bach to adore. When I conducted the music, I tried to do it with *more* than respect—the 'do-not-touch' approach. Then I realized that I had killed this music, because all the respect and thinking should be in the preparation and the study. In the performance you have to *be* the composer: 'This is *my* music, part of my body—it belongs to *me*.'

"Since then (1945), the next time I conducted Bach was only last year when I did the B-minor Mass. I had a bad conscience, such deep *dolor* that I did this to Bach. I had not the courage to love Bach and to give him myself out of the respect and study. I did him this bad service by not giving my heart to him. When I finally did the B-minor in Edinburgh, I worked very deeply on it, stopping all activities for three months to prepare it. At the first rehearsal, I told the orchestra and chorus that we will perform one of the high points in music—and that I want the audience not to *admire* this work, but to *love* it!"

Carlo Maria Giulini, who is counted among the greatest opera conductors of our time, has applied the same kind of deep, painstaking and demanding habits to this area of his work—with results that have aroused the anticipation and excitement few other operatic maestros have brought to their work since Sabata and Toscanini. After a long series of brilliant operatic productions under his baton at La Scala, Rome, Covent Garden and elsewhere on the Continent, he announced his decision to desert the operatic stage for the concert platform. "I say maybe, not forever or always—these words are not for man. But I will stop now for four or five years and do only concerts. 'Why' is delicate to say. First of all, I feel that I need a period of change. I was born into symphonic and concert music and grew up in this. I came to opera only later, after I had begun to conduct. Now I feel I need a period to concentrate on symphonic music. Yet I love the human voice and the great masterpieces written for it, the requiems and masses and so on—and these I will do. So there will still be the voices and chorus for me.

"But for my personal feeling, two composers who completely realized the idea of combining the text, music and action are Mozart and Verdi," two composers who have all but dominated Giulini's operatic endeavors, wherever he has agreed to collaborate on a new production. "Today, it is possible to have a very good Mozart cast—but it is almost impossible to have really the right Verdi cast. The real Verdi singers with stature are so few and they are so engaged and have so much to sing everywhere that it is hard to cast a Verdi opera with the *complete* right cast—not just one or two—and to have enough rehearsal and preparation work, too. I am not ready to accept the idea that an opera performance should be less prepared than a symphonic concert, because there is no reason for this. A singer must do a Mozart or Verdi opera with the same attitude as he does the Mozart or Verdi Requiem. Too often in Verdi opera you must accept compromises. I suffer too much this way. I try, but I can't. I must be happy with myself and my work. It is true that music is too great to be happy in it—you *must* suffer. But I cannot be too unhappy in it!"

Giulini, too, has found problems in the operatic productions themselves. At Milan's La Scala, where he was permanent maestro for four historic years as the immediate successor to Sabata, he fought for the importance of production and direction. "Today, there is a new generation, and it is a great mistake if opera does not follow the development of acting and the visual thing that has happened in movies and theater. We do not go to the theater or movies and still see old-fashioned actors and sets of 80 years ago. We don't accept this," and his arms spring out in semaphoric gestures to demonstrate. "I was one of the conductors who fought to give great importance to the scenery and production in opera."

This fight for a complete and overall conception led to significant collaborations with Luchino Visconti (whose production of *Marriage of Figaro* was seen here with the visiting Rome Opera) and Franco Zeffirelli. With Visconti he created a highly controversial *Traviata* at La Scala with Maria Callas in 1953, as well as an impressive *Don Carlo* (1958) and *Trovatore* (1963) at Covent Garden. His work with Zeffirelli has encompassed Rossini's *Cenerentola* and *L'Italiana in Algeri,* as well as Verdi's *Falstaff.* "Visconti was born into the melodrama atmosphere. He used to breathe the air of melodrama in the family box at Scala. I always was very close to him and happy in our work. Zeffirelli—a good friend and someone I admire for his talent and knowledge—is now, like many others, going too far. These designers and directors don't have enough confidence in the music. They think they will help the music, that Mozart and Verdi are not enough. They do things to support an aria, because they don't believe it stands on its own.

"It has happened, I'm afraid, that this generation is getting all its intellectual experiences only through looking. People want to *see* rather than read a good story or play. Everything is visual. The young generation places too much emphasis on the eye, on what they can see, and not enough attention on words and music. Television and the cinema have affected the young producers, who now pander more to action than to anything else. They have forgotten that in opera the actions have to be done to music. The visual part has become so important that the music of *Traviata,* for example, becomes like movie music—a comment, not the central issue. Some producers take the libretto and disregard the composer, so they can do what they want with the work."

He calls to mind a day before the dress rehearsal of a new *Don Giovanni* at the Holland Festival a few years ago—the moment he saw that the director and designer had not altered things he had felt were wrong during previous rehearsals. "I called the director, Peter Diamand, and said that the producer and designer go or I go. He said they would, because this is a musical theater. We performed the opera in costumes with lights and curtains and no scenery—and we created a terrible scandal. But this simplest way is possibly the best, since it puts the light on the music."

Still another problem he cannot adjust to in opera is "the idea of routine." After the third or fourth or fifth performance, the singers and orchestra start to go a little easy, too confident. "I hate routine with all my strength. Every time you touch the music, it is the *most* important time—rehearsals, premiere, later performances, final performance. Each one is always the best. I tell my cast that we begin now and the performances are steps going up, and each night it is more difficult. It can never be a quiet life in music—if you want this, go on a vacation to the country instead."

Giulini has had the courage to pick and choose only what he has desired in Europe's opera centers, demanding always a new production with his choice of cast and never a production already in the repertory. He has felt the importance of maintaining the idea of an ensemble opera, despite the fact that singers of high standards are few and hard to fix to one place. "Ideally, opera should be a unity of three elements: text, action and music—this is in the composition. In performance it must be the same thing—drama, production and music—and this I have demanded.

"So now I stop opera for a few years. If, after this parenthesis, I feel differently, I will go back. I like opera very much because I like the human being and the people who live on stage—Eboli, Iago, Leporello—and their psychology. The interpretation of genius is fascinating, but I need the right men. If I then have the opportunity of the right cast and time and people to do opera here and there, I will think again. I do not say 'never'—that is ridiculous. One work I have in my dreams is *Otello*, but I don't know if ever. It is very difficult. The roles are so great, what Verdi did is so great—this is the problem. For some operas you can accept a voice of not absolute beauty—if it is well used and he is an artist and interpreter, it will work. But for Verdi you need all this *plus* the essential sound. It is the same thing as trying to use a clarinet in place of a trumpet—you can't substitute."

As Maestro Giulini insists, it is primarily the orchestral sound on which he turns his efforts in this next phase of an already distinguished career. He has been Principal Guest Conductor of the Chicago Symphony (where he made his American debut in the fall of 1955 at the invitation of the late Fritz Reiner). On record he has finished the four Brahms symphonies and is at work—though in no hurry to complete—the nine Beethoven symphonies. Will he consider a full-time musical directorship? "No, I don't like this too much, being in the same place. I have no talent in administration and organization. I want to think of music only. I have lived like a bear for many years, isolated with my music." And so it is likely to remain.

★ Gary Graffman ★

After more than twenty-five years before the public, Gary Graffman remains one of America's busiest pianists, playing annually with all the leading orchestras and on the most prestigious concert series, as well as covering the world. This 1967 interview coincided with a "Great Performers" recital and the world premiere of Benjamin Lees' Second Concerto with the Boston Symphony.

Talking with Gary Graffman is a little like imbibing the profusion of the Victorian, Eastern and Near Eastern *objets* that fill his spacious 57th Street co-op apartment. Considerations of Beethoven or Prokofiev are interspersed with a galloping enthusiasm for painted scrolls of the Ming Dynasty . . . at the far left of his living room, a 17th century Chinese rooster drawing looms above twin ebony grand pianos stacked with Beethoven sonatas and works of Granados. In a word, Graffman's way of life, like his musical taste and repertory, is eclectic—in the very best sense of the word.

As is often the case, one can be easily misled in an attempt to reach conclusions about an artist, even when given the known quantities of his background, his teachers, and what he has put on record. With American-born Gary Graffman, the assumption is generally that of a Russian orientation: his parents are Russian, he spoke Russian even before English, he studied with Isabelle Vengerova (a pupil of Leschetizky) at the Curtis Institute and with Vladimir Horowitz in New York, and he has recorded major works of Tchaikovsky, Rachmaninoff and Prokofiev. But he counters with the fact that much of recorded music happens "for a lot of reasons, many of them non-musical. Several recordings, in fact, include works by Haydn, Brahms and Paganini. And I play Scarlatti, Beethoven, Schumann, Mendelssohn, Schubert, Chopin and Lees."

The mention of Benjamin Lees was a reminder that Graffman played the world premiere of that composer's Second Piano Concerto with the Boston Symphony. "I learned to know his music through his First Piano Concerto and was about to add it to my repertory when I had to put everything aside to learn the Tchaikovsky Second for the recording. When I received the Ford Grant to commission a solo work, I asked Lees to write a piano sonata which I played on the Ford recital at the Metropolitan Museum in 1964 and again last season at Carnegie Hall, as well as many places in this country, South America and New Zealand. So now he has written a Second Piano Concerto for me, a concerto which is characterized by constantly changing rhythmic figurations. By electronic and aleatoric music standards of today, it will be considered conservative. But, influenced by Prokofiev and Bartók, he writes marvelously for the piano, and few contemporary composers can do this."

One work Graffman has made a specialty of in the past few

seasons is Tchaikovsky's Second Piano Concerto. Four years ago, Schuyler Chapin (then A & R man at Columbia Records) suggested several works for the pianist's contemplation, among which was the rarely-heard Tchaikovsky Second, known primarily as the music for George Balanchine's *Ballet Imperial*—and about this work Chapin was insistent. "I first saw the score in Paris, read it through many times and liked it—but I decided I would only learn it when I had the time. In the meantime, a recording session was tentatively set up with the Philadelphia Orchestra, I learned the Concerto, and it was then discovered that there would also be room for the one-movement Third Concerto, which is full of solo cadenzas," he smiles enthusiastically.

"At that time, I tried to get other orchestras to program the Second, to try it out before the recording. Most of them knew only the popular First Concerto and were reluctant, but a few showed interest. Now, since the recording has been out, all the orchestras which didn't show an adventurous spirit are anxious to have me play it." This season alone he will be playing it no less than twenty times, including the Cleveland premiere of the work which was written in 1879. The pert Mrs. Graffman, Naomi, has something less than a musical recollection of the period of her husband's work on the Concerto: "I was scraping the walls then, and I still smell paint remover at certain passages."

The handsome, high-ceilinged, white paint-and-panelled apartment, which the couple has occupied for five years, is predominantly the product of said paint remover and the hand labors of Naomi Graffman who relates that "The uncovering of the fireplace at the end of the living room was only the beginning. Once you begin, it's like a disease which spreads all over the apartment." "Many of the antiques," the pianist adds, "are from Philadelphia. In fact, one day last spring I remember that between sessions with two of my students there came a call for me to come immediately to a certain shop near by. And there was Naomi, who had found a chandelier we had been looking for. I paid the bill and rushed back to classes."

Teaching for Gary Graffman began only a little over a year ago at the Philadelphia Musical Academy. "Two years ago they pounced on me while I was in town playing with the Philadelphia Orchestra. They asked me if I were interested and I decided to take a chance, even though I had had no experience. A flexible schedule had to be worked out to fit the peculiar needs of my yearly tours. My five students [all girls, at present] are good enough in theory so that if I disappear for a while, they are all right. During September, for instance, I had a free month and taught four times—then I went away for three weeks."

One other specification he made in his teaching is a long lesson of two hours per pupil, which he feels is the only way for the proper warm-up and for working on major pieces. "I find I am learning a great deal from this experience. When I learn a Beethoven sonata, I do things instinctively. But with a student, you must explain *why* you do it this way. It helps me to re-evaluate the ways of doing things, to question the ways. Although it is not true today, in the past it was completely normal to teach and play. Liszt (to name the most successful) all the way to Schnabel and Hofmann did this. They gave concerts, taught students and composed, too. In Russia, all the artists teach a part of each year in the conservatories of Moscow and Leningrad."

As a teacher and a performer, Graffman tries to succeed on the premise that you must give the composer credit by doing what he wanted. "In the end, when you are onstage playing, you should sound as if you are composing the music —it should have spontaneity. Anyone with talent and training knows that, of course, you cannot play a slow movement of a Mozart sonata in the style of Liszt; but within the certain limits of every piece, there is the freedom for the personality of each interpreter to emerge—even in works like Beethoven's late sonatas, where he wrote in every bar what he wanted in terms of dynamics and phrasing. One mistake an artist can make is that when he is learning he will do things that are not in the music, things that he has heard others do or believed to be right. We can be tempted to copy rather than looking into the music itself. Even a great artist can have a lapse; he may give a bad performance which others mistakenly pick up as the 'right way.' Maybe that is the definition of tradition: the last bad performance, as Toscanini said. So it is crucial for any performer to begin with the music first."

As far as repertory is concerned, he states simply, "I don't specialize. A great performance of a Chopin ballade by someone impresses me no less than a great performance of a Bach partita. But in judging the Leventritt Piano Competitions over the years, I think I can speak for all the judges when I say this too: if someone comes and does something magnificent with Ravel's *Gaspard de Nuit* and plays a Mozart sonata only adequately, we will look for a third piece in that artist's stronger area. It is enough if he can play superbly in that one area. For myself, I think it is difficult to pick at all ends of the repertory, but whenever I have time I work at the weakest link."

Graffman's penchant for programming three major works for an evening, he notes as being symptomatic of what has been happening in concerts in the past few years. "When I began twenty years ago, a program always had many short pieces with one, or maybe two, large works. There were always fights between artists and management about programs for tours. Twenty years ago, if someone played Schumann's *Carnaval,* he was advised to play a cut version—and for some artists this was impossible. When William Kapell was playing the Copland Sonata, it was a rarity, but not today. The situation has improved and audiences have graduated. I like to begin with something short—for latecomers and the noise, but also for me to warm up. It is not unnatural to take five or ten minutes to warm up, and I'd rather do it with brief pieces than with the beginning of a long work."

The musical atmosphere of performing and teaching, in which Gary Graffman is now immersed, can be traced back to his father Vladimir, who had been a violin student of Leopold Auer at the Imperial Conservatory in St. Petersburg, had become Auer's assistant in New York and eventually a well-known pedagogue in his own right. At the age of three Gary was given a small violin, but because of his difficulty in handling the instrument at that age, he was encouraged to acquire his musical training at the piano—and, at the age of seven, he auditioned as a pianist at Philadelphia's Curtis Institute (where Josef Hofmann was director), after which he was

awarded a scholarship for study under the late Mme. Vengerova. At seventeen, three appearances with Eugene Ormandy
and the Philadelphia Orchestra launched his career; and, in
1949, as winner of the Leventritt Award, he made his debut
with the New York Philharmonic. While in his early 20's he
worked intensively with Vladimir Horowitz in New York,
and in the summers of 1952 and '53 he studied the chamber-
music repertory with Rudolf Serkin at the Marlboro Festival.

Guidance by these illustrious musicians seemed obviously
an outgrowth of the younger musician's admiration for them.
Today, he admits, "I don't admire all that many, and those I
do represent ,contrasting points of view. Early in life I was
drawn to Hofmann, Rachmaninoff and Schnabel, and they
stood for completely different points of view. Among living
pianists, there are Horowitz, Serkin, Rubinstein and Richter.
I suppose it's that somebody has to be completely convincing
in what he does, and that is, in effect, what makes an artist."
As for his own artistry and formidable technique, he does
not deliberately work at any one facet of his playing, such as
tone or pedaling. "I work for everything, even though certain
things may emerge, and critics will point to these as being
typical of my style—it's bound to happen. I don't believe that
an artist consciously strives for what he is known for, even
though each musician *does* have his individual point of view."

Graffman's frequent tours abroad, begun in South America
in 1955, have taken him throughout Europe, Asia, Australia
and Africa—with his first visit to the Soviet Union on tap
for this spring. These trips, as well as his yearly American
travels, have yielded the varied and extensive art and antique
collection over the past dozen years—a Tiki from Maui, a
Dutch armoire which houses the pianist's scores, a fifth-cen-
tury Greek amphora, an Indian temple sculpture, a Louis-
Philippe desk complete with secret drawers, to name only a
few. It was on a recent trip to the Philippines that he made a
major acquisition to his Oriental porcelain collection: 105
pieces found in an ancient Chinese burial site, some three
hours outside Manila. Thirty to forty of these pieces, he
claims, are of first-class, museum quality. "The Philippines
were under Chinese rule during the Sung Dynasty, from the
tenth to the sixteenth century. Through some good friends in

Manila, I was taken to this newly-discovered burial site. The diggers would clear a hole and sell the entire contents at once—so to get one interesting piece, you had to take five others."

A large glass case houses this sea-green celadon ware which dates back to the tenth and eleventh centuries. Some are rare covered jars, others are open dishes for cosmetics and sauces. "My interest in Oriental art actively began about five years ago. That North Chinese, Ming Dynasty painting over the fireplace was the first painting I bought—then I got the bug and went berserk. Two years ago I bought four works from an auction of the collection of Senator Green of Rhode Island: these Chinese and Japanese silk or rice paper paintings are my main interest. All of ours are on display, but in the proper Chinese household, the greater part of the collection was kept carefully rolled, and a few choice scrolls were hung for a few weeks at a time. These were taken down periodically and others put in their place. Like the seasons, the artwork of the home was constantly changing, and it was then possible for the occupants to enjoy each painting without tiring of it. This is one reason, too, that some scrolls over five hundred years old can look almost new today."

One of the prides of the Graffman household is a fascinating 27-foot horizontal, allegorical scroll of dozens of turtles dancing, eating, drinking saki and fighting. "In Japan, you know, turtles bring good luck and long life; a turtle symbolizes 1000 years of good life. And that crane at the end means 5000 years good life." Turtles and cranes notwithstanding, Gary Graffman is clearly leading the "good life."

★ Guarneri Quartet ★

Interviewing four men at one time must be the ultimate challenge, especially without a tape recorder—and especially if they are the men of the Guarneri Quartet. This interview with the irrepressible subjects took place during the summer of 1970 at the time of their appearances with the then newly-formed Chamber Music Society of Lincoln Center.

On a blistering Indian-summer day the windows high over Riverside Drive are thrown open to whatever breeze may find its way off the Hudson River. The Brahms First Quartet sits closed on the four music stands huddled close to the windows. The huge, disarranged black-and-white-tile floored apartment is the scene of instruments being carefully packed away after a morning rehearsal. The goateed violinist John Dalley is on the phone in one corner. Host Arnold Steinhardt (violin)—in whose apartment the Guarneri Quartet gathers daily to practice—leads a quick tour: The patchwork quilt on the bed in the far corner is from Vermont, as is the pine sea chest next to it and the throw rugs on the floor—"Oh, they were woven by Vermont nomads," he laughs. On the walls is a catholic gathering of posters, a small Miró, a Japanese silk drawing and two decorative works of Carol Summers—"Yes, he's alive and well in New York City. . . . I'd like to sell *all* of it. I'm tired of it now," Steinhardt offers half jokingly. In the midst of the general confusion sits a girl sketching in oil crayons. She is silent and unruffled throughout, but eventually she is revealed to be pianist Samuel Sanders' wife Rhoda, who has been coming daily to sketch the apartment and its musicians.

The men in question are what might politely be called "elusive," protagonists in a collage-like conversation. There

is not much the Guarneri Quartet agrees on, whether it be
Lady Bird Johnson, Pat Nixon, the width of current neckwear,
their own "in" jokes—except music. "Sometimes we can't
even agree on whether or not we disagree," says violist
Michael Tree. "We're the only democracy extant—that's why
we argue so much," cellist David Soyer offers. "No, it's not
the tie vote in decisions that's the problem—it's the three to
one," Tree smiles. "Then the minority feels ostracized and
doesn't give up for years and years. Actually, it all boils
down to a race problem—John's the only Midwesterner and
the only *goy* in the group." General amusement.

The Guarneri Quartet was formed at Vermont's Marlboro
Festival in 1965 at the suggestion of the Budapest Quartet's
second violinist, Alexander Schneider—its name was sup-
plied by Budapest violist Boris Kroyt, who had once played
with a European quartet called the Guarneri, after the 18th-
century Italian violin-maker. "It was really an accident,"
Dalley leads off. "It was a matter of finding people you respect
musically, finding personalities that get along," Steinhardt
comes back more seriously. "We were lucky, we didn't re-
cruit players. We were all known quantities. Three of us
had studied together and played together. Then we met David
at Marlboro, and he had played trios with John. It emanated
out of that." Michael Tree, the violist, was originally a violinist.
"I had an operation: I went to Denmark and became a . . .
a trans-instrumentalist," he rears back laughing. "Actually, I
had to put up a fight because we had three fiddlers and one
cellist—but I wanted to experience the other." "Maybe we
should reconsider," another chimes in.

The four players hasten to acknowledge the influence of the
long-prominent Budapest Quartet, but if you mention that the
Guarneri seems to create a warmer, more homogenous sound
as opposed to the four more contrasting personalities of the
Budapest, they are quick to disagree. "On recordings," Tree
volunteers, "there *was* an homogenous style because the fiddles
—with Gorodetzky and Roisman—were so alike." "Our ways
of playing stick out too—but's a different kind of ensemble,"
Soyer interjects. "Sasha [Schneider] is a different kind of fiddler than Roisman, and they made a different ensemble. Sasha
was different from Jack [Gorodetzky]," Tree reasons.

As well-informed musicians of today, they are aware of the historical changes in instrumental playing. Listening to famous quartets of thirty or forty years ago on recordings, they note: "There is nothing like it today. The character has changed and evolved like soloists did."

"Just listen to the Flonzaley Quartet."

"There are not the same kinds of slides and vibrato."

"All string playing has changed."

"Instrumental playing standards are higher today, man for man."

"There was a time when the emphasis was on the first violinist."

"In the Joachim Quartet, it was Joachim and three players who changed from city to city, tour to tour."

"He was the Mantovani of his time."

"Jacques Gordon too."

"It would be unthinkable today."

"We have no leader as such, except where designated by the music," first violinist Steinhardt says.

"Joachim picked up three players—it was a shoddy practice. In England he would play solo recitals and then three English players joined him as the Joachim Quartet."

"That's why we're far more serious today."

"But he did have a regular quartet in Germany."

"That was serious and occupied a good part of his time. Ysaye said that for his taste Joachim became too serious in later years when he was associated with Brahms and Shumann, when he became a spokesman for these masters— Ysaye lamented that the other gave up his claim as a virtuoso."

"Casals said Joachim played out of tune."

"I heard a recording and Ysaye plays marvelously—little trills, beautiful playing of an inconsequential piece."

Apropos of recordings, note is made of the Guarneri Quartet's extensive studio activity, which already has included the complete Beethoven Quartets on RCA. "No, we don't worry about recording works so early in our career," Dalley volleys. "We thought about it . . . briefly," Soyer smiles. "But we're always changing, so we will disagree in five years or five weeks."

"Our performances do *not* change," Dalley comes back.

"But our performances *are* different now from six years ago."

"Yes, there are the same bad mistakes, only glossed over," laughs Soyer. "I heard a record I made twenty years ago and I've changed—but it is closer to what I am now than what I was ten years ago, so I guess I've grown in a circle."

Back to Tree: "You can't become self-conscious on a disc, but some would like to consider recordings the final word on a piece of music."

"Some of the Rubinstein things we did, though, were almost without rehearsal."

"Of course they would be different the next day or the next week."

"When you hear Casals play the Bach Suites on a recording, that's the way Casals played it that day. You can't take it to mean that that is his way and that's that! Like the opening of the C-minor Suite. One day it will be . . ." and Soyer sings quite slowly and measured. "And the next it will be . . ." and he sings faster and more irregularly.

"Yes, but with a quartet the interpretation has to be more set than with a soloist—and the personality of the quartet changes over a period of years."

"I think we turned down the speed after a few years."

"After a while we were less savage, more mellow."

"We've changed for the better—it's hard to conceive of that possibility, but . . . ."

All four do, however, agree on the freedom they must maintain in interpreting music, believing that every musician has a different personality and sense of aesthetics.

"Times have changed—music is not to glorify the soloist, as it used to be."

"Yes, there's more respect for the music itself and less stress on the importance of our own egos."

"But often we run up against a composer's instruction that we don't go along with."

"First we give the printed text its full share. Then if we can't make it, we can alter."

"Markings are so imperfect: They demand interpretation."

"Some markings did not mean much to the composers."

"You can hear Bartók on records, and he doesn't pay heed to his own markings."

"Beethoven was the most meticulous all through his life. He began the overmarking stage in music—and if you take it all, like the *subito pianos,* it sounds overdone, too much."

One of the most startling facts is that the Guarneri Quartet was an instant success and international commodity the moment it began life—it started at the top. They all concur that even though solo recitals around the country have fallen off badly, interest in chamber music has in fact been growing. "We were busy right from the start—some groups have to struggle for years."

"Chamber music has something to do with rock and the interest in groups—quartets are favored over soloists."

"The rock cult at the universities overlaps with chamber music interest. Both draw young people, so we overlap."

"Yes, but the young generation is so ingrown."

"How many of us were listening to chamber music when we were young as compared to now?"

"Rock has cut into everything and pushed everything aside," Soyer laments.

"But rock has more intellectual substance than the popular music of the '40's and '50's did."

"But jazz had this too."

"Kids today do not listen to, like or understand jazz."

"Not long ago a jazz group played on a rock TV program and the moderator asked a girl on the panel how she liked it. 'I don't care for it,' she said."

"A guy in Newark—Chuck Israel, a great jazz arranger— put together a big band and it was sensational: very sophisticated with new and old tunes. When I heard it in the Village there were five people in the audience and it had to close down."

"In Europe jazz is still a big thing—the old bands still tour. We run into them."

"In Europe they're more willing to sustain what's good while accepting new forms. Here we discard things quickly and take on the new."

"I'm old-fashioned, I love the old songs," Tree confesses.

"The jazz bass players I worked with and knew, like Hinton, Haggart and Olivier, now have to play the Fender bass guitar—they had to learn it. Hinton is a legend, and he had to play this thing," Soyer motions helplessly.

All four feel that the "total experience" of sound, movement and light is just a fad that will disappear. "If people are impatient with music alone, that's their problem."

"We don't change to suit people's needs."

"The Beethoven quartets are monuments and they *last* too."

Soyer, the group's most verbal pessimist, won't let the rock thing rest: "I've read that kids are so wrapped up in the rock sound that they'll never get out. They're enveloped, segregated."

"But they're awed by the Opus 132 also. It stuns them in the same fashion."

"Some of our students also like rock and listen to it."

"I can't enjoy it easily," Soyer frowns. "My son plays the guitar and is a real rock 'n' roll fiend. He brings me all the records—Goldberg and the Gefilte Fish—and I listen and make a serious attempt. But still I ask, 'What is it, what is there?' The Beatles, yes, but the rest is faddism."

"Go back to the songs of the Fifties, of Eddie Fisher and the rest—now they're real period pieces," says Steinhardt.

"But I love them," smiles Tree.

"It's a different language today."

"I'd be happy if they left out the music altogether," Dalley offers. "I find the music superfluous in a protest song, for instance."

"The people who perform are really noodniks—they pick up a guitar and are 'great artists.' "

"Janis Joplin was not a noodnik!"

"I once saw her check out of a hotel—that was quite a scene!"

"Speaking of the bizarre, I was driving down the turnpike last night and saw a big truck with a tall van, almost like a derrick," Soyer relates. "And there were three giraffes in it."

"What drunken brawl were you at?"

"No, it was positively surrealistic—with the oil-refiners, the lights, the traffic—and three giraffes!" he bellows.

One of the secrets in maintaining this kind of rapport

among four distinct personalities is their insistence on leading separate off-stage lives. "You know," Dalley says, "that story of the Budapest was pure hokum, about their not getting along."

"They too tried to cultivate private lives."

"That photo of them sitting in separate chairs at the airport —it just happened!"

While together on tour, a preferred indoor sport is betting. Steinhardt and Tree are, by the foursome's consensus, the liveliest, and they will bet on just about anything within or without reason. "One night, for instance, our hostess after a concert was Greek and we began to bet if there would be yogurt in her icebox," Tree recalls. "We had fantastic odds: ten-to-one, 25-to-one. I was very suspicious, but the other two egged us on. The better the odds, the more nervous I got. Arnold had gone berserk—50-to-one! When the hostess opened the door, we all pounced on her, 'DO YOU HAVE YOGURT??' No, she said, and then there were four blood-curdling screams.

"In an Italian restaurant in Stuttgart we were playing a game everyone plays with those little cardboard coasters they have in every restaurant and bar—you flip it off the edge of the table with the back of the hand. Then you do two together and then three, up to thirteen and fourteen. So we began betting."

"Arnold was really bad at it—the first time he knocked over a glass on the *next* table and things were flying all over the place."

"You know Arnold—he can't even pick up a chair without knocking it over."

"Anyway, we bet and Arnold kept losing. Then I gave him 25-to-one odds—he lost five and six times. Then it was 50-to-one odds. I bet six times out of ten for Arnold—then suddenly he got eight out of ten and won $75!"

"Didn't you see *The Flim Flam Man?*—How do you fall for that?"

Soyer reminds them of the time Michael gave Arnold 100-to-one odds. "John and Michael had reservations on a plane from Chicago—Arnold and I were waiting on standby. When Michael got on the plane, he said facetiously, 'See you in New

York sometime.' I hollered back at him, 'I bet $10 I get on this plane,' and as he went down the stairs I yelled it out again —and he agreed. Three minutes later we got on, and when we came through the door into the plane, Michael began yelling 'Stop!' and bodily tried to block us."

Aside from full seasons of concerts, the Quartet fits in teaching at the Curtis Institute in Philadelphia, where Steinhardt, Dalley and Tree received their training. Elsewhere they give masterclasses, open rehearsals and seminars. Asked about the quality of string players, they pause, then, "Well . . . some are good."

"But good talents are few and far between. This never changes."

Dalley shakes his head, "I don't know where they'll go. The whole thing is so repressed."

"There used to be the cream in New York—commercial players for ads, TV, radio spots—now all that work's going to rock groups," Soyer moans.

"Yes, but there's more activity in Los Angeles."

"There are so many people and such population growth, that there are more talents; but now orchestras are collapsing."

On the immediate agenda are recordings with Artur Rubinstein—the Fauré C-minor Quartet and the Dvořák E-flat Piano Quartet. This remarkable combination of talents has to date produced the three Brahms Quartets and Quintet, as well as the Schumann Quintet for RCA. Steinhardt recalls meeting with Rubinstein in Paris: "He feeds on his own playing. At his house, he smoked and drank for twelve hours. We went home exhausted, but he was still going strong on wine and cigars."

"We hoped that after this big Polish dinner he would say that's it for the evening—but he wanted three more hours of playing."

"We played six quartets with him."

"He's a compulsive player and loves it."

"He always smiles and jokes; even when something is difficult, it comes out funny."

Not too unlike the four gentlemen of the Guarneri Quartet.

★ Eugene Istomin ★

One of the towering leaders of the middle generation of American pianists, Eugene Istomin has a unique commitment to both the standard solo repertory and to chamber music. Our talk in the fall of 1971 coincided with his first New York recital (Carnegie Hall) in several years, one that offered a mighty reading of Schubert's Opus 53 Sonata.

"Come right in, Mr. Istomin will be with you in a few moments," the voice said with just a touch of hauteur. The face, suddenly, was beaming its kid's smile—for it was Eugene Istomin himself. "Now I should be standing at the top of a great flight of stairs, making you wait a few minutes." Back in the recesses of his mind, he believes that's the way a "great artist" should behave—but in reality he couldn't, because he's not that kind. Istomin is, rather, an outgoing man of the world who organized artists for Humphrey's 1968 campaign and who follows baseball with a passion. But he also reads Toynbee and Borges, lunches in Paris with André Malraux and has been closely aligned with many of the century's musical giants, including Casals, Serkin and Reiner. Amid his crammed bookshelves, painting-covered walls and music-stacked piano overlooking Central Park, he is often withdrawn and sullen, probing, mulling and angry at much that goes on about him.

Now in his late forties, Eugene Istomin has passed through his trials of fire and water, making that leap between promising young artist and respected master. No one knows when this bit of magic happens, but critics and the public have both sensed this in his recordings, his performances and especially in his part of the Istomin-Stern-Rose Trio's Beethoven cycle —not only in New York but in Paris, London, Buenos Aires,

Lucerne and Tokyo during the Bicentenary Year. Has he felt a kind of crossing over from one artistic way of life into another?

"No, I wouldn't say so," he tilts his head thoughtfully. "I think that probably I have been crossing over from one period of my life into another in the natural way. You have to count in decades, really, rather than in the space of a season or a given situation. Quite naturally, what has happened has evolved from very original roots. There hasn't been a turning point one way or another, but there does come a time in some people's lives when the elements come together and another threshold has been crossed—and these are the periods in my life that probably I can assess from this vantage point. Certainly the last ten years have been such a period."

He is quick to note, however, that his career—which took off at the age of 17 with the Leventritt Award and appearances with The Philadelphia Orchestra and New York Philharmonic, as well as concerts with Adolf Busch—was not that of a young flash-in-the-pan overwhelmed with adulation, only to fall with a thud into some letdown years. "No, the general public nature of my career has been one of never being fashionable—even though at the beginning I was recognized as an important talent. I never had a very spectacular run at any time, so that there was always resistance, while at the same time there were dedicated friends and supporters in the musical profession. And I think I owe the continuity of my career more than anything to my fellow musicians, to my elder musicians at that period, who engaged me for important appearances on which my future depended—even though I was received rather coolly, rather antipathetically by the press. There was a kind of resistance to me for a long time. I would say, quite objectively, that I was rather harshly treated—because you would expect people to get behind a talent, follow it through its mistakes and support it. But with me it was people such as Rodzinski, Ormandy and Reiner who saw me through, rather than critics or management."

He terms his Philharmonic debut "successful, but not spectacularly so." All the signs of a major talent were there at 17 as he set out to play the Brahms Second, a rugged choice for a youngster. The feeling was he didn't do as well as he should have, and some of the critics said so. Nevertheless, he was re-engaged by Rodzinski for the following season, when again the reviews were mixed. "In almost all the major U.S. cities my first entry was a mixed bag, so that even though I was immediately known, the road was not strewn with roses. I never was one of the 'in' people who had a fashionable run. It has been a fairly steady thing, in its way rather modest—and over some twenty years I did compile a long series of appearances in every major place in the country and then in Europe. Things began to sort of pile up," he says matter-of-factly.

One of the things that made him stand apart from others of his generation was his choice of repertoire. "I made certain decisions because of my natural inclination toward the intellectual and toward the deeper aspects of playing. At a very early stage I chose the sort of repertoire that was bound to create obstacles for my success, because a man in his teens doesn't go around playing the Beethoven Fourth and expect to be recognized as a great Beethoven player. He's bound to be criticized. So it was natural that I just had to fight upstream —but it gave me the strength to last the fight. You either drown or learn to swim. I was fortunate in being able to last long enough to overcome this. There was a lot of confusion at this early phase because of the breadth of the repertoire with which I was involved. I made my original debut with the Philharmonic and the Philadelphia in Brahms and Chopin, and I played Beethoven. Well, when you add Mozart and Bach, you've covered a large area of the repertoire—and in those days the divisions in an artist's image were far more narrowly defined. Schnabel and Serkin were Beethoven players. Rubinstein and Hofmann were Chopin men. Someone else was a Brahms player and Gieseking was a Debussy player. The idea of an artist who could cover a larger area and be acceptable—and particularly for a young man who didn't have an established reputation—was hopeless. You were bound to be resisted. But in actual fact I played this repertoire out of my own inner necessity. It wasn't arrogance. It was born of the fact that intuitively I knew I had something to say about these composers—and in the actual event of my career this turned out to be true."

Today, of course, this kind of rigidity has been broken down and Istomin notes that we have a still further perspective about the 19th century today than we did in 1940. "It gives us more of an air view about things, in that we realize that between the time of Mozart and Haydn and that of Schubert and Chopin is merely a matter of fifty years. It was once considered epochal. Now it's a matter of an understanding, an affinity for the subtle, very urgently important, but very subtle differences in idiom and style between these composers. They're really of one piece—relative to our new world."

As for the pigeonholing he experienced, he relates that if he would play Chopin in one town and it was well received, he might be re-engaged to come back. If he would then play Beethoven, a critic would write that he plays Chopin beautifully but has no understanding for Beethoven. In another city, if he reversed procedures, a critic would write that he is a classicist and understands the architectonic style but not the self-indulgent lyricism of Chopin. "There was no way I could win. But I think the fact that I was criticized proved that there was an importance placed on me by these people—and that I was being challenged and horsewhipped along the way. This didn't happen to many—names you don't even remember today did a lot better for a while, but then what?"

He describes his style as being an offshoot of the 19th-century virtuoso musician, but with "the particular trappings of today." It does not mean the flashy Liszt school of pure pyrotechnics, but that "basically my feelings about music are what are described as romantic. I'm an intellectual, not an exhibitionist in the superficial sense of the word—with no 19th-century trappings. For me, the glamor and the patina is in the actual making of the music, not in the externals. In that sense I think that I like to practice this deception, because it *is* a deception, because what I do musically is intended to be extremely dramatic, emotional, involved and passionate—yet the exterior I like to give is that the person playing is simply a vessel for this thing to happen, not an actor. The acting is taking place through the notes."

The dichotomy of the German intellectual side (acquired) vying with the Russian emotional side (by birth) is one key to his personality as well as his playing. There have been the influences of Schnabel and Serkin, but also Rachmaninoff, Rubinstein, Casals and Toscanini. The base on which he has staked his career is a broad one. One time, early on, Virgil Thomson in the *Herald Tribune* called him "a contemporary spirit," swooning over the *Gaspard de la nuit* which Istomin had played in recital, but adding that he knew very little about other music. Thomson's later comment to the musician was, "Boy, was I wrong!"

Istomin relates that he was brought up the son of Russian parents—"with all the predilections of the Russian heart and soul and what-have-you, with melody and songs. My parents were singers, and I heard Caruso and Melba and all those people in the house. So it was a very romantic 19th-century kind of Slavic background. And the first really profound emotional impression I had of a pianist was Artur Rubinstein. How I emulated him as a child! I absolutely worshipped him! And then, when I went to the Curtis Institute, came the influence of Serkin and this very purifying, severe German thing, which was hard. It was a situation, again, of sink or swim. My own rather more lyrical and sensual temperament was under his control. What happened was that, because of a natural intellectual bent, I was able to absorb this—and it opened up an entire new area which I emulated and absorbed and revolted against too." He heard Schnabel as well as Rachmaninoff, but "I always reacted to music intuitively, as I do still today. I never hesitated to imitate what I loved, what a great artist did, whether it was a pianist or Heifetz or Casals."

Musical maturity came hard, he emphasizes: "The rules of the game were very big and it's a hard game to win. But if you win, then you've got something. It's valuable, for instance, to play a Prokofiev sonata beautifully—but it's *more* important to play a Beethoven sonata well because it's more important *musically*. I think if you play Mozart beautifully, you can play the entire area up to I don't know where, because technically it demands the kind of control that is required in the entire repertoire. For me, the most difficult, the deepest music is in Mozart, Beethoven, Schubert and Haydn. And, therefore, if you're a master in that area, what you have to say about Brahms and Schumann will be very interesting. Chopin is a special cup of tea, because of a particular international idiomatic Polish-Slavic quality in rubato and rhythms, which are intuitive and have to be understood early in life."

Beethoven, with whom the pianist communed long and hard during the Bicentenary Year, is the composer he feels one can play *without* regard for piano playing—whose ideas don't need any one particular instrument. "Sound and the sheer beauty of touch is terribly important in Mozart, but not at all in Beethoven. Some pianists attempt to extract from Beethoven a force that simply defeats itself on the piano. There are things in this music that simply cannot be done on the piano. Some of them you must attempt in order to convey the idea of Beethoven, but he does present special problems—and there are some superb players of Beethoven who are less successful in the late Romantic period for this reason."

In his more than four decades of piano experience Istomin has heard almost every one who mattered: Rachmaninoff, Hofmann, Horowitz, Rubinstein, Schnabel and so on. What are the ingredients that go into making a great pianist? "Very simply, they are the elements that make a musician to begin with: before anything, a musical temperament, the need to say something, the need and ability to communicate. Then come such things as the physical equipment, sensitivity of the ear (which comes from a general sensitivity, taste and intelligence). If you have all these qualities by nature, then you must have tremendous determination and discipline. But the foremost motivation has to be to say something to people." It is exactly this quality he finds so potent in Casals, a major influence on his life since the first Prades Festival in 1950. "His quality of communication is the most intensely developed that I have experienced. He has the extraordinary ability to extrovert something, yet with such depth and with such a profundity of feeling and a breadth that is unique among instrumentalists I've heard. It's through a deep natural intelligence, not necessarily an intellectual development, but the profoundest kind of natural intuition and general intelligence. Hearing him play a few times, I felt he reached the farthest limits of the art of interpretation. The greatest heights of musical experience were given to me by Casals. It was through those experiences that I realized what it is all about."

The Casals milieu, he nods, was awesome in its way—"but

I did not feel it. I felt smitten and just that I had to be there with him. It was a great deep sort of soul need. And incidentally, he reciprocated, because we became very close. He didn't have a son and we had that kind of relationship—and still do, as a matter of fact. It was fortunate to be around him because I learned inadvertently, involuntarily by making music with him. I never was his pupil and he never criticized me—even when I asked him to. All he did was approve, all the time. But that approval was enormously important to me, for my own self-esteem, because I would say to myself, 'Well, so-and-so says I don't play this very well, yet here this great man thinks I'm a great artist, so I *must* have something to say.' You see, it's that sort of confidence by others that I had very early in my career. This made me feel that I had only to work and develop, and that I *belonged* in this circle, this world, when my time came—and I never doubted this was what I was on this earth for. The career obstacles and managers and reviews and things like that were often dramatic, screaming problems to me, but they never made me doubt my own value —if I could only develop and exercise self-discipline."

Among the struggles that are waged inside many artists as they grow is finding that middle ground between personal subjectivity and academic formalism demanded by the music. For Istomin, on the other hand, it is different: "The struggle is one of clarification, once a work has been absorbed. And that I do within myself over a period of time. There are phases in learning and they just take time. But the goal is clarity— and that's a quote of Wagner, of all people! That is what you have to do when you play music: make it clear. Then there is the question of eloquence. As for the formal, structural things, those one takes for granted after a while. You study a work and you bring whatever a human brings to it, your consciousness, applied to the best of your ability. But when it comes to the performance and the interpretation, the giving to someone else, that is all a matter of execution. As one has more and more experience in playing a piece there is a process of etherealization that takes place—a simplification. Of course, you often have to pass through a mooning and spooning phase. But if you go the other way and decide to stick to the form and this and that, you stunt your growth emotionally. In time there is a way of compressing and clarifying, so that it becomes clear as the blue sky in that essence, so that it becomes all spirit and all sound, the phrases falling simply into place— the simplest thing in the world," and his face lights up. "That's the whole thing! But behind it has to be an awareness and the fear of technical failure too."

Istomin confesses that there is always something in a performance that is imperfect from a technical point of view. "It would be absurd if it weren't. There's no such thing as perfection. Technique is to be able to lay open the basic sense of a great work of art, to make it clear. The most extraordinary example of an artist who always did that, but who was technically unreliable and inaccurate (sometimes to the point of seriously jeopardizing his performance) was Schnabel. Even today on records I'm struck by this incredible thing—he always had the ability to give you a really in-depth sense of the work, even though details might be botched left and right. And this is the highest form of the art, particularly in the colossal works where the details are absolutely unimportant. They're so myriad that they all have to be part of the vast mosaic—so little chips are little things. The big line *must* be there!"

Among the changes Istomin has witnessed in his profession is an increasing lack of conviction on the part of many artists. The men of the past had passion, he insists, a certainty in their playing, in themselves and in their beliefs—and it all came across. "Their personalities are so much in relief today because of this passion. So many artists I hear, young ones who come to play for me, say 'I don't know what to do here,' 'I don't know what this is about,' 'I'm not sure.' Well, in my youth—today I'm less sure than I was when I was younger —but when I was younger, whenever I played something, I was *absolutely* persuaded of it. I may have been as wrong as anything and I may hate what I did in retrospect; but I find there are far fewer artists who have that quality of feeling strongly, being involved with the language, swimming as a fish in that sea of music.

"The fad phrase 'identity crisis' may have a certain grain of truth. Certainly we're getting farther and farther from the 19th century. I'm still of a generation in which people knew people

who knew Beethoven. Literally, it's as close as that. Schnabel
knew Brahms. Casals knew a great friend of Mendelssohn's
who knew all about his problems in reinstating Bach. When
you think that I played for the first time with George Szell
in 1948 at the Philharmonic, and in 1948 Richard Strauss
finished his *Four Last Songs*—and I have a recording of Szell
with Schwarzkopf of those songs. Strauss was born in 1864,
just 32 years after the death of Beethoven. And in these 23
years since 1948, this passage of time is important. Probably
there are more artists who are in doubt as to which period is
really theirs. It is only natural, because the new music must
have its new artists. Yet I'm unable to see how it's possible
to be at one with both worlds. So maybe for many it *is* an
identity crisis."

His roots are definitely planted in the previous two centuries.
His interest in contemporary music, he says, is only that of
a man who has great curiosity to know about the important
things going on in his time. "And I am equally interested in
what's going on in painting and writing and politics and all
these areas. But the curiosity and desire to know is not the
same as my desire to express and identify myself with this
music. That's why I play so little of it. For me, playing means
expression. Yes, this is a world in which I live and in which
I have something to say. And though I have tremendous respect for a Xenakis or Stockhausen, they don't provide me with
visceral, intellectual excitement. To make music is the ultimate
and the true act of love that exists in my life; and I feel very
deeply the risks, the fear, the shyness and all the things that
go with it. I *don't* feel this in regard to the new music."

Although a successful, long career has its rewards, Istomin
balks at one aspect, what he calls "the anxiety for success. In
order to function, I need a public. We all need it. And there
is none of us who is free of that anxiety for one reason or another. I'll never forget some seven or eight years ago when
Rubinstein was giving his enormous cycle of concerts here
and I called him one day. 'How are you?' I asked. And he
said with great joy, 'Well, the concert is sold out.' Here he was
at the zenith of everything, and still he couldn't get over that
fact, because he had known other times much earlier. That's
the greatest problem of the performing artist—we need an

audience and performances to refine our work. So there is a primordial anxiety that one day, perhaps, they won't want to hear me."

As for emotionally coping with the yearly crop of this new competition winner and that young dynamo out of Central Europe, he submits, "I only envy the success of undeserving artists. There has never been a great one whose success I've envied, because I'm completely aware that in this area the only enemy I could possibly have is myself—that no artist by his quality can prevent me from achieving what I want to achieve. There have been many who have inspired me, and if I hear something beautiful I'm profoundly grateful. Yet I do often feel resentment toward certain fashionable successes, and lesser artists who command higher fees. But that's the machinery of the profession. When I started, there were certain concert managements which were very powerful in influencing public taste and success. This doesn't exist anymore. What they latch onto is the most easily bookable artists, and that often is the lesser artist. In every period there are some who run through the quick fad thing and then there are those who last. Some who have success too fabulously, too early, have their strength sapped. It can be a cancer."

With all the problems, the defeats, the frustration, had he ever thought of giving up his pursuit? "Often," he laughs heartily. "But I never had any doubt that I was a musician from the start and that would never change. What prevented me was the fact that I wasn't anything else but a part of music. That was my identity, it was me. I couldn't live without music. I never said to myself, 'You *are* music,' but what I was saying was 'You are, however infinitesimal, you are a part of music. That's what you are. You can't think of giving up yourself.'" He talks of a certain conscious anguish every time he walks out on stage as being part of a loss of innocence. "But it's important to try to regain it through one's art, and that's the process of etherealization."

Does the anguish increase with the years? "No, it becomes more simple. I say to myself that this may be the last time I'll ever play. I may die. And it seems more realistic every time I play. As days and years go, it becomes more true and I gain greater tranquility inside myself. I'm able to shut out the anxieties more successfully than I used to. When I was younger, I was aware of certain gifts, but not of myself. I was much more anxious as to whether I was being accepted or recognized. How do people like what I'm doing, am I *good* enough? Well, today I have these anxieties—it's perfectly normal—but I'm much more able to credibly control them. My thing is one of reaching the stage where there isn't anything left to do *but* play. This happens more often. Come what may, I take my risks and am resigned to them. There is nothing that's gained of any value in human existence without risks. And sometimes you have to create new ones. Now I'm more aware of the limits of time left to sing my tune. And I'm more resigned to the inevitability that I *must* sing—and therefore there's nothing to do but sing, make music. You can know that intellectually for a long time, but without feeling it deeply enough to give you strength in times of stress. But there's a time in life that comes when you do believe it. And that's what gives me the courage to go on the stage, because I'm not impelled to be accepted, to have the success—that is not my ambition. I have enough of that now. My first ambition is to speak, to communicate the truth as best I can, in the music that I'm playing. After a performance that's really been what I wanted it to be, I feel a wonderful light sense of having spent myself, having fulfilled myself. The moment of truth is the doing."

And how does he handle the inevitable critics? "When the reviews are good, I'm inutterably happy for a few minutes. And when they're bad, I'm unspeakably depressed and furious for the whole day. But rarely has a review corresponded with what I actually thought about a concert. I'm enormously susceptible and anxious for observations and criticisms from everybody. And I listen and absorb any observations someone makes to me personally. But in the nature of a review, very few are constructive. They posit certain ideas which for the most part (I know through experience) are false. I mean, one will say Mr. Istomin played the Beethoven Fifth with a bright brassy tone and covered all the superficial aspects of the work —but didn't plumb the depths. How many like that have I had in my career! It's the standard review of a younger person tackling a big work. Well, I know that the depths that I *have* already plumbed are probably so infinitely greater than those that the critic is observing I *haven't* plumbed, so how can I take what he says seriously? I know perfectly well I haven't plumbed *all* the depths, but only as many as I could at that moment. And I know that I have a significant understanding, a better understanding of Beethoven than most people." Almost as a warning to his departing guest, he shakes his finger, he urges a standard of constructive criticism. "You know, few performers are as evil, as vitriolic as some critics," and he beams behind the slowly closing door.

★ *Dorothy Kirsten* ★

This 1971 tribute to Dorothy Kirsten came with the 25th anniversary of her Metropolitan Opera debut—while now she is headed towards a record for a Met soprano: thirty years of service. While she has cut back her singing activities in lieu of golfing in southern California, annual Met performances in Puccini roles and orchestral concerts keep her among America's most illustrious divas.

There was a pizza place on the fringe of the University of Wisconsin that served up operatic arias on the juke box along with the campus' best Italian food. And so, over a steaming, oily pizza, musical snobs like myself could burn the roofs of our mouths to the Puccini and Verdi of Albanese, Sayão, Steber, Kirsten, Bjoerling or Warren—while debating the merits of Callas, Tebaldi, de los Angeles, Schwarzkopf and Nilsson. For us "serious" music people, Dorothy Kirsten was definitely off-limits. How could she really be any good in the celestial world of grand opera? After all, she had besmirched her art with radio, television, movies and pop recordings! Could anyone who had traded quips and songs with Frank

Sinatra and Bing Crosby come to grips with the world of opera? Dorothy Kirsten was glamor, Hollywood, dazzling blonde and honey-minked (as I had once seen her come through a stage door). And we chose to turn up our noses at her, barely hearing what she had to offer.

But the truth was—and still is—that to hear her in a variety of roles, pitted against the reigning competition on stage, is to come away with a respect for her consummate professionalism, acute intelligence, unswervingly fresh vocal estate and unstinting dramatic effectiveness. It's strange how history works its ways. Dorothy Kirsten began making her way in the operatic firmament during World War II, while planting the seeds for simultaneous careers in radio, recordings, films and operetta. Although she had a single year in Europe, working with Gigli's teacher, she is purely an American product. And just as the proverbial prophet goes unsung in his homeland, so her own generation of Americans were too willing to turn up their noses at a domestic vintage, while glorifying the import—just *because* she had such unique versatility!

But history has a way of meting out its justice too. Dorothy Kirsten is now celebrating her 25th anniversary at the Met— a mark few singers achieve. If the records are correct, she is the first American soprano ever to achieve this landmark, and she is the only soprano still on the roster 25 years after her debut. At the same time, she has become the first singer ever to celebrate 25 years with the San Francisco Opera, her second operatic home, which she opened as Tosca in September and which honored her with the company's first medal awarded in recognition of distinguished achievement and service. For the sake of vocal history and for all of us former pizza-loving musical snobs, Dorothy Kirsten has been vindicated.

Her mentor, the glamorous Grace Moore, also had found many unwilling to accept her as a "serious" opera singer because she had found such success on Broadway, on the screen and as a devastating personality. The Grace Moore tradition, in fact, has clung closely to Kirsten's own career. Both were typical of the American singer born and bred at home, extending their artistry and personal magnetism to operetta, popular music, radio and TV. They also shared many roles—Mimi, Manon, Louise, Marguerite, Juliette, Flora and Tosca. Miss Moore—who had heard the young New Jersey-born soprano through the machinations of *The New York Journal*'s Dinty Doyle and then arranged to send her to Italy to pursue singing studies—sat up in Box One, close to the proscenium of the old Met on the night of December 1, 1945, when her young blond protegee bowed as Mimi (the same role of Miss Moore's own debut 17 years earlier). Even before, when the soprano sang her first Mimi, her mentor presented her with an autographed photo: "To the new Mimi, and may she be the greater."

When the Met on 39th and Broadway was to bow to what was called progress in 1966 (the memorable year of Kirsten's own 20th anniversary as *La Fanciulla del West*), one critic noted at the Gala Farewell program: "For Dorothy Kirsten, the 'Depuis le jour' she performed (more beautifully than anything she had sung on this stage in a twenty-year span) was not for her alone, but also for her benefactress Grace Moore. She sang it well enough for both." And later the diva was rewarded with two chairs from the special Box One. As late as the summer of 1970 the Moore link remained unbroken. During one of the Met's park concerts a man with a large bouquet rushed to the footlights after Miss Kirsten had sung a touching *Bohème*—and as he handed them to her, he said, "In memory of Grace Moore." Looking back on that vanished age, the soprano notes: "Grace was so unique in those days; and there was so much extravagance then. Singers aren't idols anymore. They're too close to the public. When they go on the talk shows, they become too familiar, too much the good Joe and the girl-next-door. I've tried to maintain the image of the prima donna all through the years, wherever I was."

Up until the time she met and auditioned for Grace Moore, the young aspirer had not sung anything but "light" music and had had no thoughts of an opera career. She had been studying in New York, supporting herself by frequent radio appearances with choral groups, including Kate Smith's. The future was not bright until Doyle began to look after the singer's interests. She learned "Musetta's Waltz" and "Mimi's Farewell" and so impressed the great stage and screen star that Miss Moore immediately decided to send her to Italy to

study with Gigli's teacher, Astolfo Pescia. "He developed a
rough voice," she reflects. "But he thought I could be a dramatic voice and began forcing it out of shape. He wanted me
to sing the things Tebaldi eventually did. Actually, it was
Ludwig Fabri in New York who brought me back vocally and
gave me a technique. He was a master and he completely con-
structed my voice. I worked with him for over ten years before he died."

What prefaced Dorothy Kirsten's 25-year run at the Met
prepared her well for what was to follow. Returning home
during the war, she made her stage debut at the Chicago Opera
as the supporting Poussette in *Manon* and sang no less than
17 "second lead" roles—within a year however, she was singing the title role of Manon! Two years later she sang with the
San Carlo Opera and made a highly successful New York
bow in Lehár's *The Merry Widow,* followed by a debut with
the New York City Opera (*Manon Lescaut*) and the Mexico
Bellas Artes ánd a run on Broadway in *Blue Moon.* Not long
after her Met debut she became the first opera star to appear
on the cover of *Life,* and later she shared similar honors with
Eleanor Steber on *Newsweek.* Since then there hasn't been
a single American city with anything resembling an opera
season that she has not visited and revisited time and again.
In San Francisco alone she has opened the season over half-
a-dozen times. She has no regrets for never having sung in
Europe (outside of Sweden). "I'm lucky because I can be very
grateful for what I've been and done. I've been so busy here.
At the Met a real American company was formed during the
Forties and the war years. I was asked three times for La
Scala, but always I had the good excuse of being busy here."

But it was a tour of the Soviet Union in 1962 that provided
one of the capstones to her career. Sent as a cultural ambassador on the State Department Cultural Exchange Program,
she sang *Madama Butterfly, La Traviata, Tosca* and *Faust*
in Moscow, Leningrad, Riga and Tiflis. In this last city she
earned 28 curtain calls for her Violetta and at a dinner, after
many warm toasts, the director of the opera raised his glass:
"You are an important link in the chain of friendship between
our countries. We hope you will come back and sing with us
soon again. We shall wait your return with all our hearts, but

please don't make us wait as long as poor Cio-Cio-San had to wait for her Pinkerton." At that same four-hour banquet of caviar, shashlik and Ukrainian wine, the music began and suddenly came a request for America's newest craze, the twist (remember the twist?). And so to the music of ragtime, Russian-style, the diva brought the twist to the U.S.S.R.

Hundreds of Russians stopped her on the streets wherever she went, calling her *attrice,* actress, because they had seen her in *The Great Caruso.* Fame had preceded her to Russia because of the movie she had made with Mario Lanza—a film in which she played the Met's entire soprano roster rolled into one, from Destinn to Farrar singing everything from Lucia to Aida! Her experience making the film was not exactly a happy one. "I have to be honest and say that Lanza was dreadful on the set. When we began, he had a stream of dirty Italian words which he used until he realized I understood Italian. He was spoiled rotten by the studio. Anyway, it was too bad. He desecrated his art and I think it was the fault of the studio. It was difficult for everyone. I had done concerts with him, so I was ready for it."

Even before this she had made *Mister Music* with Bing Crosby, with whom she had worked on the radio and who had become something more than just a musical colleague. She was also a regular with Gordon MacRae on *The Railroad Hour,* sang operetta with Nelson Eddy on the *Kraft Music Hall* and co-hosted the *Chevy Show* with John Raitt. And there was Lucky Strike's *Light Up Time* with Frank Sinatra, every day, five days a week. It was this that put her temporarily into hot water with Mr. Bing and the Met, because she refused to cancel her radio appearances for Met performances. "But it was here I learned how to sing popular music—it was Frank's timing and phrasing, no one else's. He always called me 'diva' and still does when we see each other."

As a pop singer, Kirsten was not alone among opera stars. Grace Moore, Gladys Swarthout, Helen Traubel and many others had their fling on radio and records. But as the musically knowledgeable dance critic Walter Terry notes: "Dorothy Kirsten, more than any other opera star, can change the timbre of her voice to suit the music. She is no prima donna slumming. There are no opera-concert accents and mannerisms—only a

gentleness and ease of delivery. I find her a little like Mary
Martin, who is the greatest lieder singer in America. Kirsten's
Gershwin things are heaven! She is a real singer with a voice,
singing in terms of the popular idiom—throaty and through
the nose and just right. I could listen forever."

All these facets turned Dorothy Kirsten into a remarkably
rounded artist—and she especially believes in her extensive
experience in operetta. Her advice to young singers is to get
experience in things other than opera. "I did 500 operetta
performances before I ever became an opera singer. It not only
helped my singing, but it gave me a feeling for the stage, how
to walk, how to dance, aiding the figure and providing all the
other requisites for grand opera. The trouble today is that too
many young singers want to race to the top without being sure
of their footing."

As a colleague she has been described as "a superstar, but
no antics." Despite its glamorous patina, opera for her is a
no-nonsense profession. She has long been admired for warmly
shouldering a nervous newcomer on the scene—she has lost
count of exactly how many tenors she has pulled through the
terrors of first nights on both coasts—and for the unfaltering
professionalism of a marked trouper. But neither is she the
kind of colleague who eagerly runs off to see another's performance: her confidence in her own handling of a role is
that strong. Once she was badgered into seeing Maria Callas
when she came back to the Met as Tosca. When she returned,
the question came fast and breathlessly. "Well, what did you
think?" She shrugged, nonplussed, "I picked up one or two
good things from her."

Her work is a craft, so that on the day of every performance
and during each intermission she is quietly occupied with the
words and music of an opera she may have sung 200 times. Her
last-minute saving of performances has become legendary.
Who can forget her third-act entrance on galloping horseback
during an ill-fated Leontyne Price *Fanciulla del West* performance?—after Kirsten had already retired for the night in
her hotel room with a sleeping pill.

And life today? Cross-country tours to all reaches of the
U.S., Canada, Hawaii, singing opera, recitals and orchestral
concerts. There are her annual stagings of opera at Los An-

geles Greek Theater, for which she is director, producer and star. There is a happy marriage to Dr. John French, director of the Brain Research Institute at UCLA. There is golf, fishing, painting, interior decorating. There are occasional master classes at UCLA. And there is committee work in L.A.'s cultural life.

And so, now a time to celebrate and salute Dorothy Kirsten's 25 years at the Met. She is a woman so much of the moment and so unpreoccupied with the past that when queried about career highlights, she simply states: "The satisfaction of what I got in San Francisco—the standing ovations and the hundreds of bouquets after all the years there. A great evening with a splendid cast . . . and then the medal. This is really *something* in the 'twilight zone' of a career, to know your work has been important and appreciated." A former pizza-loving snob can only nod in agreement.

★ *Evelyn Lear* ★

The recent emergence of Evelyn Lear as a heroine of traditional Mozart-Strauss repertoire has come as a surprise to those who knew her only in Lulu, Wozzeck *and other modern works. I first spoke with her before the autumn 1969 opening of the Juilliard School, of which she is an alumnus; and later in 1970, following a serious vocal crisis and reconsideration of her career. The two pieces have been combined.*

The svelte figure in black velvet at the piano was nimbly making her way through one of Charles Ives' more difficult songs, in preparation for a Columbia recording. Suddenly, in mock fatigue, she collapsed on the keyboard. "God, I hate modern music," she moaned. But then she smiled as if to say, "I don't really mean it"—in a gesture, the duality of a soprano named Evelyn Lear, who has achieved all she once set out to accomplish, but often by the arduous means of a Berg, a Schoenberg or a Levy. Looking back on the blood, sweat and tears that have been poured into this music, she can't help but longingly look at the others who have risen to the top of the heap on the lyrical waves of a Puccini, a Verdi or a Wagner. We were chatting about the "new" Evelyn Lear being readied on the launching pad—the new Evelyn Lear who is banishing Berg, Bartók, Blacher, Schoenberg and what-not from her domain after enduring their rigors since her European debut over a decade ago. Now the determined New York-born singer has decided to do an abrupt about-face and take her career down a more traditional lane. She has given up the role of Berg's Lulu which catapulted her to instant fame in Vienna in 1962, she is avoiding Schoenberg's *Erwartung,* she is staying away from tempting offers to create roles in new operas with cruel vocal lines. Instead, she is happily at work on Puccini's *Tosca* for the first time, she is refurbishing Mimi in *La Bohème,* she is returning to the wellsprings of Bach, Mozart, Haydn and the lighter Richard Strauss.

But this has come about only after serious self-assessment and intelligent perception as to what direction her career had traveled. After a concert of the Final Scene from *Salome,* her throat did not feel right—she knew she had pushed her voice beyond its natural capacities to achieve the right effect in the music. She had already experienced what nearly every singer goes through at least once in a career, a "Crisis," as long ago as spring of 1969 during performances of the taxing *Erwartung* in Europe. So she found a new teacher . . . and she found out how to say "no," unless the music suited her particular vocal instrument.

She beams, "I'm so happy that the only modern music I'll sing is *Wozzeck* at my La Scala debut— but I would only go if I could sing Mimi there, too. So they will be able to see both sides of Evelyn Lear." Thinking back over the years, she reasons: "I got into the same trouble as Callas did. I revelled in the idea of being a 'singing actress,' to the detriment of the voice. Fortunately, I pulled out. With Callas it was not so. She became an actress . . . and I feel I am becoming a singer. If I should ever feel that a dramatic part is more important, then I would give up my career as a singer and become an actress too.

"Both of us ladies are basically sopranos with dramatic temperaments. But if the temperament begins to rule the voice, then forget it. Callas had a Greek temperament to contend with—I my Russian. She had the saving grace that her kind of music was not contemporary, but more healthy for the voice even though she sang it dramatically. I was called on to sing dramatically *in* contemporary music, music which is not written well vocally for the most part. A young voice can handle it well until around 35—then you must be careful."

Miss Lear now feels that her life has taken a new direction: "I'm thrilled about and happy to say my stress is now less on my abilities as an actress—well, it's always there, yes—and I can work more from a vocal point of view. People only heard me do *Lulu, Wozzeck, Erwartung,* and now they say they didn't realize I could sing this other kind of music. I feel that I'm embarking . . . you know, when you go down a road you reach the first landmark—that's the fame I've achieved as a leading exponent of Berg heroines. Now I could continue further on this road and explore all the ramifications of contemporary music. But there is another cut-off—and that is to return to the womb and start fresh to be reborn. I now see that when we don't have our voices, we are no longer singers, and so one reaches the point of taking stock—was it to be *Wozzeck* and *Lulu,* or Tosca and Mimi? I cancelled performances, I sat down and studied, knowing I had fallen into bad vocal habits singing modern music."

Regardless of what people say, Evelyn Lear believes contemporary music is not vocally demanding, "because it does not demand purity and spin. You can create effects to make people think you are marvelous, but the test comes in Puccini, Verdi, Bellini and Donizetti, the traditional classical and bel canto works, in other words. What I needed was a disciplined form of vocal study. It is as if a pianist who had been playing showy, dramatic pieces such as *Pictures at an Exhibition* was suddenly confronted with a Mozart sonata—you find the necessity of doing little fine things. Now my advice to young

singers would be not to lose your technique and your spin.
But since I gained my fame with the others, I guess I can't
knock it!" she shrugs.

"Now I am falling in love with my voice: I want to pamper
it, treat it well and not abuse it. Callas, for instance, was her
own worst enemy. With too much talent, she always gave and
kept nothing in reserve. That drove her audiences into hysteria. But you must sing with the cool part of the brain. You
can't be emotionally involved with what you're doing. At
least for me, you must approach it from an intellectual point
of view. Now," she pauses thoughtfully, "this is *not* exactly
100 percent true. I *am* emotionally involved, but not *too*
much. I am an emotional person. I can give and spend so
much if I don't watch out! Yet you need reserve in the technique of singing. The seat of any emotion is in the throat.
When you laugh or cry or are afraid and so on—the minute
you become tense—the throat closes, and you can't sing with
a closed throat."

Evelyn Lear, now firmly established as an opera and con-
cert force of international import, has been a practicing musi-
cian since the age of five. Born into a Russian-Jewish family
of musicians, she called home the Prospect Park section of
Brooklyn, while schools included PS 241, George Washington
High, NYU, Hunter and Juilliard. "My grandfather, Zavel
Kwartin, was one of the great cantors of the world, and my
mother, Nina Quartin, one of the great singers of her time.
[She had sung in Europe, in New York concerts and at the
Brooklyn Academy as Micaela to Castagna's Carmen.] I knew
I wanted to be a singer from the time I was three years old.
But my parents were smart and insisted that I study music
first."

So, she studied piano and the French horn. Though she
dreamed of becoming a great singer and, perhaps, of fulfilling
some of her mother's aspirations, her father—a lawyer who
had immigrated from Siberia at 19, a self-made man who held
broad, intensive learning as the highest goal in life—tried to
discourage her career (and the limitations imposed by it) by
refusing her singing lessons. Miss Lear did, however, have a
solid musical foundation when she turned to singing "on the
side" at Juilliard. It was there that she realized her love for

German lieder. Her father had already set the scene for a fascination with poetry and literature, for he had given his children a dime each time they learned a poem.

"The desire to sing must have been instilled in me from the womb, and somehow I had this feeling inside me that I must be a singer. Unlike the instrument, your voice is part of you and it is the most personal form of expression. So, although as yet I'd no thought of taking up singing professionally, I used to go through works for my own satisfaction. When I was fifteen, I could sing and play my way through *Die Winterreise*. The first song I ever learned was 'Heidenröslein' of Schubert—I heard my mother singing it and learned just from listening. I was five at the time. Later, because I wanted to be a singer from the time I was able to walk, I went to many concerts, my mother's included. My first lieder recitalist was Lotte Lehmann, and then I avidly followed all recitalists thereafter: Seefried, Schwarzkopf, etc. Later I studied lieder with Sergius Kagen at Juilliard and privately with Leo Roseneck, the accompanist for Elisabeth Schumann for almost twenty years."

The fact remained, however, that a feeling and capacity for the song literature was hardly the "open sesame" for a young American singer on the threshold. Doors were not that easily opened and, after a number of abortive attempts at a career— "and the realization that I would never make it"—Miss Lear enrolled in the Opera Workshop of the Juilliard School. In the meantime there had been marriage at 18 and two children in seven years, during which she did almost no singing at all. "Since Juilliard is where I met Tom [Texas-born baritone Thomas Stewart], it is a very special place to me. It was there that we worked with Dr. Frederick Cohen and Fred Waldman, who advised us to go to Europe and make a career. The house on Claremont Avenue holds fond memories for me—student recitals, operatic performances (me as Despina in *Così*!) and for me the stepping stone in the professional world."

What followed included in a 1955 Concert Artist's Guild Award and a Town Hall recital, an appearance with the Little Orchestra Society and a lead role in Marc Blitzstein's *Reuben, Reuben,* which never made it past out-of-town tryouts in Boston. For both there had been endless auditions and singing in choruses, on TV, in summer tent work in *South Pacific, Kiss Me, Kate!* and *Kismet*. The aspiring soprano had been turned down for the role of Maria in Bernstein's *West Side Story*—Stewart had been set to alternate in *The Ballad of Baby Doe* at the Greek Theater in Los Angeles, and this did not materialize. There had also been a recording of Kurt Weill's *Johnny Johnson* with Lotte Lenya. Enough capsule versions of Broadway musicals for women's clubs and Hadassah groups might have led to a long career as "The Singing Stewarts." On the advice of Dr. Cohen, they both applied for Fulbright grants in 1957, received them, sailed to Bremen (when asked by customs officials what they had to declare, all they could honestly offer was their talent, *à la* Oscar Wilde) and settled in Berlin to study at the Hochschule für Musik. Not long after, Stewart was asked to audition for the Deutsche Oper Berlin, and the then-director Carl Ebert hired him for a three-year contract.

Miss Lear experienced more of a struggle. With no manager looking after her interests, she noted in the telephone book every music agent in Berlin, called them up and introduced herself—telling them she was good and could learn lots of music and very quickly. Some radio engagements were the net result and some offers to join opera houses elsewhere in Germany, but she did not want to leave her family. In Berlin she auditioned three times for an administrator of the Deutsche Oper, choosing the Composer's scene from *Ariadne auf Naxos:* "I've always been known for doing something a little bit off-beat. I mean for me to have gotten up and sung the standard repertoire . . . I'm not a standard person in that respect. I suppose that it's my musical background, or something like that. I was about to give it all up and just be Mrs. Stewart, but Tom—even though we had sworn always to remain separate artists—said he would intercede with Ebert. He asked him to hear me and advise me. I again sang the Composer's music because I knew they needed a Composer, and I was hired."

That was 1959, the year that also took Evelyn Lear to London to sing Richard Strauss' *Four Last Songs* in Royal Festival Hall with the London Symphony under the baton of Sir Adrian Boult—as a last minute replacement for Elisabeth

Grümmer. The manager of the orchestra had failed to relate Miss Grümmer's indisposition to Sir Adrian and, as the maestro was introducing the singer to the orchestra as the famed German soprano, the nervous Miss Lear (she had learned the music in five days) tugged on his sleeve. "But, Sir Boult, Sir Boult, I am not Miss Grümmer." "Well, who the devil are you then?" he demanded. She told him, he rather suspiciously carried on, they rehearsed, and she was well on her way out of the web of obscurity.

The following year, the soprano truly was thrust into international prominence when she sang Alban Berg's provocative *Lulu* in a concert performance for the Vienna Festival, conducted by Karl Böhm, on only three weeks' notice. The most modern music she had sung up until then was Barber's *Knoxville: Summer of 1915,* "and when I received the score in the mail, after having already agreed on the telephone to sing it, I almost dropped dead, because it was the most difficult thing I'd ever seen in my life." Yet the long-implanted discipline, ability to learn virtually overnight (she once learned Micaela in 24 hours), energy, strong will to achieve and hard-core musicianship earned her a triumph in Vienna—so much so that she was invited back for a staged version of *Lulu* at the rebuilt Theater an der Wien in 1962.

The rest is history: opera at Munich, Salzburg, London, San Francisco, Buenos Aires and, finally, New York at the Metropolitan for the world premiere of Levy's *Mourning Becomes Electra* in 1967—in a diverse repertoire that stretches from Monteverdi's Poppea and Mozart's Pamina, Cherubino and Countess, Donna Elvira and Fiordiligi to Strauss' Composer, Octavian and Marschallin, Berg's Lulu (seven productions) and Marie, Klebe's Alkmene, Berlioz' Dido and Lehár's Hanna, the merry widow. Concert assignments have encompassed Bach's *St. John Passion,* Brahms' *German Requiem,* Haydn masses, Berlioz' *Damnation de Faust,* Weill's *Seven Deadly Sins* and Berg's *Altenberg Lieder.* "Karajan asked me to do Salome, but I had to turn him down because I feel it isn't really my thing." No wonder that the Germans call her category *"interessantes Fach."*

Despite the recognition earned from opera, Evelyn Lear has often said she would be quite happy to forsake the opera house in a few years and spend her time in recitals. "Great lieder singing," she feels, "is Romanticism in its purest form, and I feel a great resurgence of the Romantic movement in the trends of youth today—free love, pot, style of dress. Lieder singing is the highest and most demanding art form there is, for in a matter of two or three minutes the essence of a thought or an emotion must be born, live and then die. And it is in the hands of an artist to create the moods with subtlety and passion. I never sing a song the same way twice—an interpretation must vary from concert to concert, depending so much on the mood I am in or the atmosphere stemming from the audience. The challenge for a lieder singer is greater than in opera, but the rewards are even more wonderful."

Evelyn Lear is one of those rare artists who can appreciate, and even expound on, the merits of her colleagues both past and present. After Montserrat Caballé sang Bellini's *La Straniera* at Carnegie Hall, Miss Lear was heard to marvel in awe at the beauty of Caballé's voice and her ethereal *pianissimo*. When Jennie Tourel joined Leonard Bernstein in recital, the soprano expressed wonderment at Tourel's powers of communication and unique vocal timbre. She still recalls with delight a night some years ago when Renata Scotto gave true *bel canto* utterance to *La Sonnambula* in Rome. At the final curtain of Britten's *Peter Grimes* at the Met, she could be found standing and cheering the cast (headed by Jon Vickers) and the opera, which she found "even greater than *Wozzeck*."

"Naturally," she confesses, "my greatest idol in lieder singing was Lotte Lehmann, who never became the slave of the 'arty' way of singing that exists today—but delivered her lieder in genuine, simple, warm and human way. Never mind what she wrote in her books! My idol as the most perfect all-around concert singer, one who included German as well as Russian, French, Spanish and so on, is Jennie Tourel, who incorporated all the qualities so essential to lieder singing: a great voice (I think this is very important), great musicianship, good taste and great depth of feeling. I found no models in Europe that I had not already found at home in America."

As for repertoire, Miss Lear has always preferred Wolf "because the intellectualism of his songs—his fusion of poetry and music—found a very sympathetic chord with me. Every note he wrote had meaning as far as the text was concerned, whereas Schubert's emphasis was more on the melodic line. Also, Wolf is a more contemporary composer. I also love Strauss, less for the poets he chose (most of them poor), but more for the exquisite melodic lines he wove and interwove, sometimes presenting almost insurmountable obstacles in a simple song—and obstacles have always been something which fascinated and challenged me."

In building programs over the past decade, the soprano consciously sought out "the least-known songs to do in a concert rather than picking the most famous chestnuts. This was especially true when I first started making my programs. In the past year or so, in order to gain a wider audience—since lieder recitals in Europe do not have the popularity they had twenty years ago—I have included some better-known songs. Some of them are so beautiful it seems a shame not to sing them just because they are well known. I always try to include one or two contemporary composers in my recitals, even though managers here and in Europe are not too happy with the idea. Unfortunately, not enough composers understand anything about the human voice and seem to write against it, instead of for it."

Does the singer, a New York-bred, world-travelled, sophisticated woman of the mid-twentieth century, find it difficult to sympathize with and convey the meaning of songs so much a part of the past century and past manner? "Why," she parries, "cannot one simply go into a concert today and enjoy himself? Why must everything have social significance or a message? The 19th-century song literature has pertinence both for a singer and the public not because of its social significance, but because it deals with those emotions which are timeless: love, hate, sorrow, pain, death, happiness and so on. The sentiments of the past exist today in modern form, only the manners have changed. Poets of today describe love and hate and sorrow, only they do it in their own way. The basis for an interpretation of a song is an emotion which is timeless. The only thing that I must concern myself with is that I must make myself comfortable in the medium—being me—both in musical style and poetic style. Only then can I express my own emotions regarding a specific song or those emotions contained in a song which I feel must be expressed."

As for preparation, she is a believer in too much, rather than too little: "It is always wise to be well prepared, knowing every nuance that you will sing—but I always leave some little phrasing or subtlety to the inspiration of the moment. It is very important that the text be understood at all times and that it should blend with the melodic line without disturbing it. I learn the texts of my songs first, memorize them as poems, then play my accompaniment through, then tape it on a recorder and learn my songs by memory that way." A childhood of rigorous upbringing and self-sufficiency, when learning and striving already brought rewards, now would seem to be reaping rich rewards for her.

Eventually, Evelyn Lear looks ahead, "when my voice is not fresh anymore—in 20 years or so—I will do some musical comedy. Then I really will have come full circle." For now, however, she is content, calling this the "happiest period of my life, really beautiful. I have the balance of happiness, inner peace and contentment with this renascence in my career, the stirrings, the ambition and the drive I had when I started my career."

★ Rosina Lhevinne ★

One of the greatest influences on the current American school of pianism, Rosina Lhevinne was interviewed in anticipation of her 90th birthday on March 29, 1970—an event celebrated by the Juilliard School, where her eminence has reigned especially strong since 1958, when Van Cliburn won the Tchaikovsky Competition in Moscow and returned an American hero. For a current generation of pianists like Browning and Dichter, she is the last of the elder statesmen, representing perhaps the only remaining link with the late Romantic school and its composers.

Late on a winter's afternoon, Rosina Lhevinne sits proud and erect just across from the piano in her longtime apartment just a stone's throw from the old Juilliard building, quietly sipping tea, the only noise an occasional clink of the spoon against the side of the cup as she stirs. This remarkable woman has been with the school for some 48 years. Pupils first came to Josef and Rosina Lhevinne's home for lessons paid by the Juilliard estate, and then they began teaching at the school's first home on West 52nd Street. "You know," she begins, as she begins many statements, "You know, Russians are either very up or very down." Pause. "Today, I am up"—and as the tape begins to turn she proceeds to talk with but a little prompting from the sidelines. The following are excerpts from a two-hour conversation which Mme Lhevinne herself later conceded leaned more in the direction of a monologue . . . à la Russe, of course.

You know, we didn't leave Russia on account of the political situation. We left in 1906 because Mr. Lhevinne [as she always refers to her late husband] in 1905 wanted to come to America. It was the time of the Japanese war and the first Russian revolution—they did not want to dismiss the Czar, but to have a senate like here in America. Safonoff was our professor and he had come to America as guest conductor for five years. An impresario asked my husband to come as soloist on tour with the Philharmonic, Safonoff conducting. My husband, being the most unpractical person who lived on earth, didn't ask for a contract or the fee or anything. He loved America above everything, even though he had never been there. In our family they had always said that America is the country of freedom, a country . . . as it says on the French coin—*fraternité, liberté, egalité.* We had always read that about America.

So he came by boat from Bremen and I was waiting a letter from him. When I finally got one he said that when you receive my letter I will probably be on the ocean coming back. The man was not dishonest, but he mistook desire for reality and he couldn't raise enough money. So then his friend Modest Altschuler, who was conductor of the Russian Symphony—it is an organization that lived on support here and support there, but with no possibility of advertising or anything—said to my husband that, instead of going immediately back, he should play with his orchestra. He brought him to Steinway, to Knabe, to Mason-Hamlin and Chickering and all the piano manufacturers would say is "Wonderful," "Magnificent," "Let's see what the press will say." But what could the press say when he had no engagements? So he said he would play, even though they could not pay a red cent or make any publicity, and he played the Rubinstein Fifth Concerto. In 1895 he won the Rubinstein International Prize with this Concerto, which is exceedingly difficult, starting with a big cadenza solo. A few years ago, a fireman who was still alive at Carnegie Hall told me: "Madame Lev*i*ne"—he always said Lev*i*ne—"you ought to have seen that. People started to move to see if it was a real person or a pianola or something, because not a word of publicity had appeared." Before he played nobody wanted to do anything, but then Steinway told him to come the next morning and offered him a contract for $10,000—and $10,000 then was $100,000 now—and they said they would manage him themselves. He was the second person only after Paderewski.

And so then in 1906 we came together. I was pregnant with the boy, but he arranged all that. You know, he was so quiet and so placid and so out of this world that in little domestic things he let me do whatever I wanted, and people thought that I could turn him around my little finger. But all the big things in our life he arranged himself. The trains were three days to Berlin and very unhygienic—and I would never do this. So he arranged to sell all our furniture and in May go to Paris where his brother-in-law had a *sanité*—not a hospital but a convalescent home. The child was born there. Then we, with this Russian woman and my father, we all came to America in *cabine deluxe,* and it was marvelous. We arrived in 1906 and then in 1907 we had a villa in Wahnsee, a suburb in Germany, a beautiful place, while he concertized in Germany, France and England. Then we came back and he had another tour. In 1910 I stayed in Germany while he had a tour in Mexico, a stupendous success. When they are very enthusiastic, they throw the person into the air—there are thousands of hands and, really, he cannot fall. But all the next contracts he insisted on one condition—that they do not throw in him the air, because he thought it was a horrible feeling.

I gave up playing the piano seven days after we were married, even though I had finished with the same coveted gold medal as Mr. Lhevinne. Every one of my friends, our friends and so-called friends said that in one year they will be divorced, because this young girl will think of her career and she will never leave it. And that's one thing in life I remember with great pleasure, because I was only 18 and I gave myself a solemn promise that I would never play alone. I kept it until it was our 40th anniversary, and to celebrate the occasion Juilliard gave a party and a big concert in Carnegie Hall—and Mr. Lhevinne, lo and behold, said he would play this concert only if I played alone. I said we should only play together, but he insisted—and our dean and my colleagues, nobody helped me. So I was really brave when I started this concert. I played Chopin and he played Tchaikovsky and then we played the Mozart E-flat together, with Hutcheson, the President, conducting. That was 1938, and Mr. Lhevinne passed away in 1944.

I never played alone again and, in general, I didn't think that I would go on the stage at all anymore. But when I was 75 the Aspen Festival engaged me to teach and Mack Harrell —he was a wonderful singer and every two years President of the Faculty—came to say it was not obligatory but he liked the faculty to play with the orchestra. I did not have to do it, but I thought it would be great fun to play alone and I agreed —but only if I could play a Mozart concerto which I hardly taught at all and never had played myself. So I learned [K.] 497, D major, and I played in Aspen, and after it was recorded with our orchestra in Juilliard. Then every year I learned a new one and I played five Mozart concertos—and then I played the Bach Triple Concerto with the Babins, as well as a lot of chamber music. It got around that I played in Aspen, and Barnett of the National Orchestral Association asked me to make a recording.

But the zenith of my career was one day when I came with

a student who was playing for a Young People's Concert with Bernstein. So I came just to be there and Bernstein said, "Listen, I hear all around that you play now yourself. Why won't you play with the Philharmonic?" I said, "You know, that's a nice question. I would do it but nobody has ever asked me." So he said we must play together. Then Moseley called me just out of the clear blue sky to ask if I would play with the Philharmonic. I said, wait now, let me sit down, because it is so exciting. They wanted three days in succession, Thursday, Friday and Saturday—and I felt that was not in my power. He said he would report to Lenny, and Lenny said, "Tell her that, knowing her, after she plays three days, on the fourth she will not know what to do with herself and will say she wants to play again"—and it was the real truth: I couldn't find myself a place, you know. I was aching to play again. The joy I had in playing with him is not to be described. He asked if he could come to Juilliard to accompany me, so he would know my ideas, so that the rehearsal would be easier. And from the very first opening, you know, when the piano enters, I played the theme and he jumped up and kissed me and said, "How can it be that it is the third generation, not the second, the third, and that we feel so much together." So the whole Concerto he accompanied and all the time he jumped and kissed.

I entered the Conservatory when I was nine. I was very sickly and a very small child. My colleagues afterwards said that the door would open and something huge would come into the room, and my mother would take all my coats and shoes and sweaters off and underneath it was a bean. I think in three months my teacher became sick and Safonoff said to my teacher that she should take his star pupil, Josef Lhevinne, to help me until my teacher would be well. So he presented himself to the house—he was fourteen but looked like seventeen, and I was nine and looked like six. He gave me lessons for three months, and then my teacher was well and I continued. But he became a friend of the house. When we had some big parties, he would come many times and he would not look at me at all because he was a grown man and I was a child.

You know, I didn't take the regular schooling in the Conservatory. The Russian Conservatory in this way was wonderful—you didn't have to go to school like here, but they had all the subjects (in the morning it was music and in the afternoon we had all the regular school). You could either go or be tutored at home, but every year you had to pass the examination. As I was such a sickly child, my parents never sent me there, so I had the home tutors. When I was fifteen, one of my teachers said that his wife would be away and would I be the hostess for a little bridge party he was giving. So I was very honored and I went there and after dinner I thought it was my duty to wash the marvelous crystal glasses they had. So I was in the kitchen and, lo and behold, who came in but Mr. Lhevinne, who asked what I was doing there. I told him and evidently I was quite a rascal. Every time he came to my house he had always raved about Katinka, Patinka, Sashinka—you know, all kinds of girls. So I said, "It is quite a long time I haven't seen you—with whom are you in love now?" He said she has dark eyes and dark hair and she is a pianist, and I could see my portrait absolutely—but I didn't say "boo" and that's all. Then he started to come quite often to the house and took me to his friends. My mother allowed me to go even though in Russia then a girl didn't go with boys until . . . I really don't remember even. I was never a girl—I was a child and then I was a married woman. But he introduced me to some very interesting people.

One was a professor of history who every Friday had a gathering. We met Chekhov, Gorki, the head of the Moscow Art Theater. Musicians were invited to play, so Mr. Lhevinne played many, many times. One day he said, "Why don't you play something." And you know, I looked at him always that he was up there and I was down here. So I didn't feel that I ought to. But he said it would be nice because they invited me and that is the wages here, that people offer their services. So I played a Chopin nocturne and, you know, I think that one woman that night was the one who decided my attitude in life if we would be married. When we went to the cloak room to dress, she came to me and she thought to give me the greatest pleasure in the world by saying, "You know, I like your playing even better than Mr. Lhevinne's." And I thought: So that's how it is. It is so silly of people who would hear one piece that

maybe I played well—but certainly I couldn't compare to the
pianist he was at that time, because he was five years older
and already a mature artist. So I think it was then I made my
decision not to play, but this woman never disappeared from
my mind. I always thought that in playing there would be a
certain rivalry which I thought was absurd—because I didn't
put myself on the same plane with him.

So I never played, but the first year we were married César
Cui came to visit us. You know that always in Russia the
maid would answer the door and one would give a visitor's
card, very formal. He had a grey coat lined with red and a
sabre on the side and white gloves. He came and said he was
going to be the head of a certain concert given for the orphans
and widows of the musicians—and that he wanted something
very unusual. "Why don't you play the First Suite of Arensky,
who was your composition teacher. It would be wonderful,
because it is such a novelty. Nobody plays two pianos." Certainly, for Mr. Lhevinne it was a torture, but for me it was
a great joy because I had decided I wouldn't play at all alone.
So we said we would be delighted and we played and, you
know, the next day they didn't speak so much about our playing—yes, they said lovely things—or about the Suite, but they
marvelled that on the stage there were *two* grand pianos!
There was nobody who played two pianos professionally. Occasionally Gabrilowitsch and Bauer would play something
for some charity concert. But the steady team did not exist.
So gradually people knew of our playing and we played a
great deal, especially at this 40th anniversary. I remember
we played 38 concerts together and they were always called
"concerts for one and two pianos." Either we started the first
group, then the second he played alone and the third we'd
finish together—or he would start and we would play one
group in the middle. And that's the only professional work
I did.

You know, there are two things of which I am very proud—
of anything musical I don't feel proud. That's not the word
I ever used, even when they asked me about Mr. Lhevinne.
But I was proud when I was only 18 and I gave myself that

word not to play alone. And then the second one. I was a terribly spoiled child because I was sickly. Then when I married Mr. Lhevinne he brought me to reality because I always spoke of "my little hands and my little feet," and he would say "Nothing of the sort—regular feet and regular hands." One day after we were married my mother arranged a little cottage on one side of a Moscow suburb—they lived on the other side because it was better that I wouldn't be so close. So we would travel Sundays or Saturdays to them and he adored the sky. For him the sky was, I think, not only made on the same plane as the piano, but in his heart I think he liked the sky more. So he always looked and told me everything, even though I was a very bad student. He knew every constellation with the naked eye. This one time he was looking at the sky and he said, "Rosina, look, there's a million mosquitos," and really it was so humid and the air was full of them. "You know," he said, "we are one of them." And it may be hard for someone to believe this, but it really changed my character a great deal—to feel my size in the world.

As I say, I was brought up with tremendous love and care. They made me a queen in the house and then I probably formed in my head that I was not only the center of my home but the center of the universe. And here I was one of the mosquitos. You know, I received a terrible, terrible shock to realize this. But since then I became really a very different person, with the good qualities that I have—because people say that I am so very kind—but also, it is a very great gift from God that I have of forgetting the bad things. So I don't have to be so good to forgive, I simply forget, it doesn't exist.

And then I started to think a great deal about my position in life, what I am. Mr. Lhevinne was so celebrated in the beginning of the twentieth century. He was one of the five or six, I would say, that were on the same plane. Living with him all the 46 years we were married, I really became one of those humble persons, and the older I get the more I realize how much I don't know. People don't believe this, and I don't try to speak about it—but some, like Schoenberg, when he gave me a wonderful interview after I played and he said I had a very interesting combination: the greatness of Catherine the

Great and the simplicity of a taxi driver. I think it is very clever.

You know, so many people go to concerts to see what a colleague does bad . . . and the teachers too. Philipp had his Ten Commandments for a teacher—they are very interesting: one of them is to be accustomed to find the biggest ingratitude from the one from whom you would expect the most. And another is to remember that there is no jealous student, only jealous teachers. I think that is very true, because, you know, when a student comes to me I always start with a few words of greeting before I start the lesson. I cannot spend much time, but I always say, "Now what did you hear interesting this week," or something like that—and they will say, "Oh, I heard Rubinstein and he took fourteen wrong notes." I say that doesn't interest me at all—tell me how enchanted you were with his playing, or probably you didn't hear Rubinstein, you didn't hear the pieces—you heard fourteen wrong notes. And they come and tell me about a student of another colleague and how terrible it was. I say that it doesn't interest me at all. The moment a teacher says, "Yes, what did he do wrong?," you know then the student will become exactly that way. He doesn't go with a kind heart to hear his colleagues, he goes to see what he will do wrong.

And, you know, these people cannot play in public, because when they play they see in every corner all the people who are looking to see what they will do wrong. Many stop playing because they have absolutely no control, they are sick. I have played so little in my life, but the very first time I played in Aspen I remember I said in my mind, "I know you are all my friends," because when I go to a concert I really, truly am a friend of the person who is playing. That is why I can almost always, if I want to go backstage, find something very good and speak of that, I don't speak of the places that were bad.

It is interesting that Mr. Lhevinne played thousands of concerts and I played very little, but I never was very nervous. A certain nervousness must be . . . You certainly saw the horse races many times. I was only once, but I was interested to see how before a horse is let loose how every muscle is tensed—and when they let them run then they are really in full power. So it was with me just like that. I was excited, but it is a great difference to be excited or to have stage fright.

After being spoiled all my life at home and even when I was married—the wages in Russia were so low that you could have a cook for $5 a month—so that I always had a cook and a maid who took care of my clothes when I dressed and went to bed and everything. I was really a spoiled person. This Russian woman continued to stay with us, she took care of the children—and even when they went away to school, we still kept her and she had nothing to do but take care of us like we were babies. We always lived in the country in a big house with lots of space. Then Mr. Lhevinne passed away and my children said I ought to sell the house. It was the year the war ended, so in New York you couldn't stay in a hotel more than three days. There were no apartments, no rooms, and my wealthy friends wouldn't take any money—so it would be like taking charity to live with them. So after all our efforts, finally I found a room here on Riverside and then I patted myself on the shoulder. Here I had to move into a room and not even to speak about servants. I couldn't have this woman with me. I had to be on my own. I had to do everything myself to assimilate. Each time I wanted to open the cans, I had to call the janitor because I was helpless.

Gradually, people started coming back from the war, and one day the woman came to me and said, "I'm terribly sorry, but my son is coming back and you will have to leave his room." But where to go? So I asked everybody, almost on the street I was asking for rooms, because I wanted to be near Juilliard. In a restaurant I met a student whom we had known in Denver, who said she and two girls had a two-room apartment, if I wanted to live there. I said it was very kind, but I would keep trying. I found nothing and so moved in with them—and that's *this* apartment. One girl slept in the living room on the couch and the other two had wonderful friends opposite—so they gave me the big bedroom, and every night they undressed, put on their winter coats and went to their friends'. It was very lovely.

When one of the girls' husbands came back, there was no more hospitality, since they needed the room again. They offered me a cot and I had to accept, asking one favor: that a screen be put around the bed. So I lived this way. We had a German superintendent and I bribed him to find me something—one winter, some people went away and I lived there. Then another apartment I took above the janitor—it hurt my children when I told them about this. The girl I mentioned became my assistant and she had so many students and became so rich that she moved to Riverdale—and I got this apartment for myself.

You know, all my friends are young people. I love young people. I love to live with the time. I find myself having more in common with young people than those my age or those 65 or 70. Students at 20 are older than I am in mind. When they play a middle movement of a Schubert sonata I choke, I am so moved by it. They say, "Really? Oh, yes, it is beautiful," but they don't feel it inside. Van [Cliburn] was responsive. I would tell him and he would see that it is very beautiful—he'd get up and walk around and around, saying "I can't stand it, I can't stand it." His music was all emotion before. Now it is combined with the head. Others have the analytical mind first. I use and preach this too: one must analyze and think of the length and climax of a phrase, there must be an awareness and approach to tonalities. I ask my students, "How do you memorize?" Most say they play it until they know it. This is a very insecure way. You must live with it so that you feel the richness of certain colors. John Browning is one of the pupils that gives me the greatest satisfaction—friendship and a student together. He has great intellectuality, but it does not take away from great feeling. But he almost disliked me when I told him to memorize away from the piano, merely holding the score in front of him. I told him he must play his whole program through in his mind in bed before he could permit himself to get up for breakfast. I never play a piece without playing it *away* from the piano.

I think this revival of 19th-century music is an excellent idea. With all respect and admiration for Bach, Beethoven, Mozart and Schubert, we are saturated with the same things. Richter just played the Schumann *Bunte Blätte* and I'm not ashamed to say I didn't know the whole thing, all the small pieces—and I melted at them. A student of mine, Alan Mandel, played and recorded all the Gottschalk. It is not great music, but some is good and it is refreshing to hear new things. Many things of the past are good, but not great maybe—like the Rubinstein Concertos. Hofmann made a fortune on the Fourth. Rubinstein never corrected his writing, he wrote clean manuscripts—so there are weak spots. Medtner wrote wonderful poems, too. There are 48 Preludes and Fugues, but you get so tired. . . .

I wonder how the Russian school produces all the wonderful pianists. Think of them—Richter, Ashkenazy, Gilels and now Slobodyanik came to see me. Americans think the Russian style is all technique. But the Greek word *"technika"* means art and craft. We were taught from childhood to think of the art. We are the middle man between the music and the listener, and we must reproduce the wishes of the composer. To do this we must completely possess the piano. And to do this we must acquire technique early in school. It is mistaken to think that technique is the goal of Russian pianists—it is not so. It is never a goal, but a means to interpret.

One magazine traced the thread of our tradition. It says it is from Bach. We were pupils of Safonoff, who was a pupil of Leschetizky, who was a pupil of Liszt and then back to Bach. There is hardly a university in the United States without our students now teaching. I find the names of people all over. Now I have 22 pupils with two assistants, and I give three lessons every day at home. I am my boss and I am grateful Juilliard leaves it to me. If a pupil is talented, I give the lessons —the more primitive information they get from my assistants. Exams are a difficult time, because I want to hear all the pupils play everything from A to Z. My master classes every two weeks give the students a chance to play pieces fresh from the oven. I am the master of ceremonies and introduce them. They bow and play A to Z. When they finish, I make remarks —I do not offend or intimidate. Then at the next lesson I tell

them in detail what they did or did not do. In selecting my
pupils I look for musicality and sensitivity, not the amount of
technical equipment they have. You can always teach technique, but you cannot inject or instill the other. Oh yes, up to
a point he may be able to imitate what you do, but it can never
be truly his.

★ Yehudi Menuhin ★

*Yehudi Menuhin appears in many guises each season: as
violinist with orchestra, as conductor, as leader of the Menuhin Festival Orchestra, as recitalist with his sister Hephzibah,
as collaborator with sitarist Ravi Shankar. I talked with him
in the winter of 1971 in the midst of several of these activities
spread among New York's concert halls.*

There wasn't exactly the calm one would expect to be reigning in the Menuhin suite. Citizen-of-the-world Yehudi nervously took a series of phone calls in the all blue damask
living room, while son Jeremy napped in the next room. Wife
Diana, a former ballerina and actress, swept in from the bedroom in a long brown, fur-trimmed coat, tight red cap and
high boots to shield her from Fifth Avenue winds. "Do you
know why I married him?" comes her opening line, as if the
lights had just dimmed and the curtain was going up on a collaboration between Coward and Shaw. "I asked him if he'd
heard of Garbo and he said, 'What's Garbo?' We laughed
and I said *'Who's* Garbo' and he asked me to marry him."
    The telephone rings again and Menuhin is being encour-
aged to do the David Frost Show. He covers the phone—"Do
we like him?" he queries gently, and he is awarded an af-
firmative nod from Diana, who continues: "Yehudi can talk

about anything from bee's knees to engineering without preparation in thirty minutes flat." Then with a flourish of "Loves"
and "Dahlings" she is off into the winter air. No sooner have
we settled down to talk than stirrings of scales and *arpeggios*
and smatterings of this-and-that well up in the next room—
Jeremy, who has just made his American solo debut with the
American Symphony under his father's baton, is up and back
at the piano for his afternoon practice.

No, life hadn't been exactly calm as of late. Yehudi Menuhin had been involved in a headline-making "misunderstand-
ing" with the U.S. Government over his acceptance of an
honorary Swiss citizenship as a kind of thank-you for his or-
ganizing of a yearly festival in Gstaad; he was conducting
Bartók's Concerto for Orchestra for the first time in his career
with the American Symphony: there was the expected interest
in still another Menuhin's debut in this country . . . the
phone didn't seem to want to stop ringing. He appeared visibly
relieved to sink into the deep-cushioned sofa and calmly talk.
The 54-year-old musician has dipped into so many and
diverse musical, educational and political pots that it is hard
to know exactly where to begin. Lending what an English
writer recently called his "mixture of beneficence, idealism
and common sense," Menuhin steered the conversation in the
direction of youth, schooling and musical development.

For quite a number of years he has balanced his own career
between playing the violin and conducting, often combining
the two in chamber orchestra concerts. "I still love each for
what it gives. Personally, I still call myself a violinist, not a
conductor. I still think of myself as a violinist. In fact, I have
begun to think of myself *more* as a violinist in the past ten
years than I did before. It's partly the school I have in
England [the Yehudi Menuhin School at Stoke d'Abernon
in Surrey] and the teaching there and the learning there. I
think that nothing teaches a teacher as much as his effort to
teach. And I'm bringing out a violin method in April in book
form and on film in a series of six half-hours. The first lesson
is preparatory exercise, because it is so important to learn to
use your body and your lungs for breathing before picking
up the violin. Then comes handling the bow without the

violin, and the violin without the bow; then the use of the bow and the use of the left hand, and finally the coordinating of the two."

Menuhin agrees that having to teach basic technique made him look at his own playing more objectively. "But I had always been aware of basic technique, possibly because I started out as a musician, rather than as a violinist. My teachers were Persinger, Enesco, Busch—I mean very, very great musicians—not the violin teachers like Flesch, Auer and Sevcik, not people who only concentrated on technique. Besides, I played fairly well at a very early age, well enough so that none of my teachers felt they wanted to say anything about it. And I still feel today that when I see a child playing well and getting around the violin, I leave well enough alone . . . unless I feel there are specific dangers that might develop over the years—I just guide it and don't try to do anything that might damage. It can work itself out if it is guided along main lines, which are simply the maximum results for the minimum effort and smooth transitions and a pleasant feeling in the body, with no constraint—that kind of basic approach. Obviously, if you see something like this," and he throws his arm into an awkward fingering position, "you try to correct it. All this has given me a great deal to work with."

His boarding school for young talent is considered unique of its kind outside of Russia. Its foundation is based on the Russian educational techniques the violinist found in the Central School of Music in Moscow. "It was my ambition when I first saw this beautiful school—I think it was in 1945—to start something along the same lines. I finally got to it in 1963, which was a long wait," he smiles. "The Russian school was the inspiration, but, of course, it is an entirely different atmosphere. I don't say it is better or worse—but it is an atmosphere geared to our Western ways of thought, our Western values. In other words, the idea isn't to create virtuosi at any price and to aim at the first prize in Brussels . . . though if we had a child that could win it we would be quite pleased. It is to create a whole generation of well-balanced human beings who are excellent musicians; who are equally at home in chamber music or orchestra; who have a good basic knowledge of theory and composition and history; and who also can teach. I think it is more important to penetrate deeply into society than produce the one performer—and I can say, in all honesty, that we have succeeded. We have only been going for seven years and anyone who visits the school finds that it is quite extraordinary.

"The children are extremely well balanced in the sense that they know the values of life. They know what comes through work. They know that things don't happen overnight. They know the time and dedication it takes. They are really incredibly musical—I don't think that in any other school in the world you would find children of nine, ten and eleven playing, say, the Mendelssohn Trio with that degree of musicianship *and* proficiency, not even in Russia. You might find in Russia many individual players of nine and ten who play the Tchaikovsky Concerto very well . . . better than ours . . . but you wouldn't find the human being with that depth —no, the depth of feeling you would find—but the sophisticated application of that depth to individual expression, to the understanding of the piece.

"And every one of these children composes," he declares like a proud father. "About a year ago I spent a delightful day at the school listening to them perform all the compositions they had written. It was quite amazing to hear these pieces, each so true to its author. Some were very classical and very prim, others very modern and aggressive—absolutely the mirror image of their composers. And I think *that* is so important today, again, because we are living in a world where the individual must learn to command the raw materials of expression. He mustn't be dependent all the time on the ready-made, you see, which I think is one of the problems in our country: we've gotten used to the finished product, to the ready-made —and we've lost the savor and the flavor of life, which *only* resides in the raw. It's the transferring, the changing of the raw into what is the expression of your own self—the whole joy and satisfaction and frustration of life is built into this. But if you are surrounded by packaged, finished products with the money to buy them, that is the end of life."

These children, Menuhin continues, are entirely different because of the way they have disciplined themselves. "Most of them get up at six in the morning. In fact, there is a rather exaggerated zeal—almost like in some monasteries where the monk who has flagellated himself more than the others feels he is holier. But the headmaster had to discourage it and say, 'Now, you can't fight with each other over who is going to get up earlier and put in more work.' But they are very good to each other . . . it's like a family. Competition is not encouraged exactly, but it is there naturally, in a healthy way. When I teach and someone is doing a particular exercise well, I tell them to show it to another who also needs it. And whenever they can, they do help each other out." As for applicants, he believes that the actual audition, to the extent that it is only what they can play, "is often very inconclusive. It is their approach, their enthusiasm, the feeling one has as to what degree they are willing to give up everything for music—and then their coordination, their memory, their ear, their sense of pitch, whether they can carry a melody, many things. One of the cardinal conditions also is that if at any moment the child should give up music, he can continue with regular schooling —so they have to take what they call their O Levels and A Levels as well." He is happy with the fact that the school is self-propelled—"not financially, but self-propelled. I am not indispensable, which is the way it should be."

Beyond the confines of the school in Surrey, on a larger scale, the violinist-conductor believes that putting music into the education curriculum from the beginning would lead to making music more an integral part of people's lives. "I want to see music in the kindergarten, in the same way that painting is. You see tremendous, extravagant expression of painting all over, and interest in painting. There is real interest because everyone is painting, every child has painted from the time he can remember. The same thing must happen in music. I would like to see the children in kindergarten not only making music and singing, but also making their instruments—primitive instruments like certain African and Indian tribes make, from whatever they happen to lay their hand on. I think that's terribly important, along with improvisation and composing, which I am encouraging at the school. The regular instruments are forbidding to youngsters, because of the expertise needed to play them. That's why it should come by degrees, from the simplest first. And there are some delightful works for simple instruments."

He also stresses that each country should foster something like the Kodály method in the schools. "Only I don't like to see a method transplanted, you know, lock-stock-and-barrel from one country to another. The wonderful chorales that Kodály wrote for the children are their birthright, their heritage. This method could be adapted with compositions written by composers in each country. It seems rather silly for American children, let's say, to sing Hungarian chorales —they don't suit them. Why should they? We want variety in the world. The Orff method, too, is wonderful to the extent that it coordinates mime and dance and music—but musically it's a little bit thin, for the simple reason that it confines itself exclusively to one pentatonic scale. There's no reason why the Orff method couldn't be multiplied and enlarged by providing the children with a variety of pentatonic and other scales on their xylophones—and then give them their names as they exist in Africa and India. This way they could get used to the characteristics of each particular kind of scale and know that this scale belongs to such-and-such tribe, which has such-and-such habits and lives in such-and-such climate and has evolved this music because it expresses something peculiar to that environment. Adding the dances of the tribes, or at least dances synthesized from those tribes, suiting the music and the rhythms, would fire a child's imagination at the earliest level."

One reason for the present gap between the young generation and the older established concert audience, Menuhin feels, is that "music has become so evolved—they coin this awful phrase 'esoteric music'—and it's too far removed from the ordinary child, unless that child has been born into a composer's family and has been around it. Therefore, music must begin with the elements, the simplest forms, right away with dance and song and the simplest of instruments." Music, he notes, represents the age to which it belongs—"and we do live in a violent age, a time which is becoming increasingly violent. The antidote is the practice and discipline of the arts." He sees that today, although the very conception of melody has, to a certain extent, given way to rhythm and percussion, "melody will not disappear from the face of the earth. I can't imagine that it will disappear, because melody is continuity, the continuity of the individual and of society. And sooner or later, if we are to survive, some form of continuity will find its way.

"The religions which provided continuity of thought, whether it was reincarnation or sojourns in heaven and hell —they all dealt with eternity over the cycle of lives. Well, today we've lost that idea and that is why there is also a great deal of anxiety . . . because no one feels that it is worth living for the future. Parents feel frustrated, people don't plant trees that might take a hundred years to grow, children live on the brink of crisis—this is true of our day. Yet I can't help feeling that, barring fundamental holocaust (which may well take place), if we survive there will be some basic new morality, new conception, new continuity and therefore melody—the expression of continuity, just as harmony is an expression of society and rhythm the pulse of life. Now the pulse is frenetic and hectic, but sooner or later melody must come back. Melody is line. We have so many jagged edges and fragmentary bits of this and that, and we are so overwhelmed with a thousand impressions and a thousand fears. But the long line must surely one day restore itself. What is more, the people are longing for it. I mean, if they hear something that conveys a sense of direction, of serenity and of unity of life, they are restored and are grateful for it."

Continuity—that word crops up again in his fascination with Eastern philosophies and music. "I have always been interested in Eastern thought," he states, "but I don't really know a great deal about it . . . nor am I a believer in the sense of *literal* interpretation of belief. I see in all interpretations of infinity and eternity a great element of the symbolic. I love the symbolic for a variety of reasons, but I don't despise the symbolic because I find it to be untrue in the literal sense. I'm not a fundamentalist that way at all. I can't bear that sort of childish approach to liberal values in the Bible or any other holy book. When I was in India quite recently and spoke in Delhi where I received the Nehru Medal, I referred to the theory of reincarnation, saying that it seemed to be the most practical way in which the two cardinal elements were joined in assuring continuity: that is, the principle of heredity and the principle of merit. Heredity is what you are born, and you will be reincarnated as a human being or an animal or a human being on another level, depending on the merit you deserve in life. The fact that you have gained a little upping in one life doesn't guarantee a further upping in the next—you might fall back. That is an extremely clever contrivance to ensure the maintenance of the two cardinal principles alongside each other."

When pinned down to his belief in reincarnation, he shakes his head, "No, I can't say I believe in it because I don't know any way . . . how shall I say it? . . . to prove it. I am still sufficiently Western to want to understand a thing more, in greater tangible reality. On the other hand, I do believe with Shakespeare that, as Hamlet speaks in reference to the ghost, there is more strangeness in life than the mind can grasp. There are mysteries which are nonetheless true for being mysterious, but which we cannot explain. And so with reincarnation—there is obviously some continuity . . . we cannot just pop up for a second, we wouldn't be what we are were it not for the millions and millions of generations that have preceded us. This is obvious to anyone."

The most substantial contribution of Eastern thought to Menuhin's own life has been the practice of yoga, which he simply calls "the answer to many physical requirements. It is a form of exercise which doesn't require great spaces or a great deal of time. And certainly it is not aggressive in its content. It is meant to prepare the mind and the body for concentration, not for attack or defense. Even before I went to India for the first time about 20 years ago, it appealed to me on these grounds. I had learned a few of the stances, the postures and then our Indian friends introduced me to the various gurus, most of them very ancient men with long white beards, practicing on leopard skins, praying. Yoga has, to a certain extent, given me a sense of serenity. But without time to play tennis or swim a great deal, it has given me the opportunity to maintain a physical form in the minimum of time and with the least cost of effort."

Yehudi Menuhin the violinist has been playing since the

age of seven, when he made his debut in the Lalo *Symphonie espagnole* with the San Francisco Symphony. At 11 the prodigy undertook the historical Bach-Beethoven-Brahms debut in Berlin, followed by success in London and New York, as well as violin-piano sonata evenings with his sister Hephzibah. Born in New York in 1916, he began his violin studies at five with three great teaching influences coming from the American violinist Louis Persinger, the Rumanian George Enesco and the German Adolf Busch. Musically, he recalls, one of the deepest impressions was hearing Bach's *St. Matthew Passion* in Amsterdam conducted by Willem Mengelberg in 1938. A lasting memory as well was the first time he heard Beethoven's *Eroica,* when he was 11 in Paris. Of his own career a singular experience was his work with Wilhelm Furtwängler, with whom he played the Beethoven and Brahms concertos.

"But, personally, I never felt more wrung out, more deeply moved, as if I had gone through a catharsis with the audience and understood what the purpose of the *Passion* is than when I did the *St. John* at Windsor. I realized what it was to provide human beings with the whole gamut of human experience from its most hideous to its most sublime—and for them to share it. It's an archetypal story: human beings are as hideous as all that, as wonderful as that. Every person brings to it what he himself has known of the human experience, leaving the place, as it were, purged and clean. You can't ask for much more than that. Even if people don't go to church today, music can still do it—and the people who attended that *St. John* in that chapel, together with me and the singers and the orchestra, when it was all over we were different, we were renewed. I have experienced this kind of thing individually before with other pieces of Bach, but never on that scale, never together with the multitude, never together as one in front of something as tangible as the *Passion.*"

As a violinist describing the course of his playing for nearly five decades, he pauses to reflect, summing up: "Well, I think I have achieved . . . how to put it? . . . certainly a far better understanding of the violin and of the approach to it and the technical approach than ever I had as a child. When I began I had flair and talent and could get away with a great many things—but then what I knew was not sufficient to gap what I didn't know. And I feel *that,* more or less, has come around. Now it's a matter of old age catching up. I played absolutely instinctually, instinctively. And I remember my first awakening was not a technical one, but a musical one . . . characteristically. It was in 1936, traveling back to Europe from Australia via South Africa. It was on a long sea voyage from Perth to Durban in an old blue funnel coal-burning boat.

"The family was, as usual, together. My sisters had a piano in their room and practiced. And I realized that I was playing a great many works which I could not explain—just like the reincarnation. I couldn't explain *why* one note followed another, not in terms of dominant recapitulation, development and so on, which never interested me a great deal—those are just words denoting great lumps of music. But what interested me always is the cell, the individual cell that constitutes the life of a particular work. So then and there I began taking apart the Leclair Sonata I was playing at the time. Then gradually followed all the works I had been playing. The approach I evolved at that time was quite simply stated: never to take anything for granted, never to accept any note in a piece that is not explained by a previous note. The rule of the game is that you cannot explain a note in terms of the same sequence in another composition, or by saying that that's a C-major scale. If you go to Beethoven and say he has written down a D-major scale, you won't get anywhere with the music. You have to see how the whole is related to that scale, how it evolves and what makes that D-major scale special in terms of that particular composition. It was a very interesting game I played.

"Then technically, the same thing happened—but much later. I began to say, 'Well, why do I do this, and what makes this stroke and why, and what is the difference between a *détaché* and a *staccato'* in terms of the actual muscles and joints we use—things to which I had never given a thought before. And I dare say that if I had *not* given thought to them, I would by this time probably have been a cripple. I have that kind of mind that is not satisfied unless it really understands a thing. It's got to be satisfied and if it isn't, it's probably doing it wrong."

Although Menuhin did not stop playing certain works after giving them such reconsideration, there are certain works, he reveals, which he is not playing as frequently as he once did. "One is the 'Perpetual Motion' of Paganini which I played every night on tour. I dare say that I could still play it were I willing to give up a thousand other things and practice the violin eight hours a day—and I don't think this belongs to a musician at the age of 54. There's nothing sadder, I think, than to see a violinist who is 60 or 70, trotting around the world with his violin case and playing the pieces he has always played before. That's not the future as I would like to think of it. But once in a while I enjoy playing the old things. Just the other day on BBC television in London I did the *Symphonie espagnole,* which I hadn't played in nearly three decades. It was rather fun. I had time and worked on it and enjoyed doing it. And from time to time I may do that kind of thing again . . . especially with recording changes—now they have four-track instead of two-track and all such nonsense. Anyway, under the persuasion of the company, who said my Paganini Concertos will come off the market unless there is a new ten-channel stereo recording version, I may have still another fling with that, you see."

His conducting career began some twenty years ago when he performed Bach and Mozart concertos with a small group of musicians in Paris. "Anyway, now it's already about 12 or 13 years since the orchestra which was known as the Bath Festival Orchestra was put together in London for the Bath Festival and for recording. Now since I moved to Windsor we've given up the name Bath and called it the Menuhin Festival Orchestra—it's the same ensemble, of course, and I'm bringing it here, as you know." Gstaad specializes more in chamber music, with occasional blending of the Menuhin Festival Orchestra with the Zürich Chamber Orchestra. "We try as far as possible to coordinate. Windsor and Gstaad are what I love to do . . . but they are hardly what maintain me."

It was at Gstaad that still another Menuhin career was launched in 1965. Son Jeremy was then 13—now he had made his New York debut and his father talked of his son's burgeoning musical career as any sane parent would talk about

his child's decision to pursue medicine, teaching or law. "Whatever comes, it will be Jeremy's own launching. In fact, all
his life he's launched himself in that sense. He was very determined to give himself up completely to music. He was at Eton
for nearly two years, doing well but—although they had given
him a special room where he could work every day for an
hour or so and he would go every week to Marcel Gazelle,
who is the music master of my own school—nonetheless he
felt he wanted only music and he took the reins into his own
hands. After two three-month leaves, we knew he was really
determined to go ahead with music in Paris. He was studying
with Nadia Boulanger for composition, theory and so on, and
with Marcel Ciampi, who was my sister's teacher when we
were all young in Paris. I didn't want to burn the bridges behind Jeremy at Eton until he'd proved himself in music. He
had been trained since he was four, and he played the piano
and wrote notes before he wrote the alphabet. Now at 15 he
had a room adjoining Nadia Boulanger's apartment, so that
she could keep an eye on him. And if he didn't lay on sixty
hours of work a week, he wasn't satisfied. It was absolutely his
own initiative."

Has his handling of his own son been considerably different
than that of his own father's of him? "Oh, it couldn't be more
different—nor is it so by design or necessarily principle, because the circumstances are so entirely different. Actually,
you could still find common denominators of devotion and
tremendous desire to see the child do well and express himself, and protection. Only it takes an entirely different form.
The protection today, at least in my wife's and my experience,
has taken the form of exposure rather than protection. The
boarding school is both a protection and an exposure, in the
sense that it is a complete little world of its own with its tradi-
tions and habits—but where the child receives an uncommon
degree of freedom. Eton has the tutorial system—quite free,
with no one hounding them to do their homework. If they
don't do it, well it just isn't done and they don't pass. Up until
then at home he had been so closeted that he had to be pushed
out of the house into the world to make it on his own, draw his
own conclusions and gain his own experience. He was in a
tall fury, but he has a wonderfully live temperament—the

fury was over in about five seconds, leaving the sky quieter
and purer and more serene than it was ever before.

"Although everyone has assumed I watched over him musically and nurtured him, that is far from the truth. The fact is
that he was naturally in a musical household . . . during the
summers in Gstaad and where we were doing chamber music
rehearsals he was naturally in the house and heard it . . . and
there was always a piano. And there were always musicians.
Actually, I didn't begin to do anything for him musically
until we were performing together. Every year now for about
five years he has played concertos and chamber music in
Gstaad. Of course, in connection with the works we discuss
them very specifically. But he has probably gotten more from
Hephzibah than he did from me because she was often in the
house and playing, and she's taken him through quite a number of works in the repertoire. There is no question that he is
born a musician. For me all this is tremendously interesting
because I am cast in the role of father, and I feel I'm beginning to imagine what my father must have felt when being
interviewed."

Asked about Jeremy's statement to *The New York Times*
that "classical music is going steadily downhill. Its great days
are over. Before very long, no one will be interested in it anymore," Menuhin the elder swallows hard before relating:
"Well, when he read it and showed it to me he was rather
upset by the categorical . . . shall I say by seeing the words
in print and having them take on a firm meaning. He was
probably speaking spontaneously and said these things as coun-
ter-weights to certain arguments and with a certain measure
of conviction too. But it wasn't the way he felt about it and
he didn't wish to give so exclusive an impression, because he
adores classical music as he loves contemporary music. He
was upset to read that it had been presented without its . . .
how shall I say? . . . without all the exceptions and limitations. These are important, I told him, because people tend
to crystallize, especially a man trying to make a portrait of
you. If he has caught onto something which seems definite, he
will present it as such. I think the important thing is not to
let anything crystallize too soon. As soon as you have said one

thing, immediately give the conditional clauses almost in the same breath.

"The same thing—Jeremy was a bit upset by the presentation referring to his background as claustrophobic. Well, I said, 'But you were perfectly right. Every child must feel claustrophobic in the presence of his parents.' There is no question of that. On the other hand, compared to most children, when you think he has been independent since he was 12 or 13, that he has seen half the world, that he has had his own apartment in Vienna for two years now and had his own room in Paris for two years before that, there is hardly anything confining about that. But what he meant to convey was that he feels freer when his parents are not around—which he has every right to say . . . but didn't say."

One of the things Yehudi Menuhin is undoubtedly passing on to his son is a philosophy regarding an artist's responsibility to his public. "Oh, that's a very great thing," his eyes light up almost beatifically. "And that responsibility can only be fulfilled by the artist being true to the music, to the composer and to himself. I'm always touched by the response, the emotional and the intellectual and the human response of the audience, when I feel that something Bartók or Beethoven or Mozart or Bach wanted to say is sensed by the audience—that they know something is either grand or serene or deeply touching or moving or speaks of the broken heart or represents a deep human experience or stands for a moral conviction. And I feel that the audience *can* respond to it if the work is played in the right way. Then I feel how important it is to give the audience that—to go beyond yourself while bringing what you can of yourself to it. But I am invariably very grateful to and very moved by an audience who feels with me. There's nothing nicer than to know or sense that during a performance the audience is with you . . . that's a wonderful thing."

★ Sherrill Milnes ★

Already in the winter of 1970, Sherrill Milnes was recognized as "the" Verdi baritone of his time, a stature he maintains with a growing artistry. We talked before he opened the New York Philharmonic's eighth season of "Promenades" concerts. He has since gone on to sing Macbeth and Monforte in I Vespri Siciliani, *as well as Don Giovanni at the Metropolitan.*

The white-turtlenecked Sherrill Milnes had just returned from two rehearsals and was about to sing a benefit concert for Boris Goldovsky, as well as attend the annual Grammy Awards (he was up for two himself) that evening. His wife, soprano Nancy Stokes, was busy in the kitchen preparing a dinner to refuel her husband's sagging energies, but quickly produced drinks and cheese. Two Met *Traviatas* remained on his home schedule before he would be off for Vienna for his debut at the Staatsoper as Verdi's Macbeth. From there his months were heavily charted: *I Vespri Siciliani* at the Teatro Colon in Buenos Aires (another debut), recordings of *Don Carlo* and *Ballo in maschera* and the Met opening come September in *Ernani*.

One thing was immediately evident (if it hadn't already been clear all along): Sherrill Milnes had "made it." He has been emerging as the current leading Verdi baritone, following in the largish footsteps of Lawrence Tibbett, Leonard Warren and Robert Merrill. As for his concentration in this area, he shrugs: "Well, it's going that way and I don't mind. There is a shortage of Verdi baritones and I can fill in the gap. The way Verdi uses the voice is really rewarding, especially the way he goes in and out of the top voice. To vocalize I often use phrases from an aria in different keys as a vocal massage."

Just for the record, he has already made a full-length *Tro-*

vatore and *Aida* for RCA with Leontyne Price and Placido Domingo; *La Traviata* with Montserrat Caballé; and he is about to begin an album of duets with Domingo, including scenes from *La Forza del Destino, Don Carlo, Vespri* and Bizet's *The Pearl Fishers*—the first such pairing since Bjoerling and Merrill. Then there will be the opening night *Don Carlo* in 1971 at the Met, where he has already sung in *Ballo, Trovatore, Simon Boccanegra, Traviata, Aida* and *Luisa Miller*, etc. "In fact," he concludes after a moment's thought, "I've sung everything early and late, from *Giovanna d'arco* to *Otello*, the entire span of Verdi. It's too bad about *King Lear*—there are only a few informal sketches, but it would have been fantastic!" he says almost hungering after the prospects.

As for the up-and-coming *Macbeth* in Vienna with Christa Ludwig and Nicolai Ghiaurov, Milnes was setting out with typical determination. "I hope to bring it back from being called 'Lady Macbeth,' which has been the case for the last ten years," he insists. "There are many reasons for this. The two different versions give trouble, both the original and the revised. In Vienna we will have the best of both. For instance, the final chorus is ridiculous . . . dic-a-dic-a," he mocks. "But we will include the arietta 'Mal per me,' which was not in the original but in the Paris version. Before he dies, he tries to say that he didn't do what he did for selfish reasons, but that he was caught up in the circumstances and did it for Scotland—'This vile crown caused my death,' in other words.

"But I've seen it and I can see why the opera is called 'Lady Macbeth.' Part of it is Verdi's fault, for the words of Macbeth in the play are given to Lady Macbeth in the opera. But I think you can equalize with the right physical approach: he's a strong man who becomes fearful, yet he has got to be tough. The fall is longer when a man totally in charge goes astray. The opera is full of theater, and the Shakespeare here has enormous potential—but I've seen Macbeths just looking out front to the audience during the Procession of Kings. I'm mad when people don't look at the people they're singing to," he slams his hand down, shaking his head. He is also quick to admit that "especially in the last twenty years there's been more of the 'publicity thing' for a woman, it's true. Now, of the many famous names, many more are sopranos, more

women than men. I take it as a fact of life. In the hierarchy
of bows and dressing rooms, the baritone is always third. I
look to it as a challenge—I'm third *here,* but let's see what
happens out *there.* I know what I'm about on stage," he emphasizes almost but not quite pontifically.

A little more than a decade ago there was quite a different
Sherrill Milnes on the periphery of the operatic arena. Born in
Illinois, he had a typical farm boyhood, but his parents were
musical. His mother, a singer, pianist, choir director and conductor, had always been active in her community, teaching
voice as well as leading the choir. Her son, in addition to taking
violin and piano lessons from early childhood, also studied
voice for twelve years. He sang in choir each Sunday, and
played and sang in high school concerts. But he entered college as a pre-med student. After a year without music, he decided to enter Drake University in Des Moines, Iowa, where
he found a first-rate music course and his teacher Andrew
White. In high school Milnes had won the State Music Contest
in five categories: tuba in the brass sextet, viola in the string
quartet, concertmaster of the orchestra, first chair tuba in the
band, and as a vocal soloist. He decided to concentrate on his
voice—"I didn't like my sound in high school, but in college it
was different. It all seemed to come together, somehow. I
mean, it was all there."

He also took education courses and intended to teach music.
After graduating from Drake, he enrolled for additional voice
courses at Northwestern University under Hermanus Baer,
which led to his first professional singing job with Margaret
Hillis' Chicago Symphony Chorus, during Fritz Reiner's re-
gime. At the same time he was making ends meet with church
and synagogue jobs, and by teaching at the progressive New
Trier High School. "I taught and I will teach again. I love to
teach. Then I had sixty students a week. And I was doing jingle
voice-overs too. With my jazz background I knew more about
this than I did about opera or art songs. The companies were
amazed that an opera singer could lay out jazz rhythms." And
without prompting he belts out a few well-chosen samples . . .
"You get a lot to like with M-a-r-l-b-o-r-o-". . . . "When
you're out of Schlitz, you're out of beer—I also did Kelloggs
and one for Budweiser with Ed MacMahon."

As far as opera was concerned, he admits, "I knew a few arias, some pieces and scenes. My early years were spent on a farm full-time and I was involved in music only locally. At Drake the legit theater was the KRNT Theater where the Met played when they came on their spring tour. So I would work the show to make some money . . . and I heard the Saturday broadcasts. By 1956 I knew the general character of opera; then when the Met came I saw London and Peerce and Merrill backstage, and I was in awe. I especially remember a *Tosca* with Albanese, London and Barioni. When I worked the show, London walked by looking real scary—and I was impressed. At that point I never thought of a singing career. The Met was a famous company and I never had any thoughts of being there."

By 1960 the baritone had spent one brief summer in opera, singing in the chorus and small roles at Santa Fe. He then en-rolled at Northwestern to work with Robert Gay in the opera workshop to learn more about style, stage deportment and acting. In this way he was to gain entry to Boris Goldovsky's company, which was touring with *Don Giovanni* in the fall of that year. "Gay suggested I call Goldovsky in Cleveland. I didn't know opera from rock, and I certainly didn't know *Don Giovanni*—so I called my teachers and asked them if I could sing it and they said OK. He told me to fly to Cleveland to sing for him. I really didn't know how good I was. I was small-town musically, a farm boy who had come to opera workshop. Since I didn't know what was going on in New York, every-thing outside seemed like a big deal. Goldovsky was the big league for me. I sang for him and he didn't mention a tour, but only Tanglewood—and I didn't know what he was talking about. I thought I had failed, that I didn't get the job. I was depressed and thought my trip had been a waste of time. But I went to Tanglewood and then did 53 Masettos on tour. But how many can you do?—he's just a country bumpkin stum-bling along." Listening to Milnes describing his early years, one gets the impression that Goldovsky made the right choice.

This led to a Boston season of *Carmen* and *The Turk in Italy,* then summer again in 1961 at Tanglewood. "We had seven weeks of concentrated work with as many scenes as you could memorize. I did thirteen in one season." Goldovsky used the young singer in five cross-country tours, and in 1961 he bowed with Rosa Ponselle's Baltimore Civic Opera as Gérard in *Andrea Chénier*. From there, aided by a Ford Foundation Award, he began making the rounds of American opera companies: Pittsburgh, San Antonio, Houston, Central City, Cincinnati. A debut in Milan at the Teatro Nuovo in *The Barber of Seville* preceded his New York City Opera debut as Valentin, Figaro and the elder Germont.

In December of 1965 came the chance to sing at the Metropolitan Opera as Valentin in *Faust*—and he has since sung other such non-Verdian works as Tchaikovsky's *Pique Dame*, Beethoven's *Fidelio*, Giordano's *Chénier*, Leoncavallo's *Pagliacci*, Wagner's *Lohengrin* and the world première of Levy's *Mourning Becomes Electra*. During the Met "lock-out" (which he carefully stresses, instead of "strike"), he made his London debut on only a week's notice, singing Barnaba in a concert version of *La Gioconda* for the London Opera Society. "Caballé was to sing *Faust*, but she was sick and cancelled. So *Gioconda* with Suliotis was substituted, and I had to coach it like mad. I had my earphones on the plane and listened all the way over." Later he returned for a scheduled performance of *Chénier* in February. *Times* critic William Mann commented that he sang "with ease and power, agility when needed, all the dynamism one could wish, and beauty of tone throughout his compass and range of emotion. This was his European debut and, though his fame has preceded him, it was a magnificent one, indicative of superior gifts and unremitting hard work."

Sherrill Milnes has arrived . . . in the very best sense of the word. And, of course, his views are becoming more defined as each new experience unfolds. For one thing, he is confident about the future of opera. "Things are happening. Companies in Seattle and San Antonio are doing matinees and have school programs to prepare the kids in advance. This is healthy, for when they're out of school they come back. I feel it is growing and more is going on. But what we need is believable theater in opera. I'm amazed to see a singer who is killed on stage feel the floor before he falls—so . . . you bang an elbow," he shrugs. "I do calisthenics to keep in shape, to fall down the ramp as I do in the new *Pagliacci*. I've skinned a lot of things, but in the heat of it you can't worry. You rehearse a routine and then put yourself completely into it. You can't look like school kids playing with swords. Yes, my own stage techniques began with Goldovsky, but I also learn from colleagues. If I see something I like I steal it. How does he bend his leg or arch his spine and so on? This way I can develop a wider repertoire of gestures. I watch Norman Treigle when we sing together—he moves beautifully. Did you ever watch his thumbs? That's where you can see all the tension. Also the movies—Olivier and all the obvious names. And I've watched Gobbi and Tito Capobianco, with whom I've worked in several productions with the City Opera. Cacoyannis in *Mourning Becomes Electra* also had some interesting ideas."

He is a firm believer in caring for the voice, because "reliability is an important factor in singing. I'm amazed at all the cancelling and hypochondriacy. It hurts me to cancel if I have a contract, but a lot of big names tend to be unreliable. I think a singer must mark, or he kills his voice. I watch that I don't sing too much. If you have a busy performance schedule, then you have a big responsibility to those who hired you and to the audience—so you can't be careless. Sleep and not using the voice before a performance are beneficial—in the long run, rest is the biggest key to long vocal life. Tucker is a master at marking. If he sings one night, he won't sing for a couple of days at rehearsals. It's easy to indiscriminately beat your voice. I used to sing tenor arias at parties; now I don't fool around so much. My mind tells me to cool it. After my concerts the auspices ask me to sing at the reception or dinner, and I used to be intimidated—now I tell them, 'I gave you my all in the recital hall.' "

Milnes is aware of the problems of building a concert audience at a time when it is dwindling—"somewhere along the way many get scared off"—and in picking programs which have quality as well as entertainment quality. "An audience must be entertained and not just sit there with their hands on their foreheads. You must have ups and downs, key relations, moods. Throughout the country, recital and symphony business is off. We're not building the audience, because they are not enjoying it. I don't sing 'Home On the Range' and 'Happy Birthday' and 'September Song,' but we can do things with power and masculinity. I feel strongly about the kind of artist who feels that 'the accompanist and I are in a little shell making music: you can listen, but we don't want to be bothered.' A performer has to share with an audience—I don't talk of a nightclub act at a recital, but I have seen recitals with *nothing* in English, and that is ridiculous in this country. As for lieder, in ten years I hope to do more. When I recorded the Brahms *Four Serious Songs,* I invaded 'holy territory,' which you're not supposed to touch. But I like the lieder Bjoerling did: a full-blown approach with a full sound. For my taste, these things can get too precious. I think you can give deeper meaning with deeper sound, vocal color and inflection."

In committing a score to memory, Milnes confesses he does not have a photographic memory, "but I can read. Repetition is the only way, and it's best to know the languages. Goldovsky coached me in Yeletsky's aria for my RCA recital album. 'You're still in the United States,' he first said when we began working. Then I progressed to Europe, then Bulgaria and finally 'a suburb, not downtown Moscow,' " the baritone laughs goodnaturedly. As for the operatic stage, he reiterates before a picture gallery of Milnes in various roles, "Well, yes, I am going towards Verdi and I'm not sorry, but I haven't yet exhausted the other Italian possibilities. The Barber couldn't be a better debut opera." As for any Wagner beyond the Herald in Wieland Wagner's *Lohengrin* and Donner in Karajan's *Das Rheingold*—"That's what I call my 'Donner and Blitzen.' I don't think I can do that production again. I'm afraid of the dark."

★ *Birgit Nilsson* ★

The image of the fierce Wagnerian heroine and stories about her strong personality prompted more trepidation than any other interview I had ever done. But five minutes in her presence wiped away all these preconceptions, for she provided one of the most rewarding sessions I have had. We talked in the winter of 1973, before her annual New York recital, this one on the "Great Performers at Philharmonic Hall" series.

Although most of her things are packed away and ready to accompany her back to Europe after a lengthy Wagnerian fall and early winter, Birgit Nilsson does manage to produce two juice glasses, a considerable amount of Scotch and a vast supply of canned nuts, corn things and crackers. There was Swedish caviar, too. "I made some big propaganda at the Met for this, because it's much better than the Russian and less expensive. It comes in a tube and has to be mixed with a little onion and sour cream because it's more concentrated. Everybody loves it, but they don't know it here. We Swedes can't make any propaganda for what we have. We are very bad businessmen." The lady must be the exception to the rule, for in the past 20 or so years she has not only managed to become one of the world's most famous singers and the greatest Wagnerian of her generation but among the highest paid as well. Stories are legion about her contract negotiations, her business acumen and her shopping sprees.

Sitting in an immensely attractive, flowing at-home gown in jewel colors, she is much less severe than her photos and even stage appearances suggest. This is no Northern princess of ice nor the wickedly slashing raconteur whose published stories always seem to be at someone else's expense. No, there is warmth, sincerity and flair. Attribute it to mellowness or whatever, but the long-held Nilsson myth is just that—a myth.

Like her down-to-earth fellow Swedes (she was born in Västra Karup), Birgit Nilsson's singing career began as a sheer matter of what was practical. She did defy her farmer father's wishes by pursuing such a life, at Stockholm's Royal Academy, but once in the fray she learned roles and sang them pretty much as she was needed at the Royal Stockholm Opera. In fact, the progress of her development defined the time-tested rules of moving from the lighter Wagnerian heroines into the heavier realm by starting as Venus. "But when I was young," she recalls, "I didn't know what a Wagnerian singer was. I had never seen an opera, you know. I was born in the country and didn't know anything about opera. I wanted to be some sort of singer, but the only thing I could think of was some sort of concert or church singer—that was all I knew. I didn't even know quite what opera meant. The first Wagnerian piece I got my hand on was Siegmund's 'Winterstürme,' " she says, laughing. "But the voice was rather big from the beginning, and it turned out to be suitable for Wagner." Her first role, Venus, was followed soon after by Senta—a line of non-progression that Fremstad or Flagstad might have frowned on. "Well, it was a question of what they needed. I loved *Tannhäuser*—I was dreaming about singing Elisabeth. When it turned out I had to sing Venus, I didn't like the idea very much, but it was an order. Five or six years later I did get to sing Elisabeth." Almost all her roles, except Amelia in *Un Ballo in Maschera* and Leonore in *Fidelio,* were sung for the first time in Stockholm—even later when she had become an international star as kind of a tryout for the outer world. "But even before Elsa and Elisabeth," she smiles, "I sang Sieglinde and Brünnhilde in *Siegfried,* because our Brünnhilde couldn't sing the *Siegfried*—it was too high for her. So I learned it, and that was one of my very first roles. You know I started out with Lady Macbeth and such things. It was just that I had to sing whatever they needed there."

Her Lady Macbeth episode in Stockholm actually helped pave the way for the future, since Fritz Busch was conducting —"It was marvelous. I loved every minute of it, even though I know I wasn't ready for it. Busch sort of discovered me when nobody else really believed in me, and I got a big push from him. He was like a father, and I was very happy to work with him." He then brought her to Glyndebourne to sing Electra in *Idomeneo,* which in turn led to European recognition. Just before she went to Glyndebourne, Hans Knappertsbusch had come to Stockholm, heard the young soprano and asked her to open the Bayreuth season in 1951, but she had already promised Busch. Later she did work with the great Wagnerian in Stockholm, singing Sieglinde in *Walküre,* Brünnhilde in *Siegfried* and Woglinde in *Rheingold* and *Götterdämmerung.* "Of course we never had the chance to rehearse, so he said, 'Well I knew that Nilsson would be somewhere, but I could never guess where.' "

The soprano also credits Erich Kleiber with a certain influence on her career. "I studied *Fidelio* very carefully with him and got many good tips. It was one of his last works just before he died—we recorded it for the radio in Cologne. And he was also one of the last conductors who himself took time to work with the singers at the piano. No conductor does that any more. These men really knew their work, and they had so many wonderful ideas that one has to find out by oneself now. Of course, today it's different. Singers can listen to each other's recordings and, maybe, learn from them. I don't know if it's for good or for worse. I never listen because I'm always in a hotel and don't have a machine with me. But I know singers who travel around with a cassette recorder and tape from a record the parts they want to study; and then they play it and play it and play it until they know it. I loved so much one summer when I was in Bayreuth, staying at some sort of a hotel with a spa, and there were a few other singers staying there too. One young singer was going to sing her first Salome, and one day I was out taking a walk when I heard myself singing like crazy. It was coming through her open window. I was going to call on her anyway, so when I came in I knocked and said, 'Am I interrupting you?' 'Oh, no,' she said, 'I was just writing a letter,' " and Birgit Nilsson breaks into gales of laughter.

Like so many of the great Wagnerian singers, Miss Nilsson is not a part of the current scene at the Wagner shrine. Since the death of Wieland Wagner and the assumption of power by Wolfgang, there has been a steady exodus, leaving Bayreuth almost denuded of its great names. "If Bayreuth would have been in Salzburg, I would love to sing there, because Salzburg is beautiful and has wonderful food. But Bayreuth is so provincial. You know, I started out there in 1953 and I absolutely hated it, except for the performances. I mean there was nothing you could do—it was either cold and raining, and then you got a cold; or it was so hot that you couldn't breathe. And no restaurants, no hotels—and during the festival you *couldn't* stay in hotels unless you wanted a very small room without a bath because, no, the Herr Doktor So-and-So and Herr Baron So-and-So are coming and *they* have to have the bathroom. So the singers sacrificed.

"But, of course, when Wieland was alive he inspired us. He was the great genius and everybody loved to work with him. Now there is nothing that makes you want to give up your vacation. I sang there for 17 years, since the Beethoven Ninth in 1953, and I like to be in Sweden in the summer, which is a beautiful time. I remember my first year in Bayreuth, when I saw that house—I walked up that big hill and I looked and I thought I am going to sing in this church—my heart was beating so hard and I was so nervous. I had a fantastic respect for that house all those years. Now the younger singers just take it as another theater in which to sing. For us it was a shrine. It was the highest you could come. Of course Wagner has done a lot for me, and I would like to do a lot for Wagner—but 17 summers is enough. Wolfgang wanted me to come back and sing his *Ring,* but why go back again to another production in which you wouldn't be happy? Wolfgang's a wonderful human being, but he's missing what Wieland had."

It was actually Wieland who said of Miss Nilsson that she had become famous before she had become great. Part of this stems from the fact that initially she worked more with Wolfgang. "I didn't work with Wieland until rather late because I was a Wolfgang singer for many years. They were a little bit jealous of each other, you know. So Wieland didn't have anything to do with a Wolfgang singer, and vice versa. I think it was as late as '62 or something like that when *Tristan* came up again with Wieland. I had already done one *Tristan* production with Wolfgang, which was a rather good success, and Wieland was looking all over for an Isolde—except for me.

He tried to talk *every* mezzo-soprano he met into singing Isolde, but he didn't succeed. And finally there was no one left but me. So he asked me, and of course, I had been really longing to work with him. I well understood, too, that he thought I had sung it so often he couldn't change anything with me. We started to work, and when I met him to rehearse I said, 'I have sung Isolde 87 times.' 'Yah, yah, I know,' he answered. 'Well, listen, I will forget all those 87 performances and try like I have never done one.' 'Well, that's very kind,' but he didn't believe me. He was very sour. We worked only one week, and it was so rewarding—I was a complete other Isolde. He said afterward he didn't believe what I had said and didn't think it was possible, since I had been singing Isolde so much. He was very happy that his whole production was really beautiful—he said it was the closest to perfection he ever could come. It had a tremendous success.

"He was such a genius with lights and everything. Nothing was difficult with him, because he saw immediately what kind of person you were. He took the best things out of you and molded the role so it would fit. If he worked with three singers he made three different Isoldes. He was a painter and marvelous. Most stage directors just draw up their ideas and you have to get into it even if it hurts you, if it means having to cut your head off or your feet—like an iron costume you have to wear. The ideas of so many stage directors can be completely against your personality, against your imagination, but it is the way it has to be and *basta!* You can never get your best from it." She says her Isolde still has "the inner perspective from Wieland," no matter what productions she sings today. She also talks warmly about working with him on *Elektra* in Vienna and his last *Ring* in Bayreuth.

Asked, as one of the authentic prima donnas of the day, whether this is indeed the age of the singer or the director or the conductor, she immediately comes back: "It is absolutely *not* the age of the singer, I tell you. No, we have to bow the left and to the right and all over the place. It's the age of the director. You know in last year's *Tristan* at the Met the elevators were very dangerous. I'm sure if they would have put somebody from the chorus on that elevator in the first act—without having anything to hold on to—the union would not have permitted it. But we who are paying a fortune to the union, they couldn't care less if *we* would break arms or legs, or they think we can speak for ourselves . . . which we can." Actually she enthuses over the total result of this Everding/Schneider-Siemssen production, which originated in Vienna several seasons ago. "It was a particularly good production for America because it told you everything, it made it more clear what everything was about, and then it was wonderful to look at, too. When it's a big success then it's worth making all those efforts—but if it's a flop on top of it, it's really very hard."

Pressed as to what she considers flops in her Met career, she quickly names the Heinrich *Elektra*—"It absolutely worked against the singers. It was absolutely impossible to move around, because it was full of holes and everything was open. There was nothing that would help project the voice. That orchestra is so heavy, so big, and the whole space was open, with no doors or anything. I think it looked like a coal mine. Mr. Heinrich designed another *Elektra* at La Scala, too, and it wasn't so successful there, either. When I came for rehearsals I found the stage was full of big stones. There was not one place where you could put down your two feet—either you had to stand one foot lower and one higher, or vice versa, or crawl around on your tummy. And I said, 'Listen, I cannot sing in this production. I have been looking forward to it, but it is absolutely impossible. Maybe you think I'm too much like a goat—maybe I have a head like a goat but I don't have the feet.' Then Rennert and Heinrich said it was impossible to change, that they had been breaking their heads for two years about this production. So I said, 'How would it have been if you had given the poor singers two minutes of those two years?' They said they could not change now, and I said, 'You shouldn't change it. It's just that I can't sing it. If the other Elektra who has been rehearsing can do it, then everything is fine, because I will go home.' Then I heard that she had been complaining about it, too, but the director said, 'Oh, Miss Nilsson can do it,' so she did do the rehearsals—it was a dare, you know, poor thing. Well, they talked and talked, and of course it went against their pride—the pride was the worst thing. But at ten o'clock the next morning the stage was changed; they put in a big platform between those stones—the whole thing looked much better and half the stage came more forward (because La Scala doesn't have very good acoustics). And it was—to everyone's surprise, except maybe mine— much more beautiful. *And* Elektra had a place where she could sing without being afraid she would break her legs," she finishes with a definite note of triumph.

She wonders what director "will have us hang by our toes from the ceiling to sing," or—more immediately—how many more scrims they'll use to blanket the voice. "They use those scrims in Europe all the time, but in San Francisco I really started to think about it. When I attended *Tosca* I was sitting in Mr. Adler's box—there was no scrim, so I heard everything perfectly well. Then I heard the *Siegfried,* except that you *couldn't* hear anybody, even when the orchestra wasn't too loud. I was absolutely flabbergasted. The next week I did *Siegfried,* and there was a big, heavy, painted scrim. When I was singing I could hardly see the conductor and I couldn't hear the orchestra either, like I do in most houses. And it was so dark. It was the scrim! Then I started to fight, but it was impossible to change it. Then, you know, in America you have opera houses two or three times larger than we have in Europe. I don't think the big Wagnerian voices in the earlier days had to fight with these things. I don't think they had scrims. I don't think they had to wake up in Amsterdam Avenue—so far back! I don't think they had nothing behind them to project their voices."

She believes that the time of purely abstract productions has passed. "In Wagner we need a little bit more realism, not so naked and cold. I have the feeling that of course we shouldn't go back to 50 years ago with goats and horses on stage, but there is a certain middle way." As for the current Schneider-Siemssen *Ring* at the Met (originally directed by Karajan in Salzburg), she says frankly, "I don't like it. Where the best place for the singer is on stage, there is a big hole. That second act of *Walküre* is absolutely dangerous to life. I'm so happy whenever I discover I still have my legs and everything, because the whole backstage is pitch dark—one evening I fell together with a stagehand. I broke his glasses and hit his nose and almost broke my ankle. Then I had to sing 'Ho jo to ho' *behind* the stage because the stage was just rolling out. And then when you come in, those two half-rings have disappeared and the stage is full of cords—so when you rescue Sieglinde you have to watch every step you take. You have to be lucky and very careful not to fall on your nose. The whole second act is without imagination—everyone knows it's a ring anyway without the hole. You know, people say we have no Wagnerian singers today. But none of the earlier Wagnerian singers would have put up with such things. Absolutely not! They came out and made their one or two gestures, and they sang. These directors today say we have no Wagnerian singers, but why don't they do something to help us—instead of putting us back a city block from the audience. And, you know, when one is so lucky to come into an *Elektra* performance with a door and a wall behind the traditional yard, it's fantastic. You don't need to sing—it's incredible how you carry."

While she has become a famous Elektra in the best and worst of productions, so she also became one of the great Salomes—"I think Elektra is the greater opera but Salome is easier for the public. I started with Salome in Sweden, as usual, in '54, and my first stage director was Goeran Gentele. He helped me a lot. I couldn't think of myself as Salome, because at that time I did all these majestic roles. But he worked every step and every movement with me, so it really got under my skin that way." At that time she had just recovered from pleurisy, so she did the dance with some ballet girls who carried her in on a big platter "like a Buddha. A year later there was a strike in the ballet, and they were thinking of bringing down the curtain and just playing the music. I thought that was a little bit insulting to Salome, so I said, 'If you keep the stage very dark I will try,' and I improvised a dance by feeling the music. The music really tells you so much what to do. When I ended I saw that all the lights were on, and I had had a big success." Gentele then urged her to do Carmen. "He tried to convince me and called up every morning at seven o'clock for three weeks—they had a mezzo-soprano, but he didn't believe in her. [It was Kerstin Meyer who turned out to be an excellent Carmen, though nobody believed in her at the time.] I had been very successful with Salome and so he really wanted me to do Carmen. But I had my career outside Sweden coming, and to my taste Carmen should be sung by a mezzo. I couldn't feel that I had *anything* that was needed for Carmen, neither the voice or the other abilities or the time. So I said no."

She has also sung in Gentele's famous and controversial *Un Ballo in Maschera*—"I don't think that Verdi would have been too happy with it. But we in Sweden are not too musical. We accepted it because it was history for us, and it was a marvelous translation—which of course ruined all the Verdian cantilenas. I protested very strongly. I said I could not serve two padrones, the translator and Verdi—and Verdi is the strongest one. So I cut off many of the words, and the poet, a famous Swedish writer, *hated* me. Once he became drunk and really told me what I was worth, and it wasn't much, I can tell you."

Although she does sing Amelia, Aida, Tosca, Lady Macbeth, Turandot and other Italian roles, it still is Wagner for which she is in greatest demand—*Ring* cycle Brünnhildes and Isolde in particular. Does she become bored rehearsing still more productions of *Walküre* and *Tristan?* "Yes, sometimes, when I can't achieve anything new and when the stage director has nothing to give—then I can become bored. But otherwise not, if you can get new aspects on the role and new ideas, that's fun. This season [1972-73] has been a little bit one-sided, you know, with *Walküre* in Chicago, the *Ring* in San Francisco, *Walküre* and *Siegfried* at the Met. In Chicago, unfortunately, there were a lot of cuts, and I don't like it when it's cut so drastically as it was—you're falling on your nose trying to remember." She believes in making judicious cuts in Wagner. "You know, in our days we are a little bit more hectic, and I think there are some moments that nobody will really miss—and it would be a lot better, because the public are almost falling off their chairs by the end of a performance. I know that Wieland was very much for cuts—he wanted to make such cuts as I would never dream of, but the conductors never agreed with him. In *Götterdämmerung* he wanted to cut out the whole Norn scene. Can you believe it?"

Of the three Brünnhildes she calls the one in *Götterdämmerung* her favorite, both vocally and dramatically. "It's marvelous dramatically even though vocally the first act is very low, very broad and very tiring. The *Siegfried* Brünnhilde is so static and so concentrated, and it goes past so quickly. Ooh!

it's difficult. In *Siegfried* Brünnhilde is also three kinds of woman. She wakes up as a goddess and then gets motherly feelings towards Siegfried. Then all of a sudden she discovers she loves him. It's hard to make these things clear in such a short time." Of the *Walküre* warrior she says, "First of all she has to sing those high '*Ho jo to hos*' before she's warmed up, which absolutely kills everyone, and then the rest of the second act is so low. Wotan's '*Erzählung*' is so beautiful, but Brünnhilde has something to sing every ten minutes—very short, you know, and so after the '*Ho jo to hos*' the second act is not too exciting.

"I remember my first years as the *Siegfried* Brünnhilde. I was always absolutely paralyzed from nervousness—it was terrible. Now I am a little more relaxed. You know that was my first Brünnhilde, because, as I said, our Brünnhilde in Stockholm couldn't sing it. It was too high. In the general rehearsal I felt so stupid and so impossible that I just ran from the stage, crying. We had very little rehearsal, and the conductor was Swedish and had never conducted the *Ring* before. I felt everything was absolutely impossible—and I was the *most* impossible one. The manager followed me to my dressing room and said I should forgive and have patience with the conductor, 'Oh, no, it is not the conductor, it is me. I don't know it, and I don't want to do it. I am absolutely impossible.' He said I was gorgeous and made me feel happier. So, anyway, I had to sing, and I went on singing it for many years. But this was one of my worst moments. I felt hopeless when I came on stage with all those funny feelings one has. It was an old production, very traditional. One should do lots of *big gestures,* greeting the *earth* and the *light* and the *sun* and all these things"—she grandly demonstrates with heroic arms. "I felt so uncomfortable. Then the chains from the cloak got hooked, and I had the cloak trailing after me—it felt like a horse."

She is also amused by an incident in Florence during a *Siegfried* in which she wore a white gown with hooks instead of zippers. "I felt somehow that the dress was very loose. So while I was singing I put my hand in the back to feel—and it *was* really open, the whole back down below the waistline. I had to sing with one hand holding my dress. But I was singing with a marvelous colleague, Wolfgang Windgassen, and he

had eyes for everything. So while we were singing he came just
behind me and hooked up every hook, 75 or something like
that. When we were doing *Tristan* in Vienna in '58 there was a
big football match between Sweden and Germany, the world
championship. Windgassen was very much involved with the
result, and the game was on during the second act. King Marke
is the last to come in, so he had the last results. But Marke and
Tristan don't have anything to do with each other, because
they are rivals. Marke was sung by a marvelous bass, Ludwig
Weber, and before he left the stage he just made a hopeless
movement, went over to Tristan, put his hands on his shoulders
and said, 'Germany lost 2 to 4.' And then Tristan came to me,
Isolde, to kiss me on the forehead, and he said, 'Congratula-
tions. Sweden won.' " Immense laughter. "And Sweden won
more than one way that evening because Sir Rudolf was at the
performance, and I got my first Met contract that very evening.
Early in my career in Berlin, I auditioned for him, and he just
said thank you. That was all. In 1955 he heard my Salome in
Munich, and I didn't hear anything from him there either.
Later I reminded him of Berlin, and he told the Met Auditions
that we all make mistakes: 'I turned her down at an audition
and couldn't regret it more, because if I would have had her
at that time she wouldn't have been so expensive.' " More
laughter.

Basically Birgit Nilsson seems satisfied with the conditions
under which she works in most of the world's major opera
houses. "Oh, of course there are many things about a career
that I don't like," she shrugs. "I don't like the business all
around. That part is very difficult. In Europe we sing and that
is that—our time is for rehearsals or for ourselves. Here there
are so many other things involved for publicity and these
things, and I think it's nonsense. It takes time away from
my work. But this is a big country, and it has to be built up in
another way—I understand that . . . but I don't like it.
There's a bit of truth to what I say: 'Singing, that is the least
difficult thing. All the other things around it, all the struggling
to get time for this and that, that is the hardest thing.' But I
love the American people, they are so warm and open. When
you go on the street and somebody knocks you on the shoulder
and says, 'You are Miss Nilsson, aren't you? Oh, I loved your

performance.' I think it's very nice . . . except when you aren't dressed and look absolutely ugly and don't expect anybody to recognize you." She laughs again.

Asked when she knew she could rely on her voice and then go on to pursuing interpretation and the rest, she tilts her head: "It comes gradually. I remember how difficult I thought it was in the beginning to sing absolutely in the right rhythm and with the conductor—preferably," she laughs. "And then one should sing beautifully too, thinking about high notes and everything. And then one should act and try to cooperate with other singers and all that. Oh, I thought it was terribly difficult to put my mind to six different things. For me the singing came first—a lot of singers just leave the voice and get involved with acting, and so the singing suffers. When I started out and tried to act, I did everything so realistically that I was always killing myself. So an old colleague came to me and said, 'Listen, Birgit, you will never make it. You will kill yourself in two weeks. You shouldn't make all those things hard—you should only make them *look* hard.' And of course what I was doing hurt the voice; when you are acting that much it goes into the voice. You must know how much you can act without hurting the voice, and that's very hard. There are singers who can act wonderfully with the voice, but those big chest notes and effects really hurt the voice, and it doesn't last long."

The story of Birgit Nilsson's own infallible technique has often been told—of how in the early '50s she had to find a way of singing over a cold and then came upon the singer's ideal of head placement combined with the right breath support, which gives her that ease in the top register. "Maybe people think I am ungrateful, but my first voice teacher had a reputation of killing every voice, and I was close to it, too. And my second teacher in one way helped me a little bit, but he was making me force all the time—after half an hour I was completely hoarse. He wanted me to develop a chest voice, and I refused because it hurt—I couldn't. And I don't like registers, you know, or those singers who pull one out like an organ. Now you're down in the basement and then to the mezzanine, and so forth. After a while you hear the breaks in the voice, because you get holes there. When you go from second gear to third there is a little break that gets bigger and bigger, and after a while you have a big hole and you cannot touch that note from either above or below. So I was looking for another voice teacher, but I became so scared I didn't dare start with somebody else—I really was unhappy at that time. Finally I thought I will find it myself, and I learned through good coaches, good conductors and the stage. Every evening you feel how your voice projects and how much you can give and when it's coming in the right place. Experience is the greatest teacher."

As for new roles, there is still *La Gioconda* for which she was once announced in the '60s at La Scala. "I'm a chicken when it comes to new roles, you know," she smiles. "I always have been. With every role I have done I have to be taken by the hair and convinced I can do it. I always think, oh, that will not be good, I cannot do it. I never wanted to sing the *Ring* or Elektra or Salome. Now I think I have the best roles in my repertoire, so every other role will be a letdown." She is still debating over *Die Frau ohne Schatten,* but cannot decide which role.

As for the Marschallin in *Der Rosenkavalier,* "I've not done it in many years. I did it very early in Stockholm. It was again the same reason—there was no voice for the Marschallin. Everything was OK except that I was too young. Now we'll see what happens." Much laughter. "Now maybe it's only the age that is right and nothing else. It's a beautiful role and, of course, I will be very nervous because I have had many fantastic successors. It's an opera I love to see. I go very often in Vienna, and I've seen many Marschallins. I saw Crespin's debut here, and I think she was marvelous, really beautiful. Many years ago I saw Hilde Konetzni and she was marvelous— she made me cry like a child. And I saw Christa Ludwig in Chicago—very intelligent and well thought out. Everything was absolutely perfect, every moment, every tone. She has only one thing against her: she is even better as Octavian."

Now that Birgit Nilsson is one of the world's most celebrated singers and one of Sweden's great sources of pride, did her once resistant father change his mind? "You know, he was a farmer and had only one child, and he was a bit egoistic too— he was afraid that he would lose me. He was very much against my career and told my mother, 'You have to be blamed for it.'

I got $500 from my parents the first year, and then I struggled myself. You know, I am from the country—and in Sweden we don't talk too much—and he was a very stubborn man. Even if he felt he was convinced and happy about it, he tried to hide it, in a way. But when he got older he *was* very proud. Once when I was home singing I sent a telegram to the Swedish king on his 90th birthday, and three days later I had a telegram back from the king. I sent it immediately to my father, who had been very sick, and he was *so* happy. The older generation has such respect for kings—old people in Sweden still take that as absolutely the top. So he almost jumped up from the bed," says Birgit Nilsson with a smile that could melt all the snows of Scandinavia.

★ Leontyne Price ★

Since we talked in the summer of 1968—in advance of a Philharmonic Hall recital debut in the spring of 1969—Leontyne Price has pursued her career with a careful choice of repertoire and opera houses, returning only occasionally to the Metropolitan, elsewhere adding such roles as Giorgetta in Il Tabarro and Manon Lescaut. Her annual New York recitals and U.S. recital tours have become events in the full sense of the word, while her RCA discs have sought out countless operatic heroines.

Backstage at the Metropolitan Opera House to greet a long-time friend post-performance is a "school of hard knocks" all its own. It is to be swept along in the tidal wave of pushing and shoving amidst the mob held at bay behind closed azure doors by dour attendants until the appointed "open sesame" hour. One late Saturday afternoon, the floodgates are momentarily parted and through them into the oncoming rush passes an elegant figure, skin and smile radiant. A faceless voice calls out from the waiting crowd, "Hey, Miss Price, are you singing *Trovatore* this year?" "That's what it says in my contract," she beams back, magically making a path through the throng down the fluorescent corridor. . . .

On a frigid winter's night at the comfily old-fashioned Brooklyn Academy, the American Ballet Theatre is winding up its holiday stand to the applause of all those brave enough to withstand the elements, the subway and/or bus. In the audience, making its intermission way up the aisle, is a fur-swathed Leontyne Price. When it is noted that hers has become a familiar face at New York dance events, she says simply, "I prefer it." Though she doesn't specify, she does quickly add, "I find New York scintillating when I'm not singing," and she passes with a smile into the lobby. . . .

A month later, back at Lincoln Center in the marble-and-glass halls of Philharmonic Hall, a regal Leontyne Price, all in black, is holding court just off Door 6 during the interval of the annual Elisabeth Schwarzkopf recital. "Beautiful, isn't it," she nods at those who have come over to give their greetings.

Encountering Leontyne Price on such occasions and in her frequent New York stage appearances over the years always manages to summon warm memories of a pleasant past: hearing the young soprano as Lìu in the 1959 all-star (Nilsson, di-Stefano) *Turandot*—the fountain of fresh lyric sound pouring from the rear of the vast Chicago Civic Opera House stage . . . the excitement of the soprano's first Metropolitan broadcast *Trovatore;* just weeks after a legendary debut . . . first hearing the RCA "blue album," as it affectionately came to be known, with that luxuriant outpouring of "Che il bel sogno di Doretta" . . . . priceless (or, rather, Price-full) broadcasts from the Salzburg Festival with Karajan storming the heavens with *Trovatore* (that was the year of the interpolated high Cs in the "Miserere" and a cast of Simionato, Corelli and Bastianini!) . . . the classical brilliance of the first Price Donna Anna at the old Met in December of '62. . . .

Since Leontyne Price's "avocado green and delphinium blue" Federal-era house on Van Dam Street (to quote her press book) is currently off-bounds for reporters, we sat in

neutral territory across the table at the Plaza's Edwardian
Room to catch up with the Mississippi-born soprano who has
become an international celebrity in the past decade and a half.
For the past years, the RCA Italian studios, opera at festivals,
an apartment in Rome have kept the soprano safely away from
the oppressive heat and humidity of a New York summer. This
one, however, she had spent time with her mother after the
passing of her father, and she was now relaxing and working
here before opening the San Francisco Opera season in September as Elvira in Verdi's *Ernani*.

"I like Elvira, because there are no other women in the
opera and three men are in love with me—and it lies well
vocally," she observes, sitting coolly in black with bright
splashes of pink. More and more over the past few years it has
been Verdi, along with Mozart, who has come to dominate
the Price operatic repertoire. She candidly sums up her
thoughts on the matter: "I always say that people can give a
carelessly nailed production of *Trovatore* or a bad *mise en
scène* for *Ballo* or a not-very-well-sung *Aida,* but it is Verdi
who keeps the opera houses open. That's all I have to say. It
has been going on since he wrote his first note." The singer
herself was well launched on the wings of Verdi when she sang
Alice in a Juilliard production of *Falstaff.*

Getting down to the particulars concerning Price and Verdi,
she continues: "Verdi and Mozart are the best vocal pals I
have—they like me and I like them. I can't really explain it,
but you try on a dress and it's either becoming or it isn't. For
me, there is vocal ease in Verdi and Mozart—I'm most relaxed
here, and I can therefore perform with abandon. Of course,
there are the exceptions: Lady Macbeth and Abigaille in *Nabucco* aren't for me—it's not the department of Verdi's I'd like
to wear.

"Aida has been a part of me for a long time. I don't think
of it as a role—it is something I love to do and I don't have
to think about it. And, besides, I'm saving the theater on make-
up. For a challenge and pure vocalism, I like the difference of
mood in the two Leonoras, *Trovatore* and *Forza*—both are
challenging situations. Vocally, there are no more beautiful
roles. Sometimes, when I sing certain phrases, I can't believe
that such things could have been written. I enjoy these vocal

voyages—no, not 'orgies,' though sometimes on a good night they can be this too. As a female, I also can't imagine a more beautiful role than Amelia in *Ballo* for its sheer femininity."

How do some of the lesser-sung Verdi ladies fit into the singer's future plans? "I've learned Elisabetta in *Don Carlo* and Amelia in *Simon Boccanegra,* and they're on reserve for the future. In London recently, at Covent Garden, I heard the full five-act version of *Don Carlo* and discovered that the most beautiful music for Elisabetta is cut in the shorter version. In five acts, you enjoy the femininity of Eboli and the full regal character of the Queen. I'd also like to do Desdemona in *Otello,* and it's inevitable that I'll record it. On stage, it will need special care and thought in the production by the director. I'm very provoked by this role and I have learned it."

First, by hearing the soprano in the opera house and, second, by listening to her over the lunch table points to the fact that the *spinto* and dramatic roles have slowly gained a foothold where lyrical roles used to dominate. Yes, she agrees, there has been a good deal of *natural* vocal development (as opposed to a deliberate molding). "I made a few mistakes—we all do— one or two things I might have left alone. No. *Thaïs* in Chicago wasn't one of them—it was good in my voice, but the sets were from Mary Garden's time, the year I was born!" Perhaps it was the risk of singing so demanding a role as Puccini's Minnie, *Girl of the Golden West,* in 1961 for the opening of the Met season, "My voice has grown naturally," she believes, "and I've tried to stick to the literature that is best for me— until certain exuberant demands were made. I describe my voice as a 'juicy lyric,' I think. A lyric with a dramatic thrust to it, nearly a *spinto* even though the quality is still a healthy lyric."

Watching this natural development and helping her make the necessary adjustments—since the days when an aspiring Leontyne Price came to New York to study at the Juilliard School—has been Florence Page Kimball. As Miss Price puts it, "I call her 'my ears,' because she is always aware of the change in my apparatus and can answer the questions of the growth of my voice and repertoire. I wouldn't dream of tackling a role without her. I'm very lucky to have her. Her theory is to sing on the interest, not the capital. She says that if after a performance you feel you could repeat it, everything is okay."

What had made the young potential music teacher from Laurel, Mississippi, set out on an operatic career—one that was first set in motion at Juilliard and then in Virgil Thomson's *Four Saints in Three Acts* for the International Arts Festival? "As a child," she confesses, "I knew no opera or singers. It was only in 1949, when I came to New York to study, that I heard my first operatic performance: *Salome* with Welitsch. I really got the bug after I heard Callas. I thought this idea of being in the operatic arena (for that's what it is!) was very exciting. The histrionic and vocal combined provided an electric experience. Ponselle on records is my idea of what it's all about. Callas, of course, is still on top—a legend in her own lifetime."

As she builds her own image as opera star and recitalist, Miss Price admits: "I can't function without a challenge. Now I want more recital work, because of the growth of the singer in the arms of a pianist—you must create nineteen or twenty characters in an evening, not just one. It helps in being *the* one on stage—you relearn how to shift gears. I have not done much in the way of recitals in New York for several years, and there is so much literature I've not done: Ravel, Debussy, Schubert, Schumann and more Brahms. Recitalists are also the medium for new music, especially American, and I'm on the lookout for new works and new composers. The most important thing is the planning of programs in advance. The comfortable feeling has to be there. The reflex action is needed in both recital and opera—you can't experiment."

In the way of operatic challenges to keep her future busy, some names and titles are tossed in Miss Price's direction, only to be bombarded with a quick volley of answers. What about Richard Strauss? "Again, I hate to run out of challenges and this is provocative music, repertory with some spice. I've not researched it yet, but in the back of my mind I have *Ariadne auf Naxos* and the Empress in *Die Frau ohne Schatten*. I once saw *Egyptian Helen* in Vienna and maybe I'll do this too—I love the one aria. No, I have no interest in *Salome*, nor in *Carmen*. People thought I had exhilarating plans to do these roles on stage after I recorded them, but they're not for me. I was glad to record them, but . . . there's a great difference vocally in singing a role on stage and on the mike. I really like the roles I can do in both places."

What about the French repertoire? "Selika in Meyerbeer's *L'Africaine* is something I want to investigate. It has been mentioned for an American revival, but not here in New York. I've looked at *Louise* with the thought that this may be something to do, but. . . ." With a wave of the hand, she also rules out *Adriana Lecouvreur* and *Der Freischütz*—"I love the *Adriana* arias, but that's all, just the audience-milkers."

And Wagner? "I haven't the slightest interest in it or a desire to do it. I do not get the Wagner message. I just don't. Roles have been suggested, but I say no. I think that no matter how much effort you put into a role and a performance, you must have a lot of fun doing it—at least as much or more than the audience—and I couldn't have fun with Wagner. If I don't, then I'm not giving my audience an exciting experience. Verdi has the same kind of worshippers as Wagner does today, but he's so much more touchable." As for Puccini—"I would like to go back to Puccini, but I don't know. Two roles I've avoided like the plague are Mimi in *Bohème* and, back to Verdi again, Violetta in *Traviata*. I'm just too healthy for coughing spells. I'm not the type, except for the *tragedienne* scenes and the *legato* passages. I would, however, like to take a stab at *Suor Angelica* and *Il Tabarro*, both fascinating characters." And *Norma?*—"*Norma!* That's the gravedigger of all time! I won't go near it! I'm not bright sometimes, but I'm not dumb!"

Having played armchair impresario with the soprano, there is wonderment how she manages the never-ending stream of suggestions that flows from the world's impresarios. "Yes, they are always asking. I just say thanks, but no, sweetie. They can ask and I give the answers. It's really very easy when they ask me for new things: we talk very nicely and I smile and say 'No.' Yes, it's true they offered me *Nabucco* at the Met, and I offered it right back!"

What was the most unusual production she ever found herself involved in? "Without a doubt, Zeffirelli's *Antony and Cleopatra* for the opening of the Metropolitan. [Remember the collapsible pyramid, the mobile sphinx?] If I had any blood left, I'd let you have some! The most unusual, that's the only word for it—that's it! I think the most *exciting* production was probably the Salzburg *Trovatore*. Everything about it was fantastic: the cast, the costumes, the decor. The emphasis was on the voice and the grand heroics."

Where, when she is not travelling and sinking, does she prefer to be? "I've never become disenchanted with Italy, which I really love. I have a small apartment in Rome near Piazza Navona in the Argentina area. Everything in it I got at the gypsy market and painted myself. Maybe, that's why I like it so much. There's nothing in it worth over five dollars."

Since the 1968 political candidates were being polled this question last summer, Leontyne Price was asked for a parting thought: When history is written, what would you like your contribution to have been, what would you like to be remembered for? "It would be that I've been as true to the art form that I found myself in as possible—that I tried to do my artistic best at all times and maintained as high artistic standards as possible."

★ *Artur Rubinstein* ★

By now Artur Rubinstein has had the last word on the life of Artur Rubinstein via his own autobiography, published in the spring of 1973. I visited with him in 1967 just before the New Year, in time for a heroic cycle of nine recitals in New York during the winter of 1968. This legendary pianist, now over 80, shows no signs of ever leaving the public eye.

Artur Rubinstein—age 78 by his own admission, yet understating that venerable figure according to the record of his birth in 1886 in Lodz, Poland—has returned to New York from Europe in the weeks before Christmas. Several musical matters occupy his thoughts: one is an imminent recording of the Beethoven First and Second Piano Concertos in Boston with the Boston Symphony and Erich Leinsdorf, thereby putting the finishing touches on a new cycle of the five concerti with that orchestra: another is the cycle of nine sold-out recitals which will be shared between Philharmonic Hall and Carnegie Hall.

There is also his yearly American concert tour, the many old friends to see, dinners savored in the city's most fashionable restaurants and even the chance to refuse an appearance on one of television's leading late-night chatter programs between Christmas and New Year's. Yet, high up in one of the East Side's most elegant hotels, this exuberant citizen of the world makes time in his schedule to preside over a late afternoon chat, comfortably relaxed in an easy chair next to his piano, wearing a blue coat and grey slacks and smoking one of his favorite cigars.

Such cycles as this are nothing new for Rubinstein. During the 1955-56 season, he undertook a series of five concerts each in London, Paris and New York, encompassing seventeen piano-orchestra compositions (all the Brahms and Beethoven concerti, Chopin, Mozart, Grieg, Tchaikovsky, Rachmaninoff, Liszt and Schumann and works by Franck and Falla). To celebrate the 25th anniversary of his association with S. Hurok and his return to America in 1937, Mr. Rubinstein played an extraordinary series of no less than ten recitals in forty days in Carnegie Hall from October 30 through December 10, 1961.

"I'm always the great effort maker," he boasts mockingly. "But this time it is most important to tell my public this: In my young years, I'm proud to say I was a violent fighter for the music of my contemporaries, which I was incredibly eager to bring to the public so that they could understand and appreciate it as I did. Often I fought against strong public opposition for the compositions of my young colleagues when I played works of Scriabin, Debussy, Ravel, Szymanowski, Villa-Lobos, Shostakovich and Prokofiev. I was hissed in Milan for playing a Shostakovich prelude and in Warsaw when I played Debussy there in 1904, for these were then novelties. I did this for half of my life, but more recently new names have not appeared on my programs.

"Since I was married [to Aniela Mylnarski in 1932], I took

up a personal approach to the piano and piano literature. Since then, my great desire has been to give better performances of the classics and romantics, and always to improve on them. And I think this is the only thing I can do in my old age. I do not feel able to fight now for Stockhausen or Boulez or Nono—this I leave to the young people. I feel out of touch with new developments of music and so I dare not criticize it either; one has no right to do this about what one does not understand. One can criticize only the music one knows well. Therefore, I ask my public not to be astonished not seeing new names on my programs. My endeavor is to improve on compositions in my repertoire. It is not my time to play new things now."

What he plays is, of course, the familiar and impressive repertoire that includes Chopin, Liszt, Beethoven, Schumann, Debussy, Prokofiev, Brahms, the Spaniards and many others with the tonal beauty, virtuosity and emotional clarity we have come to expect from him. "I feel that each concert is a good lesson for the next concert. This is different from studying at home with the distractions of the telephone, visitors and my own thoughts that I can put off working. A concert is like a bull fight—the moment of truth. All my senses are wide awake. I give one hundred per cent of my attention during that time. I learn what not to do the next time. From concert to concert, experience is built up.

"Recently, I played the Beethoven Third, Fourth and Fifth Piano Concertos in London in one evening, and the public did not recognize them. They thought my interpretations were better than before, improved with experience. I've played Beethoven's *Appassionata* Sonata a thousand times before, but in Spain recently it was suddenly a new experience: I was astonished with my new approach. Beethoven himself interpreted his own works differently each time he played them. Czerny wrote that it was hard to recognize a piece at each performance, so different were his tempos and his general humor. When I sit in Paris in a café, surrounded by people, watching people pass by, I don't sit casually—I go over a certain sonata in my head and discover new things all the time."

This picture of today's Rubinstein perfecting the repertoire, which he has spent a lifetime harvesting, offers a fascinating contrast to his own description of Artur Rubinstein the youth: "I made a great impression then with my musical memory and feeling, *not* with my repertoire and technique. I was impatient to give all the music then, not just that for the piano. Actually, I was educated by the most severe classical background. The pedantic Professor Heinrich Barth, who, as you know, was my teacher in Berlin and a pupil of Bülow, Tausig and Liszt, prohibited me from hearing Wagner. But when he did this, I was already privately playing by heart the scores of *Tristan und Isolde, Lohengrin* and parts of the *Ring* tetralogy.

"I had a revolutionary musical mind even at 15. But my training was only in Bach, Mozart, Mendelssohn, Weber and the classical literature—even Chopin was given to me piecemeal. Yet on my own I was buried in the Strauss tone poems, I knew Mahler with a passion. And when I was in Berlin at age 15 I knew Scriabin and Debussy on the piano. When I came back to Berlin later in my 20's and played Debussy in a concert, my Professor was spitting blood with rage—'*Schweinemusik*' he called it. I had jumped in with both feet.

"In Paris, I played everything by heart—all the violin concertos, Schubert and Schumann and Wolf songs, Fauré. I knew all the chamber music. but I was poor in my own repertoire. When *Salome* was new, I was very enthusiastic about it. My manager in Paris brought Strauss and a German company to perform it there in 1908. At that time it was dangerous to bring anything German to Paris, since it was not long after the Franco-Prussian War. Emmy Destinn was the Salome and I played for the rehearsals. I could play the whole opera through, and several times I did it in private for 500 francs, playing the score, explaining the opera and even singing some parts by heart." Mention the fact that one renowned conductor claims his stunt was to play Strauss' *Till Eulenspiegel* on the piano and Rubinstein twinkles, "Oh, that I could do with my left hand."

The reason for this spell as a rehearsal pianist was simple: "I was having a hard time then, with few engagements, except some in Poland. Like all youngsters, I had a hard time.

It took a long time to establish a career. I always had good luck with people, with artists and writers—but I didn't have much contact with money. The long struggle lasted until I was thirty, but until then I was in debt and difficulty. Part of this was my own fault. I didn't run after engagements: they had to come by themselves. I never pursued, my conscience is pure. I never bothered anyone, not like some artists who are always calling managers and conductors and other artists asking for recommendations. My career came out of itself thanks to miracles, some unforeseen *deus ex machina* which always managed to appear."

All this discussion of his early life led to talk about Rubinstein's work on his life story. "Yes, I am writing my memoirs [completed in 1973]—autobiography is a rather big word. I have a good memory and I want to tell a truthful life story. What I don't want is a eulogistic book; that I find nauseating. I am old enough not to worry what people will think. I am telling what my life really was like, because it has been so adventurous and unusual. Already I've written over 500 pages and I'm still 20 years old!

"Because my mind is filled with musical things during the season, I can write only in the summer. Last summer I wrote 150 pages in Marbella in Spain, and I never touched the piano. Though I speak eight languages, I would give away seven for one good one. To help my English I have ten dictionaries all around me to find the right words. People tell me to use a dictaphone or a tape recorder to tell the story—and actually I do like to talk—and then let someone else put it into a book. But writing must have a certain style and movement, otherwise it is sloppy. With an editor, it would have a foreign style with his shape, not with mine. My style may be primitive, but it is mine.

"I think the first volume will be of my young years, when I was poor, always in trouble—I was no good. In this volume I will open the window on hope: something *might* happen to a no-good bum! Later the writing will become more difficult, in my 40's and 50's. I face the choice of suppressing some feelings or hurting others. It is also difficult to criticize—can I criticize Horowitz, Richter or Gilels as I can speak my mind about Nikisch, d'Albert, Schnabel and all the others of my past? I will treat my later life as an epilogue to remind the public of what they know of me. What can I tell?—that I signed with Sol Hurok and made a lot of money? Or that I made many records and again a lot of money?"

A revealing recollection of his own career, published in an interview some years ago, was his confession that, "When I was young I was lazy. I had talent but there were many things in life more important than practicing. Good food, good cigars, great wines, women. . . . When I played in the Latin countries—Spain, Italy, France—they loved me because of my temperament. When I played in Russia there was no trouble because my namesake Anton Rubinstein, no relation, had conditioned the audiences there to wrong notes. I dropped many notes in those days, maybe thirty per cent, and they felt they were being cheated." Today he admits that "at each concert I will play some wrong notes. But if the performance is great, it doesn't matter. The psychological and emotional performance is what counts on stage."

His suave and poetic approach to the music of Frédéric Chopin, of which he has been considered the sovereign master for decades, has followed in the tradition of Tausig, about whom was written, "He relieved the romantically sentimental Chopin of this *Weltschmertz,* and showed him in his pristine creative vigor and wealth of imagination"; and Josef Hofmann who also overthrew the exaggerated and mannered Romantic excess. In 1960, on the occasion of the Chopin sesquicentennial, Rubinstein wrote in *The New York Times* about his own development as a modern, yet Romantic, Chopin player: ". . . I heard quite a bit of Chopin during my childhood in Poland—mazurkas, polonaises, nocturnes, the whole beloved repertoire. All of it was played, interminably, and most of it badly. Why badly? In those days both musicians and the public believed in the Chopin myth, as do many people today. That myth was a destructive one. Chopin, the man, was seen as weak and ineffectual; Chopin the artist as an irrepressible romantic. . . ." At his next recital, he continued, he included Chopin in a manner that was noble and without sentimentality and affectation. His conscientious effort was adjudged "dry," for both the audience and critics preferred the "good old Chopin" they knew. In America, too, he was chastized for his "severe" interpretations of Chopin. "Only very much later was the validity of my interpretation granted. Only then was I permitted to have my Chopin and to give him to audiences. . . ."

In the recording studio, Rubinstein has given us the complete works of Chopin—"except for the Études. I am scared to death of them, technically and musically. But, maybe before I die I will do them. I have heard some very musical performances of the Études, but it is very rare for both to happen together. Records are different from a concert in the ultimate product. If I were dishonest, I could record them bar by bar: I could tape three bars and have coffee, then play three more and have tea, and then three more and lie down. Then the producers could splice all these together and have it all of a piece. I find that the young wizards of technique are afraid they can't play as well as their own recordings, for in a performance they are exposed—on records, nothing can happen to go wrong."

As our time draws to a close Rubinstein adds: "One thing I warn my young colleagues—not to play music that doesn't talk to them. Never play anything just because the public wants it or because it has become fashionable. A performance must have conviction, an artist must have contact with his music or he should leave it alone. To communicate a piece of music to others, you must feel it ten times stronger in playing it."

The time has come to say our farewells, but noting the Legion d'Honneur rosette on his lapel, Rubinstein counters a query with, "I don't deserve it, but I wear it with pleasure. And in France it is very helpful with the police and in getting a taxi. Paris, of course, is the town where I live, since I was seventeen. Sometimes it consisted only of leaving an old bag there. First I had a room, then a bungalow in Montmartre, and since 1938 a house on Avenue Foch off the Bois de Boulogne, on a private square closed off by an iron gate. There are twenty-four houses there and mine is next to where Debussy lived and died. I like the feeling that he had to cross the front of my house before going in and out every day."

He then scrambles through a partially unpacked suitcase, coming up with a full-dress color photograph in which he is bedecked with the full ribbon of the Commander of the Legion d'Honneur and the many decorations he has received—Commander of the Order of Chile, Grand Officer of Alfonso XII of Spain, Officer of Santiago of Portugal, Officer of Bologna Restituta, Honorary Member of the Accademia di Santa Cecilia in Rome and many others. "I had this photograph made for my children who say that they never see these decorations which I keep stored away. Today," he wistfully and humorously notes, "there are only a few opportunities to wear them, maybe in England or France on the right occasion. The day of kings and royalty is over," says the man who has played for and dined with the greatest of them—and as the door is closed, you are reassured that with the presence of such an artist as Artur Rubinstein still vibrantly alive in the musical picture, a true pianistic artistocracy does live on in an age which the late Jan Holcman once described as "this Spiritless Musical Epoch."

★ *Leonie Rysanek* ★

Leonie Rysanek's honesty and candor about herself made her a most fascinating and rewarding subject, even more so because her intensity and commitment on the operatic stage had long been admired from afar. Since we talked, in the wake of her first Salomes, she has gone on to add Ponchielli's Gioconda with great success in Berlin during the winter of 1974, while returning to San Francisco after a long hiatus.

Greatness is a thorny word to define, but in the opera world one measure is whether singers can put their stamp on two or three roles. Can they claim a Chénier or Otello, a Leonora or an Elektra for their very own on the international circuit? In the case of Leonie Rysanek, she has put her personal stamp on so many parts that the word *greatness* compels capitalizing the term *Prima Donna*. For Wagner openers, one thinks immediately of her haunted, neurotic Senta in *The Flying Dutchman*—but Sieglinde in *Die Walküre,* Elisabeth in *Tannhäuser* and Elsa in *Lohengrin* are easy entries as well. In the Straussian stratosphere, Rysanek has literally cornered Ariadne in *Ariadne auf Naxos,* the Empress in *Die Frau ohne Schatten,* the Marschallin in *Der Rosenkavalier,* Chrysothemis in *Elektra* and, more recently, the title role in *Salome*. Add to this her intensely moving Leonore in Beethoven's *Fidelio* and, simply because so few others dare it, the title part in Cherubini's *Medea,* another new acquisition. And she is a leading contender for Tosca and Desdemona honors—making a sum of at least a dozen roles which bear the Rysanek Seal of Excitement.

Excitement is almost too ordinary, too mild a word to describe what Leonie Rysanek creates on stage. But it's one on the tongues of most opera-goers when they come away from a Rysanek performance. Today, having once passed through what can politely be called difficult times, she possesses all that is needed: a striking presence, an intuitive sense of the stage (given to very few), an Olympian voice of dramatic flexibility and range, an extraordinary use of dynamic levels (from a radiant *pianissimo* to a shattering forte) and that uncanny power to make people listen, pay attention, respond (both positively and otherwise). Like any true great, she inspires more heated argument, more provoked conversation, more buzzing undercurrent than any singer of our time—except Maria Callas. The resemblance is striking, especially in that exceptional gift of commitment, of giving to the public beyond the full measure.

Casually dressed and sitting very much at ease in her luxurious suite high over Central Park, Miss Rysanek had just made her New York debut as Salome. She leans back, smiles and says, "I love voices. I still think the human voice is the most beautiful, heavenly instrument." As to the ingredients that go into making a successful singer-performer, she immediately responds: "First I want to hear beautiful singing. But almost at the same time I want to have excitement, personality! That was the success of Callas—the excitement and the voice and absolutely believing in what she did. I probably feel this way because I originally wanted to be an actress, and I *love* the theater. If I have an evening that has both the singing and the excitement, then I stand and scream. I don't understand it if singers who are no longer performing can't take the success of a younger singer on stage. Zinka Milanov said of Nilsson, 'A good top, a good middle, a good bottom. But who cares?' I told her I do and so do two million others."

Leonie Rysanek is enormously demanding of herself without ever comparing herself to other singers. "I am Rysanek. The other one is the other one. There are no two singers alike. I would never say, 'Well, I'm not as good as she is in this' or 'I am better than she is.' But I measure against the best I can do. I judge myself. It's not saying 'The performance was good!' or 'It was better than the last one.' I always say, 'Well, it was very good tonight, but I sing *much* better performances.' One shouldn't do this . . . not always. But every serious artist does make these comparisons with what *he* can do.

"You know, in the past everything is beautiful. I know, I remember. I always think I was much better ten or fifteen years ago, and then I hear a tape or recording. It wasn't *that* great! It's the same as forgetting sad things. It is beautiful to remember only the good things."

The past for Leonie Rysanek began in Vienna, where she was born to a simple family with six children (a younger sister, Lotte, is currently a singer with the Staatsoper, having grown from lyric to dramatic roles). "We always made music. My grandfather from my father's side was Czechoslovakian. Vienna and Austria were always the melting pot of the monarchy—Hungarians, Yugoslavians, Czechs and so on. You see my face—I'm Slavic. My grandfather was a military conductor, so probably my musicianship came from him. We sang at home and played a little bit. But I wanted to become an actress, not a singer, and I studied as an actress. I always liked to sing, too, and then someone—I don't remember who— said, 'Why do you want to be an actress? You have a beautiful voice. Try to become a singer. There are lots of good actresses already.' That was the reason I changed to a singing career.

"But I must say," she continues, "that nobody really believed in me in the beginning—but *I* did! I was so secure and

so sure I would make a big career. I don't know why, but I
think it is very important in the beginning to be very *sure* of
yourself, to let nobody tell you what to do . . . but, of
course, to learn. At least ten famous managers and people
said when I auditioned for them, 'Oh, come on. Go home
and marry and have children.' Only two or three people really
believed in me—and *I* did. And that's important—because
criticism of yourself comes with fame. Almost the same time
that I became famous—or let's say *known,* well known in
Europe—I started suddenly to be nervous, to have stage
fright and doubts that I was not that good. If this would
happen in the beginning, many big singers wouldn't be around,
I'm sure."

For the record, Mme Rysanek studied at the Conservatory
of the City of Vienna with Alfred Jerger and later with Rudolf
Grossman, whom she eventually married. In the early student
days she stood to hear performances at the Staatsoper, particularly admiring Hilde Konetzni and Maria Reining, the latter
a prize Strauss singer much in the Rysanek vein. She made her
debut in Innsbruck as Agathe in *Der Freischütz* ("I always
hated it, a terrible character. Mr. Bing asked me and I said,
'Are you joking?' "), spending two years in Saarbrucken and
coming to the Bayreuth Festival in 1951 for the first postwar
Ring. Then she appeared with the Vienna State Opera in
1954, America via the San Francisco Opera in 1957 and the
Met in 1959 as its first Lady Macbeth.

Asked how her voice has progressed over more than two
decades of steady, strenuous singing, she smiles. "I must be
very honest. I always had a very easy, good, secure top. In
the beginning I sang the Queen of the Night's aria with an F—
and easily. I still sing an F in scales when I vocalize. In the
beginning I had a very easy top. I could sing piano, I could
do everything. Nature gave this to me. If I look back, my
voice was almost *only* top then. I have to be honest and say
my middle was cloudy. One critic wrote—I'll never forget
this—of my Aida for the opening of the rebuilt Opera in
Vienna: 'It's a pity. She has brilliant top and beautiful *tessitura* up there, but if she comes down in the middle, her voice
sounds like an airplane that moves in the fog.' I think Wechs-
berg wrote this, and he was a fan and still likes me very much.

Now with my Medea, he was surprised that I made a big middle voice. I think my voice now is broader, darker. In the beginning I had a lyric, but powerful, voice, especially the top. Now it's bigger. Nature does this, the voice comes down. That's the big mistake many sopranos make; if they don't have a good top in the beginning, they think it will come. I don't think so. One can work hard on it and have good evenings—but you will never sing it really because you are waiting for a high note. *I* always *like* to sing high notes—I am looking forward almost always. My middle voice is much better now. I always said that this will come. And Birgit Nilsson, whom I very much adore, always said to me, 'Don't push your middle and lower registers. They will come. If you do, you have to pay with your top voice. It always goes.' So, with the time and aging, it really came to me. Also I worked a little bit on it. I do things differently, but I don't *push* it."

The soprano, who had led a golden life during the Fifties, gaining a fabled reputation, suddenly found herself in trouble, particularly after starring in the Met's first production of Verdi's *Nabucco* for the opening of the 1960-61 season and again the following year. "I must say I had a bad time after thirty. It was my idiocy to lose that much weight, first of all. Then I was sick. I had trouble—but *never* with the vocal cords, never with the voice. But if you are physically ill and in your mind you say to yourself that you can't do that anymore, it's worse—believe me! I was so scared. I wanted to quit, to stop. Many things happened with the record company and . . . ach! My luck was that I was young enough and certain. It started with Abigaille—a difficult part that took away all my confidence—the whole trouble: mind trouble, singing trouble, private things, everything came together. If it's bad, everything is bad. For a while I wanted to quit. But there was Mr. Bing. He sat for hours and kept me in his arms and said, 'You will not leave here. You will stay and appear and tell me what you want to do when you want to do it. If you leave here now you will never be back on the stage anywhere. I know you.' So I stayed and had a rest for five or six weeks. And my first performance was *Elektra* with Borkh—the broadcast. Mr. Bing stood in the wings. I was half dead, but suddenly I was in a *glorious* mood—and secure in myself. The top, everything was there. He smiled at me and grabbed me after my first exit. So from this time on—not that everything was good—but I felt I was coming back again. I had gained confidence. Not always, and I must say that shortly before I was married [she had divorced Grossmann in the meantime and married Ernst Ludwig Gaussman in 1968] I could almost do everything again with the voice. It took me quite a few years to rebuild, and they were hard years. It took me four or five years to get back—I think almost to the premiere of *Die Frau ohne Schatten* in 1966, although I was not as good as I wanted to be, as I was later. I know that, too!"

Her marriage was the turning point in realigning her life and career. "One critic," she notes, "wrote that something had changed in me with the new *Fidelio* in New York. Something has changed in the voice. Happiness—I am very happy and I hope he is—means a lot. It makes you quiet. I am not so unhappy if a performance isn't as good as I would have liked it. I am still unhappy about it, but in former days I was *destroyed*. I was always afraid to think of what will be when I retire. I thought I would die without the stage. I know I won't be happy without it, but I don't think I'll be *that* unhappy."

Boasting of happiness and good health, she reflects, "I think there hasn't been one performance—let's be very modest —in the last two years that I could say, 'Boy, you were *bad!*' Some phrases I didn't sing as I wanted, but it wasn't like the years before when I was *depressed*." The most recent roles have been unqualified triumphs: her first Salome at Munich in the summer of 1971 and her first Medea in Vienna later that winter. "When I started Medea I thought this was the biggest mistake I ever made. The problem is that the orchestra is thin—you can't lean on it. Look, in Salome of course you have the voice. But even if you are not well (it can happen) for several moments, one can do something crazy or move or keep the voice back. In *Medea,* whew! You have to always be a hundred percent personality and there! Everyone is looking. The other characters are only cue-bringers. It's not that great as art, but it's a great prima donna part."

Of all the things in her large, wide-ranging repertoire, the soprano finds the Strauss roles the most grateful. The composer's son, who lives in Garmisch, near Munich, has often told her it's a pity his father never met her because of the *heilige* tradition she carries on. Many feel that Strauss' long, arching, high, sustained music is a voice-killer—especially if it is sung for as long as Mme Rysanek has sung it—and with such passion. "It is not," she contends, "if you sing right. If one has the necessary *tessitura,* a good top, then there is *no* other composer who really wrote as brilliantly as Strauss did for a soprano." Not only has she become a famous Ariadne, Marschallin, Empress and Chrysothemis, but she's also sung *Die Aegyptische Helena, Die Liebe der Danae* and *Arabella.*

Now she admits that Salome is her prized role, one she played in a new production at Christmastime 1972 in Vienna. "Well, if one has success with an opera, then one tends to say it's a favorite. I had the feeling, when I did it in Munich, that the people *wanted* my success. They were waiting, and I was waiting, too. I had made my career there; then I had fights with the management and went away for years. So everything was right on this evening: the orchestra, the artists with me on stage—Fischer-Dieskau, Varnay and Stolze. When the curtain came down, there was dead silence for ten seconds. I was so exhausted, trembling, so involved with the whole thing. And then a twenty-five minute ovation. It was unbelievable!

"Some understood what I meant; others did not." She shakes her head. "But I have to do it *my* way. I can't do a tigress or a child. Nobody would believe me." Her idea, as developed by director Günther Rennert, is that Salome starts as a girl, but by the end has lost her youth. "It's her whole life in one day." She evolves from a sixteen-year-old into Salome. She gains in sophistication during the whole experience with Jochanaan. "That's what I wanted to show and at the end it is almost Salome's 'Liebestod' because Strauss wrote for the voice of an Isolde. Then they don't even need to kill her—because she is already dead!"

After the premiere, Franz Strauss came to her, comparing her with his father's favorite Salome, Maria Jeritza. When Mme Rysanek brought her Salome to New York, Mme Jeritza was conspicuously present and later phoned to say, "Nobody sings a Salome like you . . . including Maria."

Now, of course, critics and her public are awaiting the next logical Strauss step, Elektra. Her admiration of Nilsson is one deterrent, and, as she notes, "I like to stay on the stage as Chrysothemis beside Birgit—and Chrysothemis is much easier for the same money."

One of the most staggering elements of a Rysanek performance is her total commitment to a role, to the music. Asked if she finds it hard to balance technique with personal emotion in a performance, she nods, "Yes, sometimes, when I had my bad years. It was always difficult. Now I think I don't overdo it anymore. If I overact or get over-emotional on stage, it always shows on the voice. Look, if you speak and are breathing hard, then imagine how difficult it is in singing. I have quite balanced that. I don't get as carried away as I did before. The ideal is to give the appearance without being involved, but this I will *never* reach—I can't be that cold!

"And then I'm so ambitious," she adds. "I *want* to do it. I'm not ambitious in a way that I want to be the greatest, but if I'm on stage I want to be my *very* best. That's probably why I overdid it sometimes in the past. I always wanted to do *more*. When I study I start to build a character early so that when I come to the stage to rehearse, I can tell the director, 'Don't you think you could do it this way, too?' The artist must bring something of himself."

Her roles, then, remain fairly fixed in conception, no matter whether she's in New York, Berlin or Vienna. Her red-hot Senta, as practiced in Bayreuth, is the only thing that has ignited the Met's lackluster *Dutchman* in many revivals. Of this part she says, "My first Senta was in '51 in Saarbrucken, my second year on stage. When I did the famous production in Bayreuth in 1959, which was a sensation and I had my first rehearsal of the 'Ballad' with Wieland, he did not once interrupt. I looked at him and said, 'Don't you say anything at all?' 'There's nothing to be said. That's it,' he told me. So I felt always I must be right in this part. Usually Senta is dull, thick, boring. Well, I made this part famous, and now it's known as a good part. I made her likable, believable—good and wanted."

Does Leonie Rysanek, whose life was once threatened if she sang a Desdemona at the Met (a Tebaldi or Milanov militant, no doubt), consider herself a controversial singer? "Well, I don't know. I would rather be controversial than well accepted. In Europe it's less so than here. May I tell you something? I think the trouble here is if one is a versatile artist—they don't like it. It mixes people up. They can't place you in scheme. Even more than just German or Italian repertoire, they like just one composer. It's easier that way. And then, a look, a voice, a personality is always a matter of taste." Wagner, Strauss, Verdi are approached with the same basic vocal technique—but with different styles. "I teach myself. I have tapes with different things to vocalize and work. I do it in a very odd way. I never need a piano, and I don't sing ah-ah-ah, which I think is stupid. I do my exercises only if I have to learn something new or if I have a performance. Otherwise I don't sing. You know there is only so much left. It is my capital. It's like a salami—up to a certain age, each performance is a thin slice. So you have to be careful."

Nervousness is less a problem than before. "When I had my bad years, I was scared when I went on stage. But I always discipline myself very well. I love to sing broadcasts: there is no time to get nervous," she sighs.

She finds criticism hard to take, even from her husband, to whom she carefully listens after a performance and who tactfully relays only pleasant information first. "I take it hard, but he has to tell me the rest, too. I wonder who wants to hear *only* the best. Criticism is always hard to take. All right, I take it. I have learned to do that here because you learn from it. In Vienna, the critics are cruel; they can be nasty. But here if Schoenberg doesn't like something, he is not bitter or cynical. If you don't like something, all right, explain it—but don't be cynical. At first I took criticism hard, but also it was a lesson for me. And I'll be very honest: I don't take it as seriously anymore. I know when I am good and when I am not. It's pleasant to read the next morning, 'She was great.' If it isn't so, for a little while . . . well, it is not so tragic anymore. I am secure; I know how far I can go. I want to stay on the stage for, let's say, five or six years more—if it's possible, if it goes well. I promised myself that if one or two performances go down, then I'll stop. I will know, myself."

Many European critics, having heard her Medea and Salome, now await a Rysanek Isolde. "I was already scheduled to sing it, but I was so scared, and then Dr. Böhm said, 'Don't sing Isolde, *please,* because you will never sing the Kaiserin and all those high parts if you do." But I wanted to try my voice, how much it can take. So I did the whole part only with the cues—three times! I was completely hoarse for three days. Then I realized, no, I can't sing this opera."

In true prima donna fashion, she resents the director-dominated status of opera today—and the importance of the designer, too. "Yes, they are very important people, but sometimes I tell them they are not *that* important. I love beautifully done opera, the sets, the stage. But each in its place, please. In some houses in Europe they don't even ask if a singer has a beautiful voice. Is she a good actress? Is she slender? Okay, then she sings. And the critics write first about the production, the direction, the design. But this is not opera. The most important thing is . . . the singer."

★ *Elisabeth Schwarzkopf* ★

During the 1974–75 season, Elisabeth Schwarzkopf is making her farewell tour of America; but when we talked in the fall of 1967 she was preparing to make her debut on the "Great Performers at Philharmonic Hall" series in February 1968. For many she will long represent all that is glamorous and illustrious in the Austro-German singing tradition, a fact kept vividly alive via her many Angel recordings.

If you were getting your first taste of opera at the Chicago Lyric on Wacker Drive during the late Fifties—when the great post-war musicians began to swarm across the Atlantic to show their remarkable fares for the first time—the presence of Elisabeth Schwarzkopf was equated with the summit in portrayals of *Figaro*'s Countess, *Don Giovanni*'s Donna Elvira and *Così*'s Fiordiligi. She represented that cultivated Viennese operatic tradition which today, ten years later, threatens to be swallowed up into an international style. When she was not making operatic life so memorable at the Civic Opera House on brisk autumn nights, there were other visits for recitals, and even a Vienna-*mit-schlag* operetta evening in Orchestra Hall one fragrant spring evening.

If you were rooted to New York at this time, Elisabeth Schwarzkopf emerged as one of the great post-war recitalists —annually gaining admiration for her skillful way with Wolf, Schubert, Strauss and Schumann—who, after what was considered far too long a wait, made her belated Metropolitan Opera debut in October of 1964 with her acclaimed portrayal of Strauss' Marschallin.

Today, Elisabeth Schwarzkopf, who has so successfully straddled the worlds of opera and lieder for nearly three decades, is devoting herself primarily to the concert stage.

Critic Ernest Newman once wrote in the London *Sunday Times* on a subject that has occupied the mind of just such a singer as Mme Schwarzkopf throughout her career: lieder versus operatic singing. He reasoned that, since the vocal line is determined by other than quasi-instrumental considerations, the style appropriate to lieder is not that of what we may call purely instrumental singing. "Each great song inhabits a mental world of its own. It follows that the singer, if he wishes to carry us with him, must reproduce the world for us. Standardized methods will not do here, nor does a fine voice suffice of itself. Some voices are fundamentally unfitted by their very nature to express certain emotions or certain poetic ideas."

The worst judges of lieder singing, he wrote, are the people whose sole standard of singing is the quasi-instrumental, the people who are fundamentally insensitive to that suffusion of music by poetry that is the very essence of the lied in its most highly developed form. Summing up, he said, "The truth is that there is no such thing as 'singing' per se. There are merely different styles of singing, severally appropriate to different kinds of music and words: and the critical standards applicable to one style are only to a very small degree applicable to the other."

Elisabeth Schwarzkopf whole-heartedly concurs: "The great mistake people make is that they think a beautiful voice in itself is very nice, but it really has nothing to do with lieder. A lieder voice is different: it demands great technique because it needs colors that are not always healthy to beautiful vocal production. I say forget about a beautiful sound—you need words and meaning. For a soprano this is difficult, because the voice lies high and the words of the speaking voice are low. You need to fit these two together without seams, and then the color of the poem has to come through. You can always sound beautiful, but that is not the heart of the matter for a lieder singer. Often you have to make ill or biting or piercing sounds—things that have nothing to do with vocal beauty. And the first thing is to become unconcerned about this.

"To sing lieder you need a heart, but you also need a mind to know that they are not just simple folk songs. Of course, there is the kind of popular minstrel or *Hausfrau* who can sing many Schubert songs while playing a guitar—the singing is beautiful and simple but it has no inflection, and I want to leave after hearing two songs. I want to go because this gives me nothing, no new experience. When you hear a lieder program, you want to leave a different person than you were before it began—you should receive new experiences in life and emotion, and a singer wants to alter people by giving them such new experiences."

This giving of life and experience requires many things, then, beyond the vocal instrument itself. For a singer like Mme Schwarzkopf it is imperative to know about the period of the poem, the poet and the composer. She must have an historical awareness of the style involved, and she must also be aware of the connotations that are a part of any language. "Much as I've tried to sing in French and other languages, I do not think that it is possible to sing lieder and songs in other than your native tongue. You have to grow up in the language to know the meanings behind the words, so that all the related images that create the colors of what you sing can spring to your mind. The ambiance of a word is what is so crucial. Take the word *'Wald,'* for instance—it has different connotations in a poem by by Mörike or Eichendorff or Goethe, or in a setting by Schubert or Wolf or Brahms. Each word is different for every composer, poet and poem. It has a thousand

and one possibilities—and you cannot possibly begin to learn these things. They are what you grow up with and absorb unconsciously."

In studying a new song, she describes her working process something like this: "I go to the piano to play it through and read the song first. I try to get the first impression with both the words and music together for the initial impact. Then I read the words of the poem alone, as well as playing through the piano accompaniment, too. I try all ways to approach the material and then try to put the song into my voice technically. Then starts the work of forgetting about technique and finding the *real* meaning of the song."

The fact that she has managed to keep an air of spontaneity in her ever-expanding repertoire after seasons of repetition is attributed to her confession, "I'm lucky to be married to Walter Legge who keeps me going on things. I wish you could hear us preparing programs. I try always to use the same accompanist, because everything we do depends on these rehearsals. We go over and over everything with Walter. Songs I've done for years are re-read, re-thought, re-infused with emotion all the time. I can read the words and the music of a song I have sung thousands of times and suddenly for the first time see a diminuendo that should come a fraction later than I've been singing it—I will see a difference I have not observed before, and then it is necessary to see the emotional reason the composer put it exactly where he did. And as you grow older, the experience of life and fantasy grows, too, contributing to an always deepening attitude towards the music and poetry."

Expert advice and guidance in the field of concerts has played an important part in the life of Elisabeth Schwarzkopf, even before she stepped out on stage for her first recital in Berlin in the early 1940s. "I was a beginner at the Opera and had the good luck to study with Maria Ivogün and her husband, the tenor Erl, who devised programs for me. They were enchanting programs that suited my light voice. It was then *en vogue* to have theme programs, such as 'Tanzlieder' or 'Liebe und Frühling,' and all the material was chosen for my *soubrette* voice." At that time her operatic career was reaching the stratospheres of Zerbinetta, Musetta and Oscar. "I had no advertisements and no critics for my first recitals—it was just talked around the city. I had four concerts that first season and the word of a new young lieder singer was spread just by word of mouth. What I remember, too, is that I made the public hear something really lovely when I sang English madrigals which Ivogün had found in her library. Naturally, we couldn't sing English songs in Germany then, so they were translated into German by Mörike's niece and appeared on the program as 'old German songs'!"

When the "thaw" on German and Austrian artists first began in the post-war years, one of the first artists most eagerly awaited—based on her reputation on recordings—was Elisabeth Schwarzkopf. She recalls that for her first Boston recital she had submitted the usual choice of three programs, and the management had chosen the one with the greatest public appeal: a mixed bag of Dvorák, Schubert, Strauss and so on. "I accepted their choice, but as the concert came near I got so disgruntled not to be singing Hugo Wolf in that beautiful hall that I confess here and now that I told them I had had requests to sing Wolf on that program. The requests were, of course, by me—but I didn't tell them that! And ever since that night I haven't sung one recital without some Wolf on the program."

The singer's close association with the songs of Wolf stems in large measure from the fact that Walter Legge, founder and president of the Hugo Wolf Society, has encouraged and instructed her in this literature over their years together. It has been due to both their efforts that Wolf has managed to come into his own recently in this country. "Yes," she agrees, "his songs are very sophisticated, and it is necessary that the audience fully understand Wolf's songs before they hear them in concert. But they are true to the kernel of the heart. Wolf goes right to the soul of the poem, while many other composers, in comparison, skirt the circumstances. No other composer goes to the red blood cells of human emotions.

"Though I delight in other music, too, I feel my task in life is that I am made for Wolf's music on the lieder platform. If you compare his settings of the *Wilhelm Meister* songs to those of Schubert, for instance, it is evident that Wolf exposes the nerves in his songs, while Schubert operates on the different level of an over-all sense of mood. Schubert was more instinctive, but Wolf had great psychological insight. Half-mad, but a genius, he probed deepest into the psychological recesses of the human mind, into the pulsating heart of emotions and sufferings. When I see the words of a particular poem he has set, I can hear the musical setting in my mind, because the music is woven into it as if it had always been there.

"I want to bring Hugo Wolf to the public. If I do this, I've found my place in history. Of course, I have not yet sung all the Wolf songs. Some of the *Spanisches Liederbuch,* which I recorded complete with Fischer-Dieskau, I was doing for the first time. Some of them need more of a charged voice than I had, particularly the religious songs of self-destruction and self-deprecation. They are very Catholic, the spirit of which you can see in the paintings of El Greco—that destructive feeling of humans prostrated in front of the cross. I now have overcome the barrier I had about some of these texts and feel I can take them on. But for a long time I did not want to sing them."

Though Wolf appeals to the singer and the public as much as a poet as a musician, Mme Schwarzkopf admits that certain other portions of the song repertoire are a great deal more difficult to identify with, even for a native singer. "Schumann's *Frauenliebe und Leben,* for instance, we call 'kitchen maid' poetry, and this is not being snobbish. This trait of German poetry is beyond me. I've tried it, but I know it is not for me —and, let's face it you have to believe in *Frauenliebe und Leben* to sing it. A lot of poetry chosen by Strauss, too, is in this same vein—this is the over-sentimental poetry of the Makart period, the equivalent of the Victorian period in Austria with its potted palms and salon music. Some of Strauss' songs are not so deep and you can sing them well with the necessary line and voice alone.

"There is also the question of a woman singing songs written for a man. When Lotte Lehmann sang Schubert's *Schöne Müllerin,* this was the most womanly of voices, yet she could identify herself with the music and the words. The real men's songs I leave to them, since there are such great singers as Fischer-Dieskau to sing them. It doesn't make sense for me, because the repertoire for a woman is certainly big enough. I have been asked to sing *Schöne Müllerin* and maybe I will eventually come around to it, I don't know."

Though the subject of words and music of the song literature is almost a full-time occupation today, Elisabeth Schwarzkopf reasons that singing and acting the Marschallin in *Der Rosen-kavalier* is the closest of her operatic roles to singing lieder. "You cannot do this role if you are not a lieder singer, because here you paint with the same fine brush you use in recital. Otherwise, I've found it difficult to go right from opera to lieder—it's easier to sing lieder first and then an operatic performance after. For a singer, there is one channel for singing over an orchestra on stage and another channel for small scale singing, with its degrees of colors and shadings."

The soprano recalls that the Viennese tradition—which cast her with Jurinac, Seefried, Streich and others as leading interpreters of the operas of Mozart and Strauss—came about when the Second World War secluded Austria and Germany from the international outlook. "It became inbred, and the Vienna Mozart style which emerged after the war was due to one man: Josef Krips. Later, Karajan and Furtwängler carried on this great ensemble opera style at Salzburg and Vienna. We were very fortunate, for at that time these conductors rehearsed us at the piano every day, even after the premiere, before every performance. We were always working on ensembles and tempos. These were days of great performances. The other man was DeSabata in Milan, with whom I did Mélisande for the first time—this was a great experience. When I sang the Verdi Requiem with him, he wanted a different voice. I came with a Viennese voice, but he encouraged me to change to a more Italianate sound with more vibrato.

"Today, casts have become almost the same everywhere in the world, as artists have sought international acclaim. There is hardly a home-made ensemble anymore, except maybe still in Stockholm or at the East Berlin Komische Oper of Felsenstein. When I went to his opera, I was astounded that his singers keep their voices, because they have hundreds of rehearsals for each production. Musically, it was not remarkable, but the production as a whole—lighting, timing, spontaneity—was, because of the time to rehearse.

"Unfortunately, this is not usually possible. I am a great one to rehearse, and I never can jump into a production to do a role. I could have done Desdemona and Arabella under these conditions, but I could not do a role for the first time this way. There must be time to settle artistic problems, to establish a rapport with the other principals." Perhaps that is one reason why recitals have come to dominate her present career: In concert she can control most of the artistic variables herself and be assured of a respectable result. In opera, however, a singer is but one piece in a complex puzzle, and one is rarely sure how this puzzle might be put together.

Elisabeth Schwarzkopf and Walter Legge have recently taken residency in a new home in Geneva, Switzerland, on Lac Léman, where the singer feels nearer to the center of things than she did at Ascona on Lago Maggiore. "Last year I spent only six days at home, and we were a half-day's drive from the nearest airport." Has teaching formed any part of her future plans? "I've been asked many times, but if ever I do it, it will be with my husband. I could not teach vocal technique —that you have to know yourself. But we could teach interpretation and performance style, with Walter explaining and me demonstrating. With our new house, we also have a second smaller house, and we have envisaged having musicians coming there to work." We can see the ads already, "Come to the sunny shores of Lac Léman. . . ."

★ Andrés Segovia ★

In the winter of 1973 the ageless Spanish virtuoso Andrés Segovia was celebrating his 80th birthday during an annual American tour—a grand occasion to visit with the man who single-handedly put the classical guitar on the musical map.

Like his fellow countrymen Pablo Casals and Pablo Picasso, Andrés Segovia lays claim to a place in the historic firmament

with ceaseless energy in his work, unbounding enthusiasm for
his life's mission—and a young wife. He is celebrating his 80th
birthday during his long annual American tour (his 45th!). In
early January Segovia had just arrived in this country while
his wife remained back home in Spain with their two-and-a-
half-year-old son. He sits quietly, even modestly, in his East
Side hotel suite, hands resting on his ample paunch, talking
about the past and present with characteristic calm and clarity.
"You know, I have *two* sons—one 51 and the other two and a
half. Eleven years ago I married a pupil whose family I had
known for 41 years. She was my pupil before being my boss.
She plays magnificently but has given it up. My son has been
listening to the guitar from birth and recognizes the sound.
While I was away, my wife put on a recording of mine, and he
was playing. He came to look at the gramophone—he was one
year and four months old—and said, 'Daddy, come out!' "

Segovia's desk is piled with scores and letters and a large
magnifying glass. One score, still in manuscript, sits upright on
a stand. It's a new work by André Jolivet, *Homage to Robert de
Visée,* written for and dedicated to the guitarist. Segovia explains that Visée was a teacher of Louis XIV and dedicated a
book of his own guitar and lute music to the King. "He in-
scribed it, 'I dedicate my work to Your Majesty whose hand
is more expert in carving victory in war than in playing the
guitar.' " And that reminds him of a story. "When the French
army lost a battle against the Spanish army and they came to
announce it to Louis XIV, he lifted his eyes to heaven and
said, 'God has forgotten everything I did for him.' " And a
jovial smiles crosses his face. He has just received the last part
of this Jolivet suite, the final Passacaglia. "Now I have to
adapt it for the technique of the guitar . . . and this is *very*
hard. I will play it next autumn, but it is difficult to learn. The
guitar, you know, is a difficult instrument on which to learn
something new, because of the positions and polyphonic movement of voices. But I prefer a composer who does not know
the guitar. Villa-Lobos was a good friend, and he played a
little. When he composed, he took the guitar and tried a
chord, and it was possible. Then he tried another, and it was
possible. But to go from one to the other was *im*possible!"

Life's experience has taught Andrés Segovia all that he

knows and communicates about his instrument, which goes back to the 12th century. It has made him the leading exponent of the coolly sophisticated and complex classical guitar in this century, and perhaps for all time. Yes, he admits, he is a self-taught musician, because there was no one in the mining town of Linares to teach him. "I was born in a little Andalusian village and only one man there played the guitar, and he played only flamenco guitar. I received from him this vocation when I was six years old. I listened with such attention that he asked me if I wanted to learn, and I said I did. My uncle said that I learned exactly as if I were remembering something, *not* as if it were for the first time, because I did it with such facility. The poor man taught me everything he knew—which is to say, nothing. My uncle and aunt later went to Granada. It was different there." He tried the piano, violin and cello, but the dull teaching discouraged him. So he confined himself to the guitar, almost clandestinely, since it was then an instrument of no serious pretensions. "I had friends, and they heard me play. They found some older music for me when I became annoyed with only flamenco. So they became my teacher and my pupils at the same time. A pupil is eager to know everything, and the poor teacher has to work to provide all the explanations. Then at 16 my friends pushed me on the stage for the first time. The day after, I read a review of the concert, this innocent concert, and I already felt famous. But it was the departing point, because from there I played concerts in Córdoba, Sevilla and Madrid."

From this early period came his own self-developed virtuoso technique, which he has since passed on to generations of followers. He took a look at the techniques, methods, theories and disciplines of other musical instruments "to see how to develop strength, flexibility and independence of the fingers—and then applied these studies to the guitar. When the vocation is strong, it burns all the obstacles," he says with almost oracle-like fervor. "I saw how the others worked and then invented my own technique. I heard the flamenco playing and disapproved of the technique and style—there was no *technique*. They have dexterity in the fingers to make a scale, but. . . . I asked one, 'Why do you play so fast?' and he said, 'When I began, my fingers ran so fast I could not put on the brake.'

So I made him try to play two voices and he could not. He was *furious* that he could not. All he had was speed, and in one line."

The guitar—Segovia shakes his head as if still baffled by it after all these decades—is a mysterious instrument. "The technique is complicated, and it is difficult to arrive at a theory for it. This is why it was neglected for so many centuries. Treatises of instrumentation for all the instruments were written down, so the composer has a knowledge of each one—but not the guitar." He admits there was an old tradition but only a small group of executors. "From 1778 to 1839 there was Fernando Sor, a good composer. The Belgian musicologist Fétis called him, with exaggeration, 'the Beethoven of the guitar.'" He indeed extended the expressive range of the instrument and greatly enriched its repertoire. "After him there was Francisco Tárrega, the musician who sensibilized the guitar, who gave it more delicacy. A pupil of his was a contemporary of mine. Then there was Miguel Lobet, who was the best, but who played few concerts. Then I came, and I was fortunate enough to have the energy to set for myself four tasks. One, to rescue the guitar from the folkloric amusement of flamenco. Two, to create a good repertory for the guitar, made by composers who came from the symphony orchestra. Three, to teach all over the world to demonstrate the beauty of the guitar. And four, to influence all the major conservatories and music academies to create the teaching of the guitar on the same dignified level as the piano, violin, cello and so on. These have been important works . . . Herculean . . . and successful," he says with more than a note of deserved pride.

Early on he began asking composers to write for him, to enrich and complement the repertory of 16th-, 17th- and 18th-century works (Milán, Valderrábano, Mudarra, Giuliani and others) that he found in the libraries and collections all over the world and that scholars unearthed for him—which he adapted and introduced to audiences around the globe. The first of the modern composers was Moreno Torroba, then Joaquín Turina. "Then Falla did a short work which is shy in sonority and profoundly poetical, *Homenaje: pour le tombeau de Debussy*. But it is impossible to take it to large halls because it evaporates." In Paris, many important musicians took an interest in Segovia and helped sponsor him in concerts all over Europe, the result of being introduced by the eminent French musicologist Henri Prunières. There he met Cortot, who called him his "godson," because the first concert Segovia had ever attended was one by the pianist in Córdoba—a fact he related to him when he finally met Cortot. "I knew Ravel, too. It's a pity, and I rage against myself, that he never wrote for the guitar. He wanted to, but then I was beginning and was playing many concerts in Europe. He lived outside Paris and was ill . . . and then he died. Debussy, you know, heard Lobet play and was in love with the guitar. He said it was like a harpsichord, but expressive." He came to know Rubinstein when the pianist played in Barcelona before World War I and knew Picasso, too, during the war: "They say that he chose to present one work of his in an exhibit in Paris and telegraphed his wife, who was a dancer in the Russian Ballet of Diaghilev, then at the Liceo in Barcelona. She received the telegram, took one of his canvases, rolled it up, put it under her arm and came to the French frontier. The French police asked her what she was carrying. 'A painting by my husband,' she told them. 'What is it?' they asked. 'A portrait of me,' she answered. And when they looked they said, 'This is the plan of our fortification!' It was a big joke," and Segovia is flushed with laughter.

Looking back to the music of his native Spain, he laments the commercialization of flamenco. "In my Andalucía there is the true tradition of noble flamenco. Now it is such a mess— the singing, the dancing, the playing. It's a great pity," and he shakes his head sadly. "Not every Spaniard understands the true flamenco, so it's even more difficult for an American or a Scandinavian to understand it. The result is that there are few good connoisseurs, and we lose it. You know, the guitar was never played *alone* in flamenco, but as an accompaniment to singing and dancing. Then sometimes he was so good that the public wanted to hear him alone. Flamenco guitar grew with new compositions of variations on old things . . . and with *great* emotion. But not one of them knows music today—just terrible chords without sentiment and knowledge. Still there are some singers and dancers and players in the provinces, in the little towns of Andalucía that keep the tradition. But not in the cities. Dexterity of technique has become important. In the small villages, the smith comes home from work, rests and plays the guitar to amuse himself. He has awkward fingers but makes beautiful emotional things. Something simple. The professional came and changed it, falsified it. I do not like to hear it. I tell the best flamenco players that what they do has nothing to do with the real thing, and they say that the public wants it, that they have to make a living. But these are excuses."

Simplicity and emotion are key words in Segovia's music-making. What he looks for in colleagues and younger musicians who come to him is an emotional commitment, so that "the technique is never beyond the necessity of making the fingers obedient to the most delicate insinuation of the spirit or the mind. If it goes beyond, the artist is a prisoner of technique. Unfortunately, this happens too many times. I prefer the aesthetics, the emotion to overflow—not vice versa. Now I see many young artists whose goals are technique, speed and robust sound, not to make music." The mention of another Spanish musician, Alicia de Larrocha, brings a smile and a nod. "She is direct and simple, with no vanity. Do you know the story of the Jesuit who went to a little village and asked another man who was passing by, 'Where is the house of the priest?' The man recognized the other as a Jesuit and told him, 'You cannot go there.' 'Why?' 'Because it is straight ahead.' Alicia is not like that—she can go. She is a wonderful artist, not just with technique but everything."

Segovia's methods, philosophy and dedication are fortunately being passed on through such star pupils as John Williams, Alirio Díaz, Oscar Ghiglia and the young American Christopher Parkening. Segovia has long been teaching at the Accademia Chigiana in Siena for a month each summer (Count Chigi is a longtime friend), as well as at the Academy of Musical Studies in Santiago de Compostela in Spain. "Morales, who was the Spanish ambassador to Colombia, is the father of the Academy—and I am the uncle. I go there for a month, but never every year. I have a house in the south of Spain, and when I finish my tour I go there with the desire to rest and work on new things. But the head of the class is my pupil José Tomás, who teaches and plays. He is also a professor at the Academia Oscar Esplá in Alicante."

The guitarist is proud of the current worldwide interest in

his instrument. "I say always that a third of the public in the hall when I play is filled with young boys and girls. They have come to know the beauty of the guitar in this epoch of strong orchestras and traditional music. You know, the guitar is very delicate and persuasive. It must have music inside. When Schoenberg was told that in Paris there were young musicians following his system, he asked, 'And do they put music in it?' The most important thing is to have, sincerely, the devotion for music . . . or any art. And to realize the vocation without egotism."

He defends playing his small-scale instrument in such large halls as Philharmonic or Royal Festival Hall in London, "if the acoustics are good and the outside noise does not come in and the audience is quiet and attentive. Stravinsky said to me, 'Your guitar does not sound strong—but far.' A little harmonic can fill the hall." Always prominent on his programs are works by Bach, transcribed for the guitar. During the early years of the Weimar Republic he came across Hans Dagobert Bruger's complete edition of Bach's compositions for lute. He feels that the lute and its Spanish counterpart, the vihuela, with its double strings, are not effective for the prosody or speaking of the music. So over the years he has made countless transcriptions of Bach for his instrument. "This relative of the guitar has less possibilities, so it died. Bach wrote forty or fifty pieces for lute, and then he or his sons transcribed them for solo violin or cello. The Chaconne, too, I think was written for a plucked instrument first and later adapted for the violin. The Chaconne is Spanish in flavor, and the key of D is the best guitar key. All the variations are for a plucked instrument, except one—and that is possible for a guitar. The tonic to dominant in the bass and the central part all are as if written for a guitar kind of instrument. My work with these pieces was simply to adapt from a poorer instrument to one of more possibilities. All musicians who hear this found the Chaconne has its true poetry. It's a difference of timbre and color with the guitar. I admire the Busoni transcription for piano, but the textures are too complicated, too rich. The poetry sinks in the enormity of sounds and clothing."

Segovia's current instrument is a Miguel Fleta guitar from Barcelona. "He has orders from all over and he tells them,

'Maybe you will get it in four or five years. Barcelona is damp and humid; when I take my guitar all over during the winter the heat of hotel rooms affects it. Now he's found a glue and ingredients to make it more resistant. The sound is beautiful and almost powerful, and the craftsmanship delicious." An older guitar from 1935 was created by luthier Hauser of Munich from the wood of a harpsichord. He played it for over a dozen years, "and then it developed a sickness. Two or three notes on the first string were veiled. They were not pure. I took it to Hauser's son and a German luthier. No one could fix it, so I took it to my house where it rests now."

Home, over the years, has been many places. After the beginning of the Spanish revolution, in 1937, he left Barcelona and settled in Montevideo, Uruguay. He then lived in New York for several years and now shuttles between Spain and Switzerland. He seems to have remained aloof from the political situation—"I wanted only the best thing for my country"—and has taken no strong stand à la Casals—"We disagree on many things." The word "dictatorship," he says, is dead. "Everyone is free to speak against the government and do anything he wants. We have had 35 years of peace in Spain, and now 23 million tourists come in one year. The economy is higher, so there is progress. I go every year to Spain to play and to stay. It's like the fable of Hercules and Antaeus. They were struggling, and Hercules noticed that every time Antaeus touched the earth he received new energy. Hercules succeeded in killing the giant only when he could not touch the ground. Every composer, painter, artist has from time to time to go to his country and absorb the energy there." He adds, with a smile and a shrug, that if he could give concerts without traveling he would. "Once I asked a toreador what is the most difficult thing in this profession of fighting and killing bulls, and he said, 'The train.' For me too." But Segovia reiterates with missionary-like zeal, "I am 80 years old. My life is long and large. Everywhere there is pleasure in the guitar. Then I began with my pupils and in their own right they are attracting the public. Without infatuation for myself, I put the guitar in the appreciation of the public."

★ *Rudolf Serkin* ★

Rudolf Serkin has long represented the ultimate of the Central European piano tradition. A visit in the summer of 1972 to his Marlboro Festival in Vermont produced a long-desired interview to help celebrate his 70th birthday and an engagement with the New York Philharmonic in the winter of 1973.

Rudolf Serkin isn't exactly eager to grant interviews. The Marlboro people suggested chancing it by coming up for the weekend, getting caught up in the pace, sticking around and then, hopefully, cornering the elusive pianist, who would rather play than talk. On Friday night after the concert, there was cordial backstage banter . . . but when the suggestion of sitting down for an interview reared its head, he smiled his reticent, almost nervous smile and waved his hand: "We will talk, but not professionally"—and he vanished into the night. Again, Saturday night he was full of quick smiles and camaraderie and reminiscences about Reger and Fauré (how he hated Brahms, despite the German's stamp on the Frenchman's G-minor Quartet) as he walked to his car. On Sunday, following his superhumanly eloquent reading of Beethoven's Choral Fantasy, he remained behind in the Dining Hall after dinner, savoring the last remains of his Vermont summer . . . and the word came: "Mr. Serkin said he will see you." The waiting game had been won; the persistent reporter assumed that at last he had been deemed a safe bet. And so Rudolf Serkin sat, relaxed, at one of the long dining tables as children played outside and a few stragglers busily conversed in another corner.

Serkin's seventy years have been filled to overflowing with extraordinary music-making and musical involvement, spanning the last gasps of old imperial Europe and musical romanticism, two world wars, the birth of atonality and a good deal more. Serkin has been a part of it all, for following his belief that everyone at Marlboro learns and shares, so he has learned and absorbed from several key figures—Busch, Schnabel, Schoenberg, Toscanini—and then turned around and began passing it on relatively early in his own life. A dozen years ago Irving Kolodin was to note, after having observed Serkin since his New York debut in 1936 with the Philharmonic and Toscanini: "My conclusion about Serkin's extraordinary upsurge in the last ten or fifteen years, his ever-expanding domination of the repertory that interests him, his attainment even of a status as 'box office,' is simply that he lives the art as he teaches it, and he teaches the art as he lives it."

Rudolf Serkin was born in Eger, Bohemia (then a part of Austria, now in the northwestern corner of Czechoslovakia), in 1903 to Russian parents. His father, a basso, had turned merchant in order to support his eight children, but he encouraged their talents. Before the young Rudolf had reached his teens, World War I engulfed central Europe, further taxing the family's resources. He recalls: "I started to play the piano before I can remember. My father made me play: he tried teaching all of us piano or violin. I hated the violin. It was so close to the ear." He first played in public at Franzensbad, a spa like Marienbad and Karlsbad, not far from Eger. He was only five or six and played little pieces of Stephen Heller and Schubert's Impromptu in E-flat major, Opus 90.

"I was then supposed to study at the Conservatory in Prague, the nearest large city, but I was too young for them to accept me. About this time my father took me to hear a concert in Pilsen by the much beloved Viennese pianist, Alfred Grünfeld. I played for him, and he said I should come to Vienna to study with a friend of his—a great teacher—Professor Richard Robert. So my father took me to Vienna so I could study privately. I was nine years old and Professor Robert put me up with a family. I was studying, but I was very lonely."

It was there, though, that one of his long friendships began. George Szell was also a pupil of Robert, and although he was six years older than Serkin they were "almost like brothers." He also came to know the young Rudolf Bing and Emanuel Feuermann, the latter from Serkin's own debut in Vienna. "My

first concert was with the Vienna Symphony when I was 12.
I played the Mendelssohn G-minor Concerto. Emanuel Feuer-
mann played a Haydn cello concerto and his brother Sigmund
a Viotti violin concerto. And then the two of them played the
Brahms Double Concerto. It doesn't seem possible that they
played the Brahms, now that I think of it. They were so young!
Feuermann was an incredible player, one of the greatest artists
I have ever known."

Young Serkin also went to study composition with the conservative Joseph Marx, and then harmony and counterpoint
with the more radical Arnold Schoenberg. "You may know
the name of Loos, the architect," the pianist explains. "He was
interested in me and was very kind to me. He took me to
Schoenberg, who had started the Society for Contemporary
Music, where there was no applause, no approval *or* condem-
nation. I studied with Schoenberg when I was 15, and he was
generous to me. He had seminars in counterpoint and composition. At that time he hadn't composed for a long time and
was starting the Serenade when I first met him. To play Mozart
sonatas for Schoenberg," he recalls, "was an experience nothing
else could replace. He knew them better than anyone. He was
a fantastic man, but it broke the heart of my teacher Robert
when I told him I was going to study with Schoenberg. I could
never love his music, though. I told him so, and he never
forgave me. He said, 'It's up to you to decide whether you
want to be on this side of the barricades or that one.' I studied
composition with him for quite a time," he goes on. "It was
very informal, just six or seven of us in a class. But it was also
quite technical. He taught counterpoint and had us write
variations on a theme. Once I wrote a rondo for piano and
brought it to him. He looked at it and then said, 'Serkin, I'm
going to cut out all the parts that you like best. All the extra
things, the ornamental things.' He wanted only the essentials.
Schoenberg taught that composing was a craft, that every composition should be well made."

If he ultimately could not follow under Schoenberg's atonal
banner, Serkin eventually met the man who probably exerted
the greatest spell over his career. He was teaching piano at
Schönbrunn Palace, where colonies for workers' children had
been set up after the war, and giving concerts, but at the same

time he was preparing to go to study in Paris with Isidor
Philipp at the Conservatoire and play for the dance recitals of
Elsie Altman, the young wife of Loos. "I wanted to get out of
Vienna," he explains. "And Loos arranged for me to go to
Paris along with Kokoschka. We were bitterly poor you know,
with eight children." He shakes his head. "Vienna was an exciting place, with Hofmannsthal, Rilke and Schnitzler leading
the literary life there. But at the time I was trying to get out.
Vienna was always a city of small cliques, and I fit into none
of them. It had Loos and Schoenberg and Freud, but they were
not recognized. Their ideas were a kind of leprosy to the
Viennese establishment. Now, of course, it is proud to claim
them."

Serkin managed to miss his train to Paris (a special Red
Cross conveyance that had no fixed schedule), and a few days
later a call came through that Adolf Busch was going to give a
recital in Vienna and his pianist had fallen ill. "I was then 17
and recommended to him, but they couldn't reach me because
I was out in Schönbrunn. I came back, but only when the concert was over. He called me and asked about me, and I explained about the train. He asked if I wanted to study with
Busoni in Berlin. I, of course, said yes, but that I didn't have
any money. So he gave me tickets and the keys to his house,
and I accepted." When he reached the intellectual capital of
Berlin, he found the house occupied by a housekeeper and
Busch's youngest daughter, age three. She was Irene, whom
Serkin married fifteen years later.

The pianist went off to see the legendary Ferruccio Busoni
in Berlin, but the latter was ill. "The first letter I wrote to
Busoni he never answered. Then his pupil Egon Petri arranged
a meeting, but he was nearly dead. He asked my age and I told
him 17, and he said I was too old to take lessons. He said I
should now know myself and have my own style. He said I
should go to lots of concerts and learn from the example of
other artists. I remember that when I played for him, he said,
'Don't play so clean, and press down on the pedal more.' He
felt I should play more *schmutzig*—dirtily. It was too clean and
transparent." Some time later, when Busch returned to Berlin,
the duo went to Busoni's house and played his violin sonata
for him—"A beautiful piece. I love it. When we finished, we

asked him, 'Is that the way you imagined it to sound?' He said, 'No.' We asked why and how it should be played. He said, 'I won't tell you, because that would spoil your spontaneousness.' Only later, when Busoni made an arrangement for two pianos and he played it with Petri, then we saw what it was. He played the last movement about three times as fast as we had. We had played it very German, full of soul, but he wanted it Italian."

Young Serkin took Busoni's advice, especially since he found there was no one else with whom to study. "I practiced every day for hours. I had a concert myself at the Singakademie. There were only fifteen or twenty people in the audience, but among them were Busoni and Schnabel, who came back and introduced himself," he recalls. "How he happened to come, I don't know. But he didn't miss one of my concerts after that and always came backstage. His comments were not critical, but more like, 'Why did you play such and such a passage this way? Why not this way?' Sometimes he was there for half an hour or even an hour, talking about the piece I had played, why I did it this way, wouldn't it be a good idea to do it just the opposite, did I ever think about this and so on. He was the greatest influence on us all—in every way—by the way he played, by playing all the modern music, by keeping an open house, by knowing everyone. Anything he did was so personal, really wonderful."

It had been 1920 when Serkin began his lifelong association with the remarkable Busches, a family that included, in addition to violinist Adolf, his brothers Fritz, the conductor, and Herman, the cellist. Adolf led the chamber orchestra at Serkin's Berlin debut in 1921, in which they performed Bach's *Brandenburg* Concerto No. 5—and for an encore Serkin played the entire *Goldberg Variations*. Soon he was playing in all the important European cities in sonata recitals with Busch, chamber music performances with the Busch Chamber Players and as soloist. "When I finished the *Goldberg Variations*," Serkin smiles, "there were only four people left: Adolf Busch, Artur Schnabel, Alfred Einstein and me."

Serkin joined Adolf Busch when, in 1922, he moved to Darmstadt and, in 1927, to Basel, Switzerland, where they met a little-known emigré from Russia named Vladimir Horowitz. The atmosphere of fascism had been felt early in Berlin.

"You could smell the stink very early, and Busch took a stand in the beginning. He protested the boycott of the Jews with a letter, and the stupid Germans printed it in the newspaper. Later, Busch canceled concerts in protest, even though he was Aryan and not Jewish. Our home in Switzerland was next to the German border. The Swiss government thought we should move because they could not protect us from kidnapping, but we stayed. I remember nights of hearing motorcycles all around. But this is an understatement as to what it actually was. This was years before the war, when it became worse. People you looked up to collapsed in front of you. But there was the theatrical side of it too," he adds candidly.

Busch, Serkin recalls, "was the kind of musician obsessed by music and music-making. But most musicians should be, shouldn't they?" he asks with a quizzical look. "He had the capacity as a teacher of making almost everyone play well. Here at Marlboro, all the people were not good at first, but he had them playing exquisitely. It was a tremendous musical mind." Serkin also remembers a Leipzig concert in the late twenties, in which Busch was soloist with Wilhelm Furtwängler conducting. Serkin arrived not long before concert time and was met at the station by a friend with a car who told him to hurry because Busch needed him. On the way, as Serkin changed into evening shirt and tie, the friend related: "Busch doesn't like the tempo Furtwängler takes in the slow movement of the Bach concerto, and there's nothing he can do about it. But he has arranged for you to play the *continuo* in the orchestra, and you should follow Busch no matter what." When the movement came, Serkin proceeded at the measured pace Busch preferred, which meant that the ensemble followed his tempo rather than Furtwängler's. Busch was happy, but Furtwängler never spoke to the pianist again.

After the influence of Busch, Serkin admits that Arturo Toscanini had the profoundest effect on him. "It was this idea of fidelity to the score, which I already had from Schoenberg —so it was different with me than with some others who came in contact with Toscanini. He was the confirmation of what I had learned in Vienna with Schoenberg: clarity." Serkin stresses that in the succeeding generations the Italian conductor was a bad influence on bad musicians, a good one on good ones. "He was not cold, but . . . you heard pizzicatos together. He had the basis of music. Later, others got stuck with this aspect of perfection and precision only, but this was just a part of him. I remember Zurich in 1926 when he came with the La Scala Orchestra. It was the first time I had ever heard him, and he played the Brahms Second Symphony. It was an incredible revelation. It was architecture with passion. Afterwards, at a reception in the home of Mrs. Reiff—she figures in Mann's *Doctor Faustus* and was a pupil of Liszt—Toscanini was there with the Busches and me and Furtwängler. And Furtwängler was shocked at some things in Toscanini. It was so new! Embarrassingly and painfully, he told Toscanini in violent terms what he thought. Toscanini was like a little boy and then answered: 'Look, when Steinbock came to Turin and conducted the Brahms Second Symphony, after the first rehearsal he turned to the orchestra and said, "I have nothing to do. Who is your conductor?" And the answer was Toscanini.' But why did these two worlds exist?" Serkin asks, almost as if it's the most pressing question of the day. "Both men loved music and were inspired. I never understood this," he shakes his head.

The connection with the Italian conductor led to his coming to America, although he first appeared at the Elizabeth Sprague Coolidge Festival at the Library of Congress in Washington in 1933 with Busch. In Europe he was still the passionate disciple of Busch, as well as his ideal collaborator in sonatas (or in trios with Herman) and a leading exponent of certain solo works that demanded intimate, musically refined playing. As a soloist he had begun to appear more frequently in Switzerland and Italy, becoming known to a larger public through his interpretations of such works as the Mozart B-flat Concerto, K. 595, and the Beethoven Fourth in G minor, both of which he played for his historic New York debut with Toscanini in 1936, as the final piano soloist of the maestro's final Philharmonic season. Kolodin has written: "I have a sharp recollection of Serkin as he was in those days; a diffident figure trailing Busch to the keyboard, his bespectacled, slightly inclined body and lean figure suggesting one of *The New York Times*'s Hundred Neediest Cases. Once at the piano, however, he left nothing to be desired." Nothing much has changed today as he almost apologetically makes his way to the piano, slightly bent, bobbing nervously in response to the applause.

In 1938 Serkin and Busch performed the complete series of Beethoven's violin-piano sonatas in New York, and the next year Serkin accepted an invitation to join the faculty of the Curtis Institute in Philadelphia: late in 1939 he and his family settled permanently in this country. Life since then has meant a full schedule of concerts, teaching and, since 1950, Marlboro in the summer. "I am playing less now," he admits. "I have not so much to give, and I would drop dead if I repeated myself in any way." He feels that the only way to keep playing many of the same works and remain unmannered is "to do better all the time. That is the miracle in all art, that it is new all the time. Toscanini told me. 'For me it's always the first time,' and that means all the tension and fright that goes with it. Anything we accept is bad, if it is accepted without question. Toscanini talked about tradition being the last bad performance, but he meant anything that is done unquestioned; Mahler called it *Schlamperei*."

Since September of 1968 he has been Director of Curtis, cutting back on his engagements to fit in all the demands running such a school makes. What does he look for in pupils and musicians? "First, personality. It's a vague word, but what other is there? Then talent, of course, and seriousness. The standards of training are higher here in America than anywhere else." In an audition, he looks for enthusiasm: "If they have the enthusiasm, they will have the energy." Among his innovations at Curtis have been the addition of the Guarneri Quartet to spearhead the expanding of a chamber music program, the improvement of the theory department with five teachers who are products of Nadia Boulanger and the development of the opera department.

Although married to a violinist, Serkin has not fathered all musicians among his six children. Ursula works with handicapped children, and Elizabeth tutors in the high school department at Curtis. John is a French horn player and Peter, of course, has emerged as one of the most respected of the young American pianists. Judith studies the cello, and young Marguerite attends the Friends Select School in Philadelphia. When asked how he handled the subject of music with his children, he purses his lips: "I didn't handle. We did not push music at them, and I blame myself for not doing more. Yet they were always in this atmosphere," and his hands reach out to encompass all of Marlboro. "John plays the French horn but majored in math first, and Judith is a cellist at Curtis. Peter became an extraordinary pianist without my influencing him. Sasha Schneider discovered him at nine here at Marlboro. At ten he played the Haydn Concerto and I died with fright. Then he did it at the New School in New York. He decided at 12 or 13 to be a musician and then studied with Lee Luvisi and me. Last week he played Messiaen's *Vingt Régards* for me privately, and I was very impressed. The spiritual message is so strong."

The conflict is always tremendous and constant, since Curtis and Marlboro demand time, and he could be playing as many concerts as the world's managers could arrange. He worries about his repertoire, because "if I play more concerts, it has to narrow. I need the time to work and learn." He remains loyal to Busoni's and Reger's music. "Busoni aimed for clarity and simplicity. He and Reger were friends when they were young, but then they parted in style and Busoni went forward. Schoenberg had great admiration for Reger's music, and I was just reading Schoenberg's letter in which he writes that Reger was one of the greatest composers of the century." He also looks to Mendelssohn and Dvořák as well as his Mozart, Beethoven, Schumann and Brahms. "I never played anything I didn't like," he says, shrugging his slight shoulders. Asked about the current Romantic revival, he laughs, "Why? It's *schaumartig*—frothy. It's difficult to understand. Maybe it's just me who misses something in all that doodle, doodle. . . . I played the Hummel Piano Concerto and Rondo when I was young, and this is the border of Romanticism. It used to be that playing Liszt was thought vulgar. In my early days, I used to put pieces like Liszt's *Muette de Portici* tarantella into my programs to shock people. But gradually I decided I could no longer play music that I did not feel absolutely sincere about."

When asked about his practice habits, Serkin says, "I'm old-fashioned. I practice scales and arpeggios that I might need but don't always use." He feels that "the athletic part of music," as Donald Tovey calls it, is important—"the training to be able to play everything louder and faster than you will ever need, so you will have a generous reserve. You can't over-emphasize technique, if you really love music. If you are really gifted, you can't practice technique too much—the musicality will still come through. This is the French and Russian approach. I don't know much about the German school now, but some German approaches used to be more emotion and deep feeling, and not so much technique. But what good does it do to feel deeply, if you don't have an even trill in the Beethoven G-major Concerto?"

Musically, Serkin emphasizes his striving for the "utmost variety of tone, rhythm, of everything. I believe in a unity in music. I don't believe too much in style. The words romantic or classic never had much meaning for me. Of course, what phrasing comes down to is a matter of taste, good or bad. If a performance doesn't move you, it is a poor performance. But these things are a matter of taste." He admits he had a strict and limited upbringing as far as the piano is concerned and had to make a big effort to free himself from being strait-jacketed. "Busoni was the revelation in this respect, because he had invented an entirely new technique for himself, as Casals did for the cello. So I believe that once a young player has undergone his basic training, he must work and study for himself—study, study and keep on studying. I don't believe in any method. They are like gloves, fitting one or maybe two people, but no more. If a great artist touches the piano, there *has* to be something absolutely his own. You know who it is. Otherwise it isn't great. This I have heard all my life with Horowitz, Busoni, Schnabel, Rachmaninoff, all the great artists I have had the privilege of hearing," states Rudolf Serkin with the characteristic modesty, respect, affection and devotion he brings to his art.

⋆ *Beverly Sills* ⋆

Beverly Sills has become one of the most acclaimed American prima donnas in history since her singing of Cleopatra in Giulio Cesare with her home company, the New York City Opera. I interviewed her in the winter of 1968 and then again in 1970, this profile a composite of the two sessions. Since that time, she has sung throughout the world and will make her Metropolitan Opera debut during the 1974–75 season in Rossini's L'Assedio di Corinto.

When does it happen? When does a merely excellent artist become a star? When does a singer skyrocket to the top, bringing with it all the trappings of fame?—the loyal followings, recording contracts, productions staged around you. Sometimes, overnight . . . a young unknown wins a major contest or replaces an established star in a plum role on short notice to ovations and critical nods. Rarer is the case of the "late bloomer," someone who has sung hundreds of performances, who has persevered, who has matured like a great wine—and, suddenly, bang, it happens.

So it has been with Beverly Sills, the Brooklyn-born soprano who has been performing in the public eye almost as long as she has been able to walk. First a childhood career, then time to catch up with growing-up in her teens, then a career resumed and arduous tours with travelling opera companies and engagements wherever opera happens to be staged in America. As far as New York is concerned, the name Beverly Sills has been a New York City Opera roster mainstay since the 1955-56 season—and it has meant many an evening upon the boards, too, from *Traviatas, Faust* Marguerites, Queens of the Night and Donna Annas to the title role of Douglas Moore's

Ballad of Baby Doe and a lead in Hugo Weisgall's *Six Characters in Search of an Author*. Rekindled memories even recall a single *Louise,* one or two evenings in Moore's *Wings of the Dove* and a new production of *Die Fledermaus*.

But then one night it did happen. It was September, 1967, the first fall season of the New York City Opera in its plush red-and-gold home, the New York State Theater. Annually, Beverly Sills had been called in to volley around future plans, as part of Julius Rudel's operatic democracy—and each time she wanted a "stand-up" coloratura role: but the answer was always a firm "no," with the excuse that "no one comes to hear us do that repertoire." By early 1966 she had her eye on Handel's dazzling Cleopatra, and her long-time partner and soul-mate Norman Treigle gazed longingly at Caesar—and Rudel was in search of a non-standard (but non-contemporary) work to open the season. That September night the company was finally unveiling the East Coast premiere of Handel's *Julius Caesar*. And, bang, it happened! Trills and runs and glittering agility and awesome vocal control and irresistible feminine warmth. Beverly Sills ascendant, Beverly Sills triumphant, Beverly Sills a star.

Things began to happen, too—new productions, debuts in Europe and South America, recording plans, best-selling discs on the underground market, cheering standees, columns of adulation in the national press and all the rest. Since then there have been recordings in the top-ten classical charts for months, countless new productions and enough offers to keep her going for the next decade, if not longer.

Not too many years ago, this same struggling strawberry blonde soprano was kept waiting for an appointment in the outer office of an important concert manager. After an hour, her blood began to boil and she got up and left, determined never to be caught in such an ignominious position again. Today, that same soprano has had any number of the top managers trying to buy off her current contract, and all the major record companies are knocking at her door. There was a time when after a performance at the old New York City Center, the stage hands would call out, "Nice show, Sills," and the soprano would walk out on to 56th Street with little more fanfare—she was a member of a company, she sang often, and did her bit and that was that. Today, the adoring public lines the backstage hall at the New York State Theater to greet her, and the aficionados scramble down the aisles toward the footlights to yell and applaud their approval. Her performances now bring out Bernstein, Comden and Green, Lauren Bacall, all the "right" people.

As you wait for Beverly Sills one late morning in her apartment-house lobby, you wonder whether all of this has transformed a sunny, pleasant, exuberant lady-who-sings into (unfortunately) a typical *diva nuova*. Not a chance. The elevator opens, a wide winning smile sweeps across her lively face, those big brown eyes twinkle despite the fact that she has only returned to New York at 2 that morning, and a black-trimmed leopard coat sets off that pile of carrot hair. Off we go for a nearby breakfast and some talk.

"That first Cleopatra was the great night a singer dreams about, and it helped me to decide exactly in what direction to go. But, actually, the turning point in my career goes back to the first time I did all three roles in *The Tales of Hoffmann* at the City Center. In Tito Capobianco's version, it is necessary to do all three roles—it doesn't play with dividing them up. I had tried it before in New Orleans, but it didn't fascinate me—Giulietta gave me nothing at all. Tito urged me to do it in Cincinnati, and he made a character of her. And I do believe that Offenbach wanted all three roles played by one singer—his stage directions indicate this. Olympia has four high E flats in the first episode, so you must conclude that he wanted a lyric coloratura for all the roles. Of course, Giulietta can sound more luscious when sung by a mezzo and that is what we are used to—but so can Mimi! Offenbach didn't want this quality, I believe, and so it is not off-bounds territory for a voice like mine."

"A voice like mine." How, we proceeded (in spite of her claim of being more an emotional, rather than an intellectual, brand of singer), do you describe your voice that can handle more than 85 roles? "I've always been a coloratura, even though I don't look like one. That is the problem: at auditions, I always had to convince them that I wasn't a Tosca, but a Rosina. As I recall, one of my greatest successes with the City Opera was as Philine in a revival of *Mignon* in the late 50s, but I have also done so many roles associated with the more lyric range.

"My coloratura facility is the doing of Estelle Liebling, whom I went to at the age of seven—and I've never left. I think one great blessing has been that I've always had the same teacher and never had to go shopping. It's provided a great sense of security for me. She forced me into the coloratura repertoire, even during my teens when I was bored with it. All these roles were put into my repertoire—it took me only fifteen minutes to refresh Lucia, even though I had never performed it before. Once I even learned all three roles in *Les Huguenots!*"

Since *Julius Caesar,* she has felt this repertory to be happy in her voice, and she has continued to concentrate on it. "I feel positive with the Bellini-Donizetti works, and some day I'll even try *Norma* because I have had so many offers to sing it and I think this is right, too." When asked why she had never sung *Lucia* before the spring of 1968 she shrugged, "because nobody asked." Now everybody is asking, and she quickly learned Donizetti's *Daughter of the Regiment* ("That's a fun piece I can toss off") for the Opera Company of Boston and *Anna Bolena* ("That's another story, a heavier role than I'm used to—it's no bauble!") for the Teatro Colon in Buenos Aires. At the City Opera, she will be the focal point for a rare staging of Donizetti's *Roberto Devereux* which she has recorded for Westminster.

Maria Callas, Beverly Sills acknowledged, is the one all of us have to thank for the revival and regenerated interest in the *bel canto* repertoire, the art of embellishment and a more venturesome repertory. "I heard her many times in New York and in Europe. She was the only singer I had a real fascination for. She was an extraordinary personality with everything: voice, presence, artistry, dramatic powers—everything. We were so used to seeing the demented Lucia come down the stairs to the footlights and do nothing but *sing* her 20-some-minute 'Mad Scene' that when Callas played the role we felt what great drama there really is in the music and libretto. She made me realize that acting makes you forget any vocal limitations; the opposite is never true." It was no coincidence that Lucia was an occasional visitor to the conversation, because the *Lucia* production at the City Opera was memorable for her for many reasons—not the least being that every young coloratura yearns to go "mad" to this great music. "That night Julius Rudel wrote to me on a card, 'Only you could make such a beautiful brocade out of a Scottish *schmata*,' she laughs heartily and with pride. "But my Lucy has been changing at every performance. What's happened is that my own personality has crept into Tito Capobianco's staging. I'm not an automaton, after all these years. My own character must come through. Tito wanted a Bernhardt 'mad scene,' a tragedienne performance. I wanted her more youthful. Eventually, both merged: the high tragedy and the youthful pathos. The opera is like *Romeo and Juliet,* with Lucia and Edgardo as parallels. They are not great people caught in a great political situation, but just figures in a romantic love story. The joy of working with Tito is that you can argue—his way is not a finished way. 'No problem,' he says, 'we fix,' and he has twenty ways to do a scene."

The problem of embellishment and ornamentation is one any singer faces today in preparing the 19th century *bel canto* repertoire and the music of the 18th century as well. The special problem for Beverly Sills, however, has been that all the traditional embellishments have been published and used by many singers. "I want original decorations for my roles, and so I have been working with Roland Gagnon, an assistant conductor with the New York City Opera. He devised new ornaments and cadenzas for my Lucia and is working on the material for the new recording. He has a tremendous appetite for *bel canto* and its style, as well as scholarship and enthusiasm, which is most unusual."

Julius Caesar presented even greater obstacles, since less tradition and research findings exist for this music. "Before we began, Julius [Rudel] told me to accumulate material on Handelian ornamentation and that we would then compare notes that summer at my home at Martha's Vineyard. A lady at the Boston Public Library was very cooperative and I found a good deal of material, which I had microfilmed. It turned out that the castrato ornaments were the best and had the most *bravura*—they were not merely to close in gaps but really to embellish the melodic line. I had gathered about forty pages of various authentic embellishments by the time we met. In embellishing the score, Julius didn't copy any we had collected, but used them as a basis for decorating each of the singer's vocal lines. He had the courage to do the opera as he wanted, based on the traditional manner."

The coloratura field well ploughed, the soprano was eager to talk of her success as Massenet's *Manon* in the City Opera production directed by the ubiquitous Capobianco. "*Manon* is different—it has always been a passion with me, something special. When Julius called me in and asked with what I wanted to follow the *Caesar,* I blurted out *Manon!*—without even thinking. It is like the Swedish movie *Elvira Madigan*— a lovely thing: it is what it is. You think that you cannot possibly fall for something so simple and so slight, but yet you do in the end because it is so beautiful. I must tell you a wonderful thing that happened. In the second act of the new production, there is the Parisian bedroom with pillows tossed here and there—it is a room that has been lived in and loved in, and on stage it swallows you up. During a rehearsal one day, Julius said that as a boy of 17 he had had a room attached to his family's apartment in Paris. The desk blotter had written on it the names of two people who had once made love there —and his room reminded him exactly of the one we, Manon and Des Grieux, have on stage."

When she is working on a new character, she confesses, "I talk my husband [Peter Greenough, grandson of the founder of the *Cleveland Plain Dealer* and once the financial columnist of the *Boston Globe*] deaf, dumb and blind with it. I'm too hokey to study acting. I hate noting gestures in the score at every bar. Capobianco is a great talker, too. We talked 'til five in the morning many nights after rehearsals. We talked of Manon on the farm *before* she appears in the first act. She was of low stock, this is obvious since she is sent alone on the carriage to the convent. So we took a milk-maid approach. She is physically well-endowed, not frail as some see her. She is a peasant, a bad girl sent to a convent—and the first thing she admires are three doxies who are nothing at all. Manon has no class, but she does have a merry quality and a definite longing to amuse herself in life. Her longing to have all she wishes is always positive, not wistful.

"My own body and framework may be one reason for this approach, but it is a valid one. How Manon changes physically is interesting because all these changes take place right on stage. When Guillot approaches her in the first act, she doesn't say no, she listens; Des Grieux doesn't frighten her away or give her worry either. I try to make her change, too. For instance, the flat shoes of the first act help give the impression of a flat farm walk, while higher heels give her elegance and stature for the Cour-la-Reine. *Traviata* is different—the first act ends with cries of *'Follie'* and freedom, but Act II finds her already a changed woman. The huge change has taken place between the acts. In this *Manon,* when Des Grieux is kidnapped in Act II, de Bretigny comes back with the necklace and we must see her change right there before the curtain falls—and this leads right into the third act when she has everything she has wanted. It is a Sills Manon: I am determined to leave nothing to the audience's imagination. Each scene is to be a continuation of the last note of the previous act—one continuous line of change and development."

One continuous line of change and development—with minor detours along the way—has marked the pathway of Beverly Sills' own career. The youngest of three children, she began performing at the age of three. "I was sort of a toy for my mother, who thought all girls should sing and dance and play the piano." She was launched as "Bubbles" on *Uncle Bob's Rainbow House,* Station WOR, singing "The Wedding of Jack and Jill"—and every Saturday for four years she sang one song and tapped out a military dance. Once, she recalls, she even appeared all bundled up, because even the mumps couldn't keep her home.

By the age of seven she became a regular on *Major Bowes' Capital Family Hour.* On her first appearance with Bowes he asked the little girl her age, to which she replied: "I'm seven years old and I can sing 23 arias and everyone says I have an extraordinary voice for my age." Every word was true. Eventually, she emerged from the popular Shirley Temple image to that of a performing teen, continuing a career as the singing maiden on 36 weeks of the radio serial, *Our Gal Sunday.* She hit new heights when she did one of the first singing commercials, the immortal Rinso White bird call . . . "Rinso White, Rinso Bright, Happy Little Washday Song." At 12 she retired.

The soprano admits to none of the common pressures of being a child prodigy, "When I retired, I attended public school and summer camps and did everything everyone else did before I began singing again at 15. I spent my awkward years with all the other awkward girls, removed from the public. Ours was a close-knit family where the father was the boss. He thought it nice that his little girl could play the piano and sing, but not much more than that. He wanted me to go to school, and I don't think he ever thought it would go this far. My mother did have a vision of the future. She encouraged me and always wanted me to be very thorough in everything I did."

As a child, she had listened endlessly to her mother's collection of opera records, particularly those of Amelita Galli-Curci, and eventually (at seven) began studying with Mme. Liebling, who was once Galli-Curci's coach. She was also beginning to learn French and Italian, and had a piano lesson every Saturday. At 13 she began to study stagecraft with Desire Defrère of the Met, while at the same time she was a pupil at P.S. 91 in Brooklyn, then Erasmus High and, finally, Professional Children's School, where she was graduated at 15.

The career was again launched with years of taxing apprenticeship. She auditioned for Broadway shows just for the practice of singing in public, she competed on the Arthur Godfrey Talent Scouts (under the name Vicki Lynn) and won $300, and she sang and played piano in a private club until 2 each morning, while maintaining her daily 10 a.m. lessons. She signed with J. J. Shubert for a tour of Gilbert and Sullivan and the following years for *The Merry Widow, Countess Maritza* and *Rose Marie,* billed as "the youngest prima donna in captivity." In 1950 there was a memorable tour with the Charles Wagner Opera in which she sang 63 Micaelas in 63 one-night stands (traveling days by bus), followed by 54 *Traviatas* in 63 nights the next season. "I was 20 or 21 and had strong legs, so I survived," she reflects. "It was more the mental strain, particularly with Micaela. That is one role I'll never sing again, no matter what!"

Beginning in 1951 she auditioned every season for Joseph Rosenstock, then director of the New York City Opera—always a 25-minute audition that included "Ah! fors' è lui" and "Sempre libera" from *Traviata,* "Caro nome" from *Rigoletto* and "Una voce poco fà" from *The Barber of Seville.* But each time they proved unsuccessful. After her eighth audition in the fall of 1954 she was signed and made her debut as Rosalinda in *Die Fledermaus.* And over the past decade, the career has built in intensity, from her years as merely a "good" singer to the recent series of successes—*Tales of Hoffmann, Julius Caesar, Le Coq d'Or* and *Manon.* Of course, no road is completely smooth. In the fall of 1969, when the company went to Los Angeles, the scheduled Queen of the Night in *The Magic Flute* was suddenly not in town and Miss Sills was forced to sing the role between her own performances of *Caesar:* The first act aria did not go well, by her own admission; disgusted, she declined to sing the "Der Hölle Rache," deciding at that moment never again to sing that role in which she never had felt comfortable.

There was also the period in which she gave up singing altogether, because of her two children's needs at home. When she returned, however, something important had happened. "I really stopped caring what people thought about my voice and I decided to sing for myself." She looks over her shoulder at what has happened with a typical humor, and just a touch of skepticism: "For someone whose career had been in every way premature, it's just too much that when it came to this kind of approval, I should turn out to be a late bloomer."

The "late bloomer" has become the talk of the opera world and the demands for her exceed her available time. A two-disc album of Mozart, Strauss, Rossini and Verdi is to be dubbed "The Joy of Singing," because "I've always said I have great joy in singing and if the audience has it it's a happy coincidence. We had fun finding a title for this. I wanted 'Beverly Sills Sings Mish-Mash.' When 'The Four Sides of Sills' was suggested, Peter said, 'What is it?—right, left, top and bottom?' Then we thought 'The Treasure Chest of Sills' and disregarded this for obvious reasons," she roars.

Her large New York apartment is filled with objects from all over, despite her claim that she is not a collector. An egg collection includes onyx, lapis, agate, murano glass, hand-painted eggs, and even a plastic one with thistle inside. "I got my first during my first pregnancy—a cousin told me to rub it to feel better." Fans have sent her ceramic owls ever since her dresser, Arlene, started it at the City Center. There are ceramic sculptures from Milan, brass from the Philippines, a Giacometti on the fireplace, a Ming dynasty plate and costume sketches from various productions in Boston and New York. Her bedroom boasts "the biggest bed in the world—and the smallest dog," a toy poodle who walks sideways.

"You know," she noted at one point, "New York is really not my kind of scene. Last week we were invited to a new private club and the noise was so deafening I couldn't enjoy my food. All the skinny, chi-chi ladies in their pants suits and manes of hair. Last night fifty of us who helped build a community center around the corner were at Marietta Tree's where the Istomin-Stern-Rose Trio played. After, Isaac—he lives above us—insisted we come back for coffee, and we stayed until after three. That's my kind of evening."

★ *Janos Starker* ★

Cellist Janos Starker's slow but majestic climb to the pinnacle has been watched by many with curiosity and gratitude. It all took on a new focus in the fall of 1972 when he made his long-overdue debut with the New York Philharmonic; later that season he mesmerized a full house in Alice Tully Hall with a Bach-Kodály evening. We talked the previous summer.

An air of inevitability hangs about the dark, sharp-featured man with the cleft chin and flashing eyes. He talks in forceful, primal statements that drop into *sotto voce* asides, all in a torrential rush ahead. From his early days in Hungary, Janos

Starker seemed to sense that he would spend X amount of years as an orchestral musician, and then emerge as one of the great contemporary teachers of stringed instruments, a definitive recording artist and possibly the greatest cellist now before the public. When it was announced that he would finally make his New York Philharmonic debut [1972], there were the sighs of relief among the devotees who have clamored for the last dozen years to the Grace Rainey Rogers Auditorium, Irving High School, Carnegie Hall, Hunter College— or wherever—to relish his incisive, uncompromising brand of cello playing. He nods, "Well, this *is* an astonishing thing. But I found out that every year when the list of artists was submitted, Bernstein looked—and Starker out! There was no reason for it. I never spoke two words to him. That's why. I simply wasn't interested in kowtowing. If my output is not good enough to be playing with any orchestra in the world, then I shouldn't be. I simply don't believe in friendly gestures and so on. And now this year, Boulez looked at the list—and Starker on! And I never spoke one word to *him* in my life."

"You know," the 47-year-old virtuoso-thinker-interpreter was saying one muggy day last summer, sipping a Scotch and Perrier water high over Central Park South, "I did not work hard for my career. I worked hard to learn what I know." He has come along the long, hard road to recognition, while others like Rostropovich and Du Pré have been met with instant acceptance. "It sounds funny in retrospect, but when I was nine or ten years old my definition of the goal started clarifying. It was never the question that I wanted to be the world's most successful cellist. My statement all through the years was that I wanted to play the cello as well as it's possible to be played. And only in the last five or six years—now that I am already pretty far ahead in my life—I said, well, now I should like to cash in on all the work I've done. But the goal was not defined in the sense of success. Later on I did say that eventually if I play well, somebody's going to recognize me. My burning ambition never was to become a household word. Now, at this stage of the game, I have to admit that at times it may be annoying that some little punk kid who learned three concertos comes along and throws her hair and does this and that, *and* is very gifted, and suddenly becomes sort of a semi-semi-household word. It's annoying for a second, and then I said it's only going to last a little while—and I was right. More important than being exploited is to have a decent, logical development so that you can become a functioning, important member of the musical community."

Janos Starker was born in Budapest and was performing at the Conservatory there at 11. As a prelude to his solo career, he left his country in disillusionment, spent some time in Europe and came to America to play first desk with the Dallas Symphony under Dorati in 1948. From there he went to the Metropolitan Opera Orchestra and the Chicago Symphony under Fritz Reiner. This had all been charted out beforehand, although he admits that the 1956 Hungarian revolution slowed down his course. At that time he brought his parents and in-laws out of that country. "I had to stay a year longer in Chicago than I had planned, and that's the only thing that threw off my plan. Everything else has happened exactly as I wanted. I would say that I'm three years behind schedule in the international sense—everything else is according to schedule." He does play around the globe every season and recently returned to Hungary on the 25th anniversary of his leaving. "I tried for many years to plan it in such a way. On Friday night I played near Stuttgart. I arrived in Budapest on Saturday at 4 and at 7:30 I was on the stage of the Franz Liszt Academy where I had played as a student—so I didn't have too much time to contemplate. There was rehearsing and one more concert, and I went without any kind of official recognition. I went simply to another place to play a concert, and it happened to be my home town. The audience cheered, and they were maybe the best concerts I ever played in my entire life," he smiles.

Starker reflects that there have been five great influences on his playing. First, his early teacher whom he calls a great pedagogue. "He never taught me anything wrong. It was always cellistically right. Then, Leo Weiner, whom I consider the greatest influence of all—but that's almost standard for most Hungarian musicians. Then cellistically it was Feuermann, and then far more than anybody else there was Heifetz, instrumentally. And Fritz Reiner. My teacher put the basis in my head, as far as cello playing is concerned. Weiner taught me to hear, to apply the hearing for the sake of musical discipline, to play what's written. (This is something new, this conversation—I never tried to specify these things before, strangely enough.) Feuermann was the one who showed me that the cello can be played better and better in a different and far more varied way than Casals ever did. Heifetz was was the one who produced a kind of tonal intensity, plus an entire approach for the violin.

"I was living in Paris in 1946 and there came this idiotic movie *Carnegie Hall*. It was the first chance for a musician who came from the East to see all these people we admired when we grew up: Heifetz, Reiner, Rubinstein, Risë Stevens . . . from 1941 to 1946 we didn't hear anything from the West. And what actually drove me sleepless for a week was trying to figure out why I could not see anything that Heifetz was doing. He doesn't do anything which visibly shows. And *that* became the answer. I discovered that what he does is a timing matter, with an exact distinction between the various actions, whether it is anticipated action or delayed action. Anticipated action is part of the music itself, so it has to bear all the characteristics of the music to follow. This means that if the motion is prepared in such a way that it's exactly the same as it's going to happen, then you don't see anything. You avoid any abrupt or interrupted motions—unless you use it for musical reasons to go contrary to fluent *legato* playing. I couldn't see what the heck he was doing!—how he gets there, how he covers such a distance and absolutely nothing happens, how he can play as fast as possible with repeated motion and visibly nothing happens. It is this anticipation, conscious or subconscious. But to me it meant that I had to develop conscious anticipation of every action, musically and technically."

Ultimately came Reiner, a fellow Hungarian whom Starker first worked with at the Met and then in Chicago, where Reiner built the greatest orchestra in the country—and who accomplished orchestrally what Heifetz did instrumentally. "Primarily," Starker says, "his conducting was based on complete control over the written score and of the machinery he needed for a performance. The important thing was not that he beat or did not beat or looked or what not. He knew everything, so the blink of an eye or simply looking in a certain direction could bring out the dynamic variations and all the technical perfections and exactness that you cannot find with somewhat who knocks his brains out and physically moves like an idiot. And one of the most disturbing things in my entire life is the almost untold attempt to write Reiner *out* of music history. It's disgusting that a man who has done so much —if nothing else simply by securing *standards*—should be ignored. It was because he did not gain friends. He didn't kowtow to anyone. But that was his nature, and in the meantime he produced music on the highest imaginable level with the highest intention and unchanging principles."

This, too, has been Starker's credo. He explains that in the first decades of his playing, realizing that no matter what he did he would be criticized in various ways, he decided to strive for "the maximum technical perfection I possibly can reach— with maximum attention to the written details of the score, because this can never be questioned. I wanted to be sure that, first of all, I don't use liberties because I cannot carry something off technically. I can't stand *rubatos* and agogics used not because you plan it that way but because there is a chord and you can't get to the top of it. I was constantly using extreme agogics but without disturbing the balance within the bar. Everything is planned, not theatrical, when I feel emotionally inclined. To hold a note as long as I feel like holding it is simply a lack of discipline, and that word 'discipline' explains everything that I have to say. Regardless of whether I feel in a romantic mood or not, I believe that music is one of the disciplines—therefore *discipline* is the most important element to observe. From discipline comes freedom, not freedom first and then trying to impose discipline on top of it."

But, he continues, a musician's or any artist's life does break up into various periods. In his case, there was a long stretch of maximum discipline, immaculate playing with concentration and no taking chances. "The discipline element, which is coupled with purity and simplicity and balance, prevents what I call the third-dimensional approach—which means the diagonal element in music-making. It may sound Chinese, but I define music with horizontal, vertical and diagonal elements. Horizontal—the melody line; vertical—rhythm and harmony; diagonal—the emotional content of the music, which is dynamics and color. Each person's physical characteristics define which of these elements will dominate—whether they are skinny or fat. In my life, the vertical has dominated, but I was always striving to find a combination of the three. That means that now my attention is more on the diagonal. Today I'm interested in finding what emotional messages I can get into a piece without destroying the basic structure of the piece. I am more into the diagonal period of my life."

Starker admits that not everyone goes through this kind of intellectual approach to playing, but he is more fascinated with what can be done than what the audience will think of it—and is amused to see if the reaction coincides with his view. "When an artist starts working on a piece, he views it in such and such a way, using almost a Biedermeyer kind of decorative means with every little crescendo, dynamic, every slightest thing. And then the more you play the piece you find that you can attain the same expressiveness with far less decorative means. And you go further and further, almost to a contemporary visual arts approach: that a line expresses what all Baroque art expressed. The unfortunate thing is that in music you find yourself in an ivory tower because the audience does not go through the same development that you do. It happened to me many times that I needed absolutely minimal decorative means to express what I wanted—but only those who had gone through the same process understood it. And one realizes that performing art is not pure art. The pure *l'art pour l'art* takes place only in the studio."

All this comes in response to the hint that some listeners have sensed a certain coldness or remoteness or intellectual austerity in the cellist's playing, but in recent months he has had reviews saying that his Beethoven or Bach was overly romantic. Any listener's response is dependent on his mood and preconditioning. So if a person is accustomed to, let's say, Rostropovich's playing, then there is no way he can find Starker's romantic. "But compared to the way my playing *was* —that the people expected or accepted and got accustomed to—I am far more outgoing than I used to be. I'm simply getting old, and I care less about the type of things that made me a cool interpreter, if you please to call it that—except that it was *never* cool. It was more introspective—but it wasn't even *that*. It was simply that I first sought this maximum technical perfection. As for the Russian school, it is not a cello-playing school; it's simply a sloppy, emotionally charged thing. The historian Fridell in *The History of Western Civilization*—about the most stunning history book of all time—speaks about the fact that the Russian soul or mentality is always approximately fifty years behind the so-called Western mind. Historically, stylistic changes and so on come fifty years later. That stuck in my mind because I realized this: so-called artists who do not pursue the goals of their time are on a par with the audiences who are usually about 30–35 years behind the artist who's ahead of his time. That is the reason why composers and creative artists and a great number of re-creative artists and a great number of re-creative artists do not attain the same kind of success as those who express themselves with old-fashioned ideas and expressive means. It suddenly struck me, that's the whole reason for the huge success of the Russian musicians. They basically have the mentality of the 50-years-behind lag. So they're exactly where the audience is.

"People are always putting Rostropovich and me against each other. But I simply say that he coincides with me on the instrument. We do not have the same objectives, we do not have the same mentality. I don't play his concerts and he doesn't play mine, so he's not competition. And I take my hat off that he can go around the world and get this kind of success and please the public which pays a fortune to hear him. He's a great performer. I don't consider him a great cellist or a great instrumentalist or a great artist. A great performer, *sans pareil*. It's purity, simplicity and balance vs. a haphazard use of emotional freedom."

Starker's aims as a cellist and as a musician he traces back to Casals and Feuermann, his forefathers in showing what could be done with the instrument. "People say that now is the renaissance of the cello, but there never was a nascence! Before, the excuse always was that the cello was a difficult instrument, but today we now have at least a hundred young cellists in the world whose level of playing is pretty much on a par with what we expect on the violin. From now on it's a matter of how many cellists have important things to say." He nods that Casals is the father of all modern cello playing, but states that Casals did a disservice by delaying contemporary composers in writing for the instrument for two decades. "In 1915 when Kodály sent him a sonata, he said already then that he was too old to learn the piece—now what was he, 39 or 40? The first half of the century was under the hand of Casals in the sense that he refused to play contemporary works. Therefore, *why* should composers write if he doesn't play. Bartók didn't write a cello concerto—isn't that total nonsense? Hindemith wrote a concerto and a *Kammerkonzert* because he was a violist and his brother was a cellist. Stravinsky didn't write for the cello, except for a *Suite Italienne* or something. Composers were not encouraged. They sent their compositions by the hundreds and hundreds to Casals, and he was not interested.

"But Casals did start cello playing in the contemporary sense, and any attempt to diminish that role would be childish. He was the first one who put the cello on the map as a concert instrument by playing recitals and with orchestras regularly. Being an immensely gifted artist, he was the one who brought the cello into public consciousness. And he was the first one who played in tune and with a beautiful sound. Feuermann was the one who showed the possible road for the next step, and then he died at 41 or 42. The moment I heard Feuermann —when I was nine—I saw that his cello playing was way above the Casals type. It showed a road to something more that could be done."

Although he doesn't question Casals's artistry or his dedication to art or his effect upon an audience, Starker comments that his background put him back to the middle of the 19th century in training and education. "Casals stayed where he was and others, like me, have been much more influenced by the 20th century. But music doesn't end where he is or I am. I don't expect that everything I do is the ultimate. It always has to be carried further. I expect that my students will carry on cello playing farther than I ever did. But they are lucky because they start where I leave off. Where Casals left off, Feuermann picked up. I think in some sense where Feuermann left off I picked up."

For many years, Starker concentrated on the classic repertory—the Bach suites, Beethoven sonatas, Brahms sonatas, the

Kodály solo sonata and a few others. He admits, "My acceptance came through the masterpieces. Then one day I woke up and realized that this was an idiotic thing to gear one's existence to the critical acceptance, while the audiences on any continent will be able to take only a certain amount of the so-called heavy pieces." He effected a mixture to blend Bach and Beethoven with the old-fashioned virtuoso pieces like the Popper Tarantella, the Martinu Variations on a Rossini Theme and the Castelnuovo-Tedesco *Figaro* Variations. "If I play a masterpiece, why shouldn't I play a Chopin nocturne transcription if I feel like it? You can enjoy television even though it has nothing to do with enjoying the *St. Matthew Passion*. I happen to be very fond of watching wrestling. Everyone is laughing at me for this, but it does not reduce my intellectual capacities for enjoying other things." As for new music, he uses a very simple criterion: "I only play pieces if the fact that *I* play matters. If it's a piece that any of my students or any cellist in the world can play and there's no difference, I don't play it. If it's a piece which uses the cello in a way that none of the existing qualities of the cello as an instrument come through, I don't play it." Two works have recently been written for and premiered by him, concertos by Miklos Rosza and Bernard Heiden. "Both I consider the highest order of music. They are not revolutionary, but they have individuality and are well written. They use the cello well, and it has a chance to show off in a 20th-century way."

As a teacher, Janos Starker is a Distinguished Service Professor at Indiana University at Bloomington, where he has been since 1958. He quickly defines his modes of operation —masterclasses and seminars, which he has taught all over, from Ravinia and Aspen to Rotterdam and Düsseldorf. Both are based on his *An Organized Method of String Playing*. It goes even beyond this into other instruments of the orchestra. He reasons, "I'm simply teaching the elements which are essential to obtain the maximal body control so that you can use your brain and functions far more for music-making—so that you are free to communicate, although that's far too popular a word. The idea is to teach people to first be aware of all the physical reasoning behind various schools of playing and then try to find the one which fits the individual body and mentality best. "It's a thinking process," he adds. "If they are doing something which gives them problems, by the end of the session they're supposed to have enough material to proceed in the thinking process and eventually find the solution."

After this many decades of teaching, he finds that if someone is a recognized interpreter, people will say, "How does he have the nerve to pretend to be a great pedagogue?" And those who know him for his pedagogic activities think, "Why doesn't he just teach? Why does he have to concertize all over?" But, he insists, "what is usually not realized is that my background is so totally different from anybody alive—and this is the only statement which I unhesitatingly make as a very modest statement. I was teaching at the age of eight, and at twelve I already had five students. I lived in orchestras for eleven years, and I played over one thousand opera performances and over one thousand symphony concerts as a solo cellist of the orchestra. And I think I'm nearing the one-thousandth of my own performances. I've played jazz and every kind of music there is. I was a member of a string quartet and played Bartók quartets when I was eleven. So with this training I am qualified to teach any instrument. At Bloomington I put through a project so any student can study with any teacher of his choice for two credit hours, aside from his major. As a result I've had bassoon players, clarinetists, violinists, bass players as students who came in fairly regularly and played their repertory for me. It is never a question of 'play this short, play this long because I think it's nicer that way'—but of working on what position should be held, what would be improved and so forth. All these things work for all these instruments, and the musical principles work for everything. Eventually you find you cannot teach everybody to the same extent, but they should be able to reach their maximum ability, and that is the function of the true teacher: to try to locate the things that prevent the student from functioning."

"It's much more important to have a good teacher for a mediocre talent than a big one," he believes. "A big talent will eventually find its way no matter what you do, no matter who teaches him. The teacher's job with a great talent is only to give him shortcuts. I happen to be completely opposed to the view that the so-called famous teachers are the ones who pick the great talents and make them shine on the concert stage to give credit to themselves. I don't need that kind of credit, so therefore I can afford to work with whomever I want."

What does he look for in potential students? "Brains mostly. If they are not that musically talented, I don't mind. But they must have a brain that can absorb the type of teaching I offer, the kind of mental process I believe necessary for those who are not that talented and will teach. I'm truly concerned about what happens two generations after I'm gone, or while I'm still here. I have taught I don't know how many generations by now. How many students will have the chance to hit the big time? Very few. In every era there's only a handful. If they're very good, they will have local careers of sorts, or they will become members of a string quartet or a symphony orchestra. And most likely they will teach. That's what concerns me—what kind of teachers they will be. I want to be sure that if an enormously gifted kid at a young age comes into their hands that they don't hinder that talent. That's the reason for all these mental or almost scientific-sounding approaches to instrumental playing. I want to be sure they understand every conceivable aspect. When they go away, I'm not interested in how well they play a recital. I'm interested that they have enough material to be alone—to work by themselves —and to be sure that they can cope with any situation with any student according to those basic rules in which I believe."

He admits that these principles can be questioned or argued, but defends them by the very fact that they are inclusive of all principles. "That's the whole difference. My students play almost unrecognizably differently. The only thing that defines my students is a certain freedom of their emotions. But the sound, vibrato, intonation, musical phrasings, fingerings, bowings are all different. Of course, people have come and said, 'Starker, like all the others, teaches them to play like he does.' But not one of them sounds anywhere near the others—let alone like me. Yes, there are certain elements that are recognizable—but they are mostly physical. Very few of my students fool around on stage and make a show, because I just don't happen to believe in that. If they move, the motions are parallel with the music, so therefore it's not disturbing. But they have a freedom of motion which allows them to function and play for a long time without killing themselves. It's a matter of coinciding your actions with the basic physical principles of the human body in order to produce music beyond a certain level." Janos Starker has not only gone beyond, but beyond—and the legacy he is already leaving behind is, well, by now inevitable.

★ *Thomas Stewart* ★

Texas-born Thomas Stewart is one of the great American success stories, part of a splendid American baritone tradition that includes John Charles Thomas, Lawrence Tibbett, Leonard Warren and Robert Merrill—although Stewart did it first abroad before returning home. While he had become known primarily as a Wagnerian singer, this 1974 interview was done at a time when he sought to prove his mettle in other areas.

In his eight seasons at the Metropolitan Opera, Thomas Stewart has all but dominated the Wagnerian wing with his Wotans, Wanderer, Kurvenal, Dutchman, Wolfram, Amfortas, and Gunther—as he's done in all the major houses here and abroad. This season [1973–74], along with Gunther in the new Metropolitan Opera production of *Götterdämmerung* (ending the overlong piecing together of the current *Ring*), he's offering his other cheek, that of the Italian and French repertory. Of course, he's sung Ford in *Falstaff* (his debut in 1966), a single Amonasro in *Aida* last year, and a magnificent Golaud in the new *Pelléas et Mélisande*. But now he's adding Iago in *Otello*, Don Giovanni, and the four villains in the new production of *Les Contes d'Hoffmann*. All told, these roles make him the busiest star on the present Met roster, giving him New York residence for a good part of this season.

The day we talked in his Manhattan apartment, there was

the pre-departure mayhem of ringing phones, half-packed suitcases, business meetings, and the sound of his wife Evelyn Lear coaching the role of the Marschallin down the hall in the living room. With typical composure, however, he sat relaxed —but still imposing—amid all this in a swivel chair behind a teak desk, going through a mound of papers in his modern study. Surrounded by paintings collected all over the world, he spoke with that rich baritonal sound, interspersed with hearty laughs, warmth, and an occasional spark of those mephistophelean eyebrows that give him a certain friendly-sinister dash.

Is it hard keeping Verdi, Puccini, Offenbach, Debussy, and Mozart in the throat along with his complete, world-traveled Wagner *Heldenbariton* parts? "No, not really," comes the answer. "When I did Golaud at the Met, I hadn't done it for a long time, but in two weeks the role was back. But the voice changes over the years, and so a role becomes different. My voice is now richer and deeper—I'm older—and I know more what to do with it; I just don't open my mouth and sing, like I could do when I was younger. The greatest amount of time is spent in restudying, making the vocal adjustments that are necessary. This takes more time than the actual relearning. I hadn't done Iago for six years, and this same thing happened. I don't find 'styles' per se any problem. An Amonasro or Scarpia come naturally, but they require a shifting of gears in my thinking, my approach. Both have gone well, and I have enjoyed doing them. The voice is the same in all things, but the styles are different—Wagner is not like Verdi, and you have to do justice to both. You can flavor one with the other, and it does them good. Yet, there is a big shifting of gears."

In Berlin, where he has made his operatic home since 1958, he's sung his complete repertoire, first concentrating on the Italian school and then getting deep into Wagner territory. Doing it in Germany with Germans gave him a special point of view, an approach from the theatrical standpoint rather than the Italian musical one. "I missed the accent on music in opera," he says thoughtfully. "I was in the *most* musical repertory . . . but not with the right people. It made me a singer who never looked at things purely from a musical point of view. I was always involved with portrayal and acting and the stage.

Then working with Karajan made me realize that all the repertory, Italian and German, has certain musical values that are as important as dramatic ones. He showed me that one doesn't preclude the other, that they go hand in hand. He is a theatrical man, but approaches opera first as music—the theater comes *out* of the music." The result has been that, as much as he does with a role musically and vocally, there is that theatrical commitment and personal intensity that gives Stewart performances their special flavor.

This season's shift in focus away from Wagner was dramatically mirrored this summer when, for the first time in thirteen years, the name of Thomas Stewart was off the roster at the Bayreuth Festival. "It was basically a difference of opinion between Wolfgang Wagner and myself," he says, shrugging his big-boned shoulders. "I know for a fact that there are hard feelings on his part because of my association with Salzburg—he felt it is a betrayal because Salzburg is competition. It's not and his fears are unfounded—it's just another approach to Wagner without any danger of wiping out Bayreuth's reputation. Then there was my association with Wieland, even though it was Wolfgang who hired me initially. But I worked more with Wieland and became better known because of it. Then when I asked permission to take two Hollywood Bowl engagements, he turned completely around and said there was nothing in the schedule for me at Bayreuth—despite the fact that he had said I would be the next Bayreuth Hans Sachs. These things were enough to give me the feeling that all is not kosher and put a distance between us. It may not be a permanent break and I would go back . . . but on my terms. As you know, there's been a steady exodus of the great singers, year by year. The artistic satisfaction is less, the whole milieu has changed—and since it is always a financial loss to be there, a singer has to have the artistic satisfaction. It was strange, suddenly, not to be back, because Bayreuth has been such a part of my life for so long. But there was plenty to do, many beautiful things at the Bowl, Tanglewood, London. And from a purely business standpoint, I could make five times as much money for half the work."

Working with Wieland, he calls the most successful production the producer's final *Ring*, followed by his *Tristan, Parsifal,*

Dutchman, and *Tannhäuser.* "In 1965 or '66 that *Ring* was a step into the unknown for Wagner opera. Today it's not so hair-raising because it's been bypassed by some others. I'm sure Wieland would have gone on from there. That was seven years ago!" Stewart's work with Karajan has been part of a more lyrical look at the music-dramas during the Salzburg Easter Festivals: "It's a new, valid, beautiful insight. The bellowing phase of Wagner has no place, and the music is too beautiful to be subjected to it. When that kind of singing was allowed, people could listen mainly to the orchestra and get enough. Verdi needs beautiful singing or the audience is bored to death—but Wagner has the orchestra, and the conductor can play it like a symphony, *without* the voice. In *Tristan* and parts of the *Ring* and *Parsifal,* you can shut your ears to the singing and just listen to the orchestra if you want. If I hear a lousy performance, I do this automatically . . . if there are pigs on the stage."

With slight hesitation he admits that he thinks the Wagner operas can be improved with cuts. "With this rash renaissance of Wagner, we think we have to have every drop today. I'm sorry, but this is wrong—they should be propitiously cut for the normal audience, the ones outside Bayreuth or a festival setting. It may bring in some who stay away because of the length." He says, too, that this peaking interest in Wagner is bringing too many second-class singers into the fold. "Everyone wants to do the *Ring,*" he bellows in mock disbelief. "When I went to Germany in the fifties, I had not the vaguest thought about Wagner. I knew very little about German opera until I got there. After World War II the German repertoire here was at its lowest point, so I went through my studies with a little of it. Bing did it grudgingly because he hated it—but at least he picked the right people and knew who to get to sing."

Thomas Stewart's background is Texan and distinctly nonmusical. "Well, we did have some music at home and I learned to play the guitar and sing as a kid. Eventually, music gave me a kind of identity, because we were poor and I was unattractive, full of complexes. I learned how to sing, but never in my wildest dreams did I think I'd do it professionally . . . only as a source of pleasure. Oh, I played football and baseball, but while other kids took up raising calves, horses, and pigs,

I was singing *and* raising a calf and sheep, which I enjoyed, too. Our home was religious, deep-dyed Southern Baptists. Later I found it too constricting, but as a child I went to church three times a week and sang. If one had talent, church was the first place to use it.

"When I graduated from high school, I had big plans to go into mathematics and electronic engineering. One man who had a lot to do with my decision was a physics teacher who, at the same time, conducted an a cappella choir. I had my first primitive voice lessons with him, and he advised me to go to Cal Tech. Then some friends and family said, 'Think seriously about singing and developing the voice.' We had moved to California and I was already known in the northern part for Billy Graham gospel kinds of things, and my mother dreamed that I would be what she called an evangelistic soloist—she wanted me to study for this kind of thing, but it did not appeal to me. My teacher said I could do math or music successfully. By now I was pretty cramped by the church bit, a rebellious youth chafing under the restrictions. I had heard concerts, mostly all by foreigners, and I couldn't associate with this. But when I discovered Americans like Tibbett and John Charles Thomas, this intrigued me. So with pressures from friends, I decided to give it a try."

When his family moved back to San Saba, Texas, he came with them; his Baptist background took him to Baylor University, where he found a Welsh voice teacher who had settled there during the twenties. "I went along with the Baptist thing and studied there on a scholarship, singing as a student and amateur." After a year he was to be drafted, so he volunteered first in order to get the GI Bill when his enlistment ended. That was important because it assured his studies later. "I served from 1945 until the end of the War in the medical research and electronics section of the Air Force. When I was discharged, I toyed with the ideal of continuing in IBM computer work and was almost sidetracked from music for good. I had a job as a government employee in the research lab in San Antonio. After a year of working as a civilian, I found myself again pulled into music by way of light opera, TV and so on in the area. I had to make up my mind and, with my GI Bill, I chose to study music at Baylor for four years. With a year to go, I came to New York for graduate study at Juilliard. I always tended to opera, and my interest in the theater at Baylor led me there."

Typical of his background is the story he tells about his grandfather. Stewart was home in Texas for the first time after he had left college and Texas and home. All the family—an immediate group of over a hundred—had come to his grandparents' house for dinner and visiting. "My grandfather was on the front porch in his rocking chair, digesting his meal, and we were talking—we had been very close ever since I was a kid. I was sitting on the floor beside him and he asked me this and that. Then at one point he said, 'Tell me, sonny, how are things?' Well, I told him. 'What are you doing?' I told him, 'I'm a singer, Grandpa.' Then he smiled and looked out, 'Yeah, I know that. Tell me, what do you do for a living?' And all I could do was chuckle, because being a musician was so removed from my family . . . except if you were playing or singing on the radio or with Grand Ole Opry. He was a farmer in rural America, and I had never thought about singing professionally until I had almost finished high school."

At Juilliard not only did he complete his training and sing in the American premiere of Strauss' *Capriccio,* but he also met his future wife, the soprano Evelyn Lear, who had already been the mother of two children and divorced—and who was striking out for a big-time career. "They were shaky times," he confesses. "We were kicked around, scrounging here and there. It's disgusting what you have to do—churches, borscht belt, choruses, television, capsule operas, everything. I even won a TV contest and appeared with Mae West at the Latin Quarter! Finally I said to myself, 'At this rate you're getting nowhere.' That was the decisive year that we went to Frederic Cohen at the Juilliard Opera Workshop for advice. Evvy's *Reuben, Reuben* had been a flop and my *Ballad of Baby Doe* fell apart on the West Coast. Our world was at rock bottom. He gave us one piece of advice—go to Europe. We had two small kids and no money, so we applied for a Fulbright. I was pessimistic, fed up with the whole thing. It's a hell of a lot of hard work and few make it to the top . . . or even manage to hold their own. So I went back and made an appointment with IBM in New York, and they offered me a job in Poughkeepsie. Just then

the Fulbrights came through—so fate decided the rest of my
life. It was the last grasp at a life vest by a drowning man."

Although this looks like a passive act, chalk it up to the
desperation of the time. He admits to being an ambitious person—although his wife claims that his outgoing nature is a
cover-up for a basic shyness. "But you have to have ambition
and drive in this business. It's absolutely necessary. The 'big
break' thing is a lot of crap—you need ambition, talent and
patience. You have to know what you want and be prepared to
stay with it. I auditioned ten times for an agent, and then was
prepared to go the eleventh and twelfth times, too! But without Evvy, I wouldn't be where I am—although it may sound
like a cliché. We both feel that if we hadn't found each other
we would never have what we have. She gave me the drive I
didn't have. I was prepared to drop it at one point, as I said.
My drive was to succeed, but I was willing to compromise on
how I would succeed. I could do *other* things to succeed other
than sing, I could fall back on something else. But in music I
got my drive from Evvy, since at that time I was not driven
that much to be a success as a singer. Music was slow and not
producing things. I tried musical comedy and auditioned for
shows . . . and had parts cut out of shows—like *Candide,*
for one. I had a small part in *Reuben, Reuben* and under-
studied the baritone, and then it folded in Boston. Audition!
My God! The whole bit! Our careers were not easy. We
knocked around for years!"

With their Fulbrights, they set out for Berlin in 1957. There
they studied at the Hochschule für Musik and then bowed at
the Deutsche Oper, first Tom (in 1958, as Escamillo), then
Evelyn. "Our secret was that we never said no. Whatever it
was, we could do it. We learned and faked and kept our heads
above water. The turning point—when we knew it was going
to work, when I knew I was in the right profession—was just
before going to Bayreuth for the first time. That gave me a
tremendous boost and put me into the international scene.
After two years in Berlin and enough performances and being
successful, then I knew I'd be a big success—I had been bitten
by the bug. I had gotten a lot of drive I had not had before
and my appetite was whetted."

From Bayreuth he went on to Vienna, London, San Francisco. The Met then offered a $300 weekly contract for *Figaro* and *Pagliacci,* but he said no. "I had too many things popping in Europe. In fact, we both turned down our first Met offers. We had to come back the right way or stay in Europe. I had a better offer in San Francisco—$1,000 a week and big roles like Ford, Posa and Valentin, and I was glad to take it. We waited . . . and it paid off. I made my Met debut as Ford in *Falstaff*—it was to have been Wolfram, but someone got sick and I came in ten days earlier; Evvy came for the world premiere of *Mourning Becomes Electra* the next year."

How have they managed to keep an incredibly successsful marriage afloat with two big careers? "It's hard to say," he reflects. "In our marriage the ability to submerge your own ego at times into the ego of your mate has been important. And it's hard to learn that. Performers have strong egos, but they have to suppress them at times. There are reasons why: if love is great enough, it is a great, fantastic matter you don't want destroyed—so you do it pragmatically. There has to be give and take, and partners clash if they are not willing to do this. We clashed at the beginning . . . it was inevitable. But never at any point was there a breakdown in communication between us. Otherwise it falls apart. You have to be secure to submerge your ego, but it can be learned," he nods like someone who has known the struggle.

Aside from his own drive and his wife's moral support, Stewart admits there were others who helped him while he was abroad. One was the bass Josef Greindl, who had "a beautiful voice and a tremendous personality. He helped. He was Rocco to my first Ferrando, in *Fidelio,* in Berlin. In the final scene he came up to shake the minister of state's hand, my hand. I was a beginner and scared to death. He said, 'I knew you were going to be successful from the moment I took your hand and the way you shook it—it had the right quality.' That was very sweet. Then later he recommended me to Wieland Wagner, who was looking for an Amfortas to replace George London in 1960. Wieland knew me from Berlin and asked Greindl if I was any good. Amfortas is a special character at Bayreuth and London was a pretty good act to follow, but Greindl said that I could handle it, and so tipped the scales for me."

What Stewart looks for in other singers is professionalism,

someone who knows what he's doing and does it well. "I dislike childish *prima donnas* and *primo uomos*. I consider myself a professional and today you find more and more of them than you did thirty years ago. The business is difficult, and to succeed you have to be clear-headed about what you can do and what you want." One of the things about the business that he dislikes most is the nomadic life that finds him and his wife distributed among New York, Switzerland, Berlin and with countless stops between. In fact, after a performance in Berlin last spring, they had a special Hannover guest appearance in *Tosca*, immediately after which they had to ride a night train to Munich for a morning recording sesison—with no sleep *or* dinner. "I'm basically a home person. I like to know where I am. It's impossible, of course, so you adjust. Also, I hate the politics, the petty childishness from all facets of the profession. I like someone who doesn't indulge, doesn't need this to succeed. The intrigue makes me sick!—and there's lots of it in Germany and Austria. It was a shock at first, but soon I learned the bitter truth. If you rely on talent, alone, you can be prepared to wait a little longer. If you're adept at intrigue, your talent can come to the fore quicker. We had no idea. We just kept plugging away, singing as best as possible, hoping it would come through sooner or later." It did, and it was worth the wait.

★ *Leopold Stokowski* ★

Although the 90-some-year-old Leopold Stokowski has forsaken America for England, his spectacular kind of music making is with us via his many recordings. When I talked quietly with him in the fall of 1970, he was still director of the orchestra he had founded in the early 1960s, the American Symphony. Since his departure for England in 1972, the orchestra has reformed itself as a self-governing ensemble.

Leopold Stokowski has been called "a 19th-century man with
a 21st-century mind." The seemingly ageless maestro is in his
late eighties—he was born in London in the 1880's to a father
of Polish origin—but his vast energies and curiosity, his non-
stop conducting activity and his vitality for any number of
musical and world affairs may well find him not only a figure
of the 19th and 20th centuries but of the 21st century as well.
This summer he fulfilled a schedule of conducting throughout
Europe, during which he recorded works of Ravel, Ives, Messiaen and Debussy. As fall approached, Stokowski returned to
New York to again take the reins of the American Symphony
season as its founder and Music Director. On a late September
afternoon, as the sun was setting over the Central Park Reser-
voir, Stokowski sat at his desk near the window of his sparsely
furnished old-world apartment near the Guggenheim Museum.
One gets the impression that it is geared for work, embellished
only by a few Eastern hangings and rugs, and even a huge
Chinese gong in one corner. The following are excerpts from
a ninety-minute interview taped with Leopold Stokowski.

We have all been aware of your concern with youth and youth-
development in music. Your orchestras since the 1940's have
been generally youth oriented—the City Center Orchestra of
New York, the All-American Youth Symphony and now the
American Symphony Orchestra. Could you tell us a little about
this?

There are several sides to this question. One is that the young
people come from the schools after they have finished their
studies. They wish to enter the musical life of the country but
there's no opportunity for them because, perhaps, the New
York Philharmonic has one vacancy or two, which they easily
fill—but all the rest are disappointed. I receive so many letters
from young men and young women telling me of their disappointment and their longing to really be active. Then about
ten years ago I started what is called the American Symphony
Orchestra. We started it out of nothing and we gave the first
concert. We had four rehearsals and the writers in the news-
papers said that it was a very good concert, very satisfactory
musically—but it cannot be done with four rehearsals. So I

never was able to understand how they contradicted themselves, but that's how it was. What I do to find players is this.
I tell all the youth that I know to give anybody my telephone
number. So they call here and every afternoon at 3:00 I hear
one, at 3:30 another, at 4:00 another and at 4:30 another. I
hear four players or singers and make permanent notes which
go into this book here so that I will know when we have a
vacancy for any instrument.

You then have literally hundreds of names on waiting lists in
every category.

Yes, it's all here. That is one thing, but another is this: All
over the world, in European countries, American countries and
in Japan, for example, there is a great dissatisfaction on the part
of young people who are saying: "This is the world that you
created. I was not asked if I wanted to be born and, if I were
to be born, on which planet it should be. All of a sudden I find
myself in a terrible, dirty place—or in a very beautiful place
with a garden outside the window. I find myself existing and
I love music and I love my instrument, whatever it may be,
and I would like to be active with that instrument—particularly
in the great works of the masters, Beethoven, Bach, Brahms,
Debussy, Ravel or the great Russian and American composers.
And I have no opportunity." So that is why I started the orchestra. And what is so interesting to me is that the young women
are just as good as the young men. They are not better, but
they're equal. So the question of whether it is a man or a
woman is nothing at all. It is a question only of quality—not
origin. We are only asking one thing—Music. Love your instrument, love music, be willing to make the supreme effort for
fine performance. And they are giving that all the time.

What you are providing, then, is the experience of playing
music full time.

Yes. Most of the music the players are reading for the very
first time at the first rehearsal—and that gives them wonderful
experience. Also, I have given my whole life to music. I first
conducted when I was 12 years old—it was just because I was
a pianist in a certain music hall association and suddenly at

the last moment the conductor was very ill and somebody had
to do it. I had been playing the piano for the chorus and for
the solo singers in that program and so I knew the music well.
They said to me: "Can you do it?" And at that time I thought
I knew more than I think I know now and I said, "Yes, of
course I can."

But can we talk of world conditions, because I notice that
in the United States, with all our *tremendous* wealth, orchestras
are having difficulty—whereas in the European countries,
where wealth is much less, they are having much less difficulty,
sometimes practically no difficulty. I was just working in Holland, for example, and they don't seem to have any problems
there. One reason is that they are receiving help from the state,
and we cannot do that so easily in our United States. There
are roughly 1,500 orchestras here. Some of them are completely amateur, some are completely professional, some are
partly amateur-partly professional. But we do not have 1,500
good conductors for those orchestras. We have some young
and very talented conductors but nothing like so many. Some
of those orchestras are suffering because they do not have a
conductor with experience or even with the talent for conducting.

On the other side of the youth question, what about attracting
youth audiences? Many musicians feel that rock and popular
music have taken many people away from serious music.

I don't think it has taken away, but I think it is a new growth.
And it is part of the protest which the youth all over the world
is making today because they find such terrible conditions in
their country and such terrible wars going on all over the
world. So they are protesting and saying, "What kind of world
have you made? If you have such good ideas, why have those
good ideas produced such horrible conditions? And if you have
produced such horrible conditions that means that your ideas
were pretty bad. We think we have some *better* ideas. But
when we try to explain or express those ideas, we are often
stopped. Sometimes we even are stopped by the police. Sometimes we are hurt very much and so are some of the police."

And when we are fighting in the streets that is civil war—and that's plain stupid. We had our civil war a long time ago and what was the result? Nothing very good, just dead bodies. Are we going to have civil war again? Are we going to have civil war between the Blacks and the Whites? Are we going to have civil war between the rich and the poor? Not far from here I often drive through Harlem and I see horrible conditions, filth and dirt and houses falling down. It is shameful that with all the wealth this country has we cannot do something better. The youth has something to say to the adults, something very truthful to say in protest against the horror of life and slaughter and hatred. You kill a man because if you don't, he'll kill you—but you don't know why you did it, and he doesn't know why he wants to kill you. It is really out of what we think is self-preservation. That is not the true answer to that question—the true answer is that I could be, I would like to be friends with that man. I would like to sit at a table and have some coffee with him and talk about his ideas of life or of music or of love or beauty—of everything in humanity.

Do you think they are turning away from traditional music because they associate it with the establishment?

I don't know, but I am very interested in their kind of music. I listen to it and some of it I find has originality and the talent for improvisation, which was great in the time of Bach but has become much less now. We are becoming the slaves of little marks on a piece of white paper which we call music. That's not music, that is only the paper. Music is what sounds, what goes into the ears, what goes into the heart and the soul of a person—and we are not understanding that so clearly. But many of the artists who are producing the modern pop music are improvising very interestingly. Some of it is just imitation of old jazz of a long time ago and has no originality, but some is original. It also shows the desire of the youth for action. They like to dance to their kind of music, which makes them happy. And what makes them happy is a wonderful thing. Making people unhappy by killing and slaughtering and smashing is a detestable, deeply immoral thing.

What about your long experience in modern music? You have
been associated with many world and American premieres.
And you have experienced people walking out, booing and so
on. Why do you think that music is always ahead of its public?

Well, I think it is very simple. A musician devotes all his life
and all his thoughts, all his energies to music—even in his sleep
he is thinking about music. Whereas the public which comes
to concerts perhaps once a week, or once in two weeks, they
have much less experience. Also their ears are not developed
for listening intensely; and as they listen to music very often
it penetrates their inner consciousness, their soul—but sometimes it does not. Some people tell me that they *saw* me conduct somewhere. Apparently they listen with their eyes rather
than their ears. And it is natural because in a month's time
they devote perhaps only three or four hours to music, whereas
we musicians devote all our time to it.

Have you ever felt that you were wrong in your belief in or
estimation of a piece of music?

Yes, yes, that happens quite often. Also, when I listen to some
records which I made, I'm very dissatisfied with certain moments in them. I think I was wrong in the balance of the instruments or in the tempo or in the phrasing or whatever—and I
wish it could have been better. I would like to destroy that
record and do it all over again, but the companies will not let
that happen.

You gave the American premiere of Mahler's Eighth Symphony and *Das Lied von der Erde* in Philadelphia in 1916,
long before the composer was in any kind of vogue. Why do
you think it took Mahler such a long time to find public acceptance?

I did not know Mahler, but I heard him conduct often and
particularly recall the first performance of the Eighth Symphony when it was done in Munich. Mahler's music is an intense expression of his inner life, of his longing to find what
is beautiful and what is really, in a sense, religion and the
highest forms of thought and feeling. He put all that into his

music, and it has taken time for the general public to realize that. They do now today. But, of course, individual musicians did know that and did feel that. He was not only a musician, he was a philosopher in my opinion, and all that went into his music. It was an expression of his inner life as he saw it in Vienna and in America. When I first came to America I heard Mahler conduct in the opera—it was very great, but the players in the orchestra did not respond well to him and were often quite cruel to him. So he went away very despondent in his thoughts.

Do you remember scores which you have conducted in the past, or do you have to restudy them before each performance?

I study them in any case. For example, take the *Eroica* Symphony of Beethoven. I've conducted it many, many times— but if I were going to conduct it tomorrow I would look through that score again, because I find that I constantly see new possibilities in music that I have known all my life. Something becomes clearer or there is a new angle of approach or the influence of new ideas from a different environment where I am conducting.

What would you say have been some of the most sweeping changes that you've witnessed in your long career in music in terms of the symphony orchestra?

I think it is the wide spread of talent. I remember when I first was engaged to conduct the orchestra in Philadelphia in 1912. I came to the first rehearsal and I noted that everyone was speaking German. So we rehearsed in the German language, which is all right. But soon I noted that there were only three good players in this orchestra—three only in an orchestra of about 95 players! One was a first horn and the other was a third horn and another was the timpanist. They were three Germans and very great players. But that's all. Woodwinds terrible, strings terrible. So I took years and years to find good players and gradually improve the quality and make it really American. It took years to find a good oboe and a good flute and a good clarinet, first trombone and first trumpet. We finally did find them, but it took a long time and one had to be very patient and very persistent and very determined. Today we have so much great talent among the American-born young men and women that we can find plenty of good players.

What are some of your early recollections of the great conductors you heard as a young man?

I think that the greatest conductor I ever heard was Hans Richter. At first he did little things to help Wagner—he was like an assistant who copies what the composer has written. Then Wagner noticed that he really had talent beyond such things and said to him, "Take all the brass instruments and rehearse them in this passage here and make a better balance, with the horns more here, and the trombones less there" and so forth. So the man did that, and then Wagner said to him, "Here's the score. Please rehearse the whole orchestra." And this young man then became I think the greatest conductor I've ever heard. You never heard Richter—you were too young —and it is your loss that you didn't. He was *enormous*. Very sensitive and at the same time enormously powerful. And he not only conducted Wagner but Brahms and Beethoven and Mozart and everybody. As a child, I heard him in Paris or Vienna and I had the good fortune to hear what can be done by a man like that. He was a giant.

We have a whole new world of problems and union regulations and self-ruling orchestras and increasing demands. Do you feel, therefore, that the age of the autocratic conductor is finished?

I don't think it has changed. I notice that, for example, we work with the unions, and we do completely what we should do. In a rehearsal we begin exactly on the minute. Someone who works with us and the unions gives me the sign and I begin. At a certain point he makes a sign to me and the players take a 20-minute rest according to the regulation. The union helps the players and I understand that. I try to help the players too. The gossip that goes on about these things is really untrue.

You mentioned before that as an orchestra builder in Philadelphia you had to do a good deal of weeding out and replacing of musicians. Wouldn't that be more difficult with today's new regulations?

Yes, it is more difficult. But of course there are two sides to this. One is humanity—you hate to put somebody out. On the other hand, the conductor is responsible to the composer. We are responsible to Bach, Beethoven, Shostakovich and Stravinsky—and the players understand that.

Do you feel that your early experience as an organist in London and New York helped to formulate in your ear the sound you want from an orchestra?

No. My first instrument was the violin, which I began when I was seven. It is still my favorite instrument—all the strings, in fact. Because in back of everything that comes from all of them is the human mind and the human heart of emotion and feeling and understanding and expressing something about life, which all great music does. So the idea that you just mentioned of sound—the conductor does not make the sound, the players make it.

But he fuses them during a rehearsal to achieve a certain effect he has in his ear, does he not?

I don't understand it. Many things happen. You hear and see them happening, but you don't understand what is underlying all that. But the feeling of the string vibrating with the bow and also the vibrato of the left hand technique—all these things are very important. And to give enough room for a phrase or to build a phrase to an important tone, broadening it a little on one tone—all these things are instinctive and, of course, built up by experience of many years.

When you reorganized the traditional orchestra layout in Philadelphia with the rearrangement of violins and so on, you obviously did feel that it created more of the sound you were looking for.

It is not what I'm looking for, it is what the composer is looking for. The sound of Mozart and the sound of Brahms—both

were Germans, yet how different. The conception of sound is
the profound inner quest and always is. A composer had hundreds of wonderful ideas. Now these ideas which he heard in
his inner soul he has to bring down on to a piece of paper and
make some little black marks down there which are supposed
to represent what happened in his mind. Now comes the orchestra and the conductor. They take the little black marks on
the paper and they must try to find what was that inspiration—
can I convey to the listener that inspiration from Beethoven
or Mozart or whoever it is? That is what is our great problem.
Because our writing of music on paper is extremely limited,
there are thousands of possibilities which cannot be put on that
little piece of white paper. So that has to be done. . . . I
don't know . . . by sensitivity, by imagination, all kinds of
qualities. We have to search for Brahms who had a certain
masculine power, for Mozart who had another kind of flexibility and also great humor—and a certain kind of beauty and an
expression of life of that day. Mozart understood life and met
it with humor. With Archbishop Colloredo, he would give a
stinging rebuff with his reference to "Your Highness" and "my
littleness."

Critics have talked about your reorchestrating certain portions
of scores to bring out more oboe or more bassoon or what-
have-you. How would you defend this?

I don't defend it, but I do explain it, and would like to have
the opportunity to explain it. Very often, some of the greatest
composers do not understand the instruments. They ask the
instrument to do what is against its nature—or they ask all
the trumpets and trombones and horns to play *fortissimo,*
while the second clarinet is also playing *fortissimo* and cannot
be heard. The trumpets, trombones and horns have a *fortissimo*
79 times as great as the clarinets. But on paper it is the same
thing. We players and conductors have to make it possible to
balance between those two. And that is very difficult, particularly because the publishers of music do terrible things: They
take a score and write *fortissimo* all the way down the score.
Whereas a *fortissimo* here is of a relation of one to forty, let's
say. So we have to find a way to balance it. We have to say

to the composer, so to speak—he is dead now, but to his spirit we say—"How do you want the balance of this piece? Do you want an English horn to be prominent?" If so, then he cannot play *piano* when 45 strings are accompanying him also *piano*. This *piano* and that one are totally different. He must play more *mezzo-forte* and the strings must play softer to accompany him. That's part of our duty and we feel strongly our responsibility to the composer—particularly when he's dead. A few weeks ago I was conducting a work of Panufnik, a Polish composer. He is living and I can say to him, "What would you like for this passage? It isn't good here; do you mind if I rearrange it?" And he will agree to a little more of this or a little less of that. I could have asked Ives 55 questions and then I would know what he really meant by things. As it is, we have to use our best judgment and do the best for the composer.

What about the Bach transcriptions which are so well known but which have an intellectual stigma about them. Why do you feel this has happened?

Yes, there are those who criticize them and who say we want to have Bach only in the way he wrote it—you have orchestrated it otherwise and it is wrong. I think that they have the right to their opinion and I have the right to mine too. It is a free country and we can all think any way we wish. But what is so humorous about this situation is that the one musician of all time in all countries who made the most re-orchestrations of other composers is Bach. Both Bach and Handel would not agree to this criticism. What they could say to me is: "You have re-orchestrated this but you haven't done it well. You don't conduct it well either." They could say that.

You have felt that had Bach had this kind of orchestral power at his disposal, he might have done this kind of orchestration.

Well, let's think about such things. Take the C-minor Passacaglia of Bach. Colossal music! He had his own music on a very small organ with one man pumping the air. He could not make a big *crescendo* and a big *diminuendo*—it just wasn't there. In the organs that still exist in Germany and Austria one can see clearly that Bach had tremendous understanding of what this music could express if he had had more—and the modern organ can do it. Although it wasn't possible in Bach's time, he had the imagination and the foresight and this wonderful quality of seeing what is possible in the future. But we might ask ourselves that today: What is the future on this earth which has too many people existing in the space, not enough food and so on? What is the future?—we had better do a little thinking about that, just as Bach did about the organ.

What do you think of the current Romantic revival? You have programmed both the Paderewski and Moszkowski Piano Concertos. Do you think this new-found interest in 19th-century virtuoso music has come about because of the disenchantment with what is going on in contemporary music?

I think it might be that, but also the fact that the human mind is growing. There was a time when he really was a caveman. Gradually, he developed new ideas, a new way, perhaps, of making a mark on the sand—a message to some other cavemen and the beginning of writing. The human mind is growing all the time, fortunately. The process of education is still not too good, but it is better than it used to be. So we are seeing life in new ways: the gaiety of the pop music, the very earnest music of Brahms, let's say, and there is that kind of music that Stravinsky has been producing lately. There are all kinds of new things happening and as long as men are really men and women are really women there will be romance, there will be love and there will be romantic ideas in the arts—not only music but in literature, poetry, all the arts. Some people don't like the Romantic because they have become dry like fruits which never become ripe but remain hard and dry. The more they know, the less they understand about life—it is knowledge and no understanding. Perhaps it is also a protest against so much in life that has become automatic—against the mechanical conception of life. Thank God we say we wish to remain human, we do not want to become a machine. We have computers now—we push a lot of ideas into a computer and it tells us some answers to some problems very quickly. I hope humanity will not become just mere computers, that we will remain men and women. Maybe this music is a bit of an antidote.

You have also been a pioneer in technology involved with music, in recordings and film and television. What do you see for the future in terms of cassettes, video-tape and sound? Have you become interested in them?

Oh yes, I think they are all new developments. What I would like to see is something I worked on in Holland with the Philips company. We and our ancestors are accustomed to going to the concert hall where at one end is the stage and the sound waves come to us. We listen to the music reflected from two side walls and the ceiling—and to some extent from the crowd and what comes back, what reflects from the other end of the hall. We are accustomed to that directional way of listening. Philips has started a system of loud speakers in four corners of the room—you sit in the middle and listen to the music non-directionally with the whole room full of soundwaves. It was not possible in Mozart's time or even 60 or 70 years ago. Concert halls were much smaller than they are now. The Salle Gaveau in Paris, where Ravel heard most of his music, has very good acoustics but is quite small. Carnegie Hall is five times the size and Philharmonic five or six times the size. So if we play Ravel in Philharmonic Hall we must expand it five times—otherwise we will not hear it and the public will not hear it as Ravel conceived it in volume.

Do you think video cassettes are a threat to the future of live performance? If people will be able to go to the store and buy a performance by you and the American Symphony, do you think they will come to hear the concerts?

We never know the future. It is now 6 o'clock. We don't know what will happen at 8 o'clock tonight or midnight or tomorrow—nobody knows. Some people think they know, but they really don't, because suddenly, like today, a man in Cairo dies. It changes the whole aspect of his Arabic world. There may be civil war, different generals trying to gain control until it settles down. So yesterday we did not know. Let us not think we know the future or try to control it, but let's develop it. Everything in life—let's develop it better, make it warmer, with more vitality and more vision, looking into the future.

What would you say have been the proudest accomplishments of your career—or the most memorable events?

There was never anything like that. The love of music is a continuous life of enjoying beauty and sound. Sound in three dimensions—one is frequency, another is intensity, another is duration. All music is composed of those three dimensions, whether it is our kind or Chinese or Japanese or any kind. It has been a continual effort to make music more alive, so that it is not a mechanical reproduction of what is on a piece of paper—but a real expression, as it always was with the greatest artists.

★ Jess Thomas ★

When first interviewed in 1969, Jess Thomas had just made the big plunge into the full Heldentenor *repertoire and was singing Tristan in concert with Leonard Bernstein and the New York Philharmonic. When caught up with in the summer of 1971, he was preparing to sing Tristan at the Metropolitan in the splendid new Everding-Schneider-Siemssen production, and had just appeared in the new Covent Garden production directed by Peter Hall. This profile draws on both our talks.*

Just by glancing down at his left hand, you know he has taken the big plunge. There a magnificent star-ruby ring—encircled by two gold Ts, symbolizing Tristan and Tannhäuser—tells you that Jess Thomas has tossed down his gauntlet to the challenge of undoubtedly the most demanding repertoire for the tenor voice, Wagner's *Heldentenor* breed. Just a few years ago he was saying, "In my repertoire, I must have a large mixture of styles and languages. . . . Today, my Wagnerian repertoire consists only of three roles—Lohengrin, Walther in *Die*

Meistersinger, and Parsifal—the roles associated with what is called a *jugendlich Heldentenor.* But, of course, the goal of all Wagnerian tenors is Tannhäuser."

Just a few wintry months ago, the story had been very much altered. Jess Thomas—in the intervening years during which he neared the forty-year mark—had gone for broke in the Wagnerian sweepstakes. He had made the important transition as a full-fledged heroic Wagnerian tenor—Tannhäuser, Tristan, Siegmund and, finally, Siegfried.

It is only 90 or so years since the very term *Heldentenor* came into being, with Wagner's creation of such heroic roles demanding endurance, projection and the vocal range of a tenor with the colorings of a baritone. Herman Winkelmann, Joseph Tichatschek, Alois Ander, Albert Niemann, Georg Unger, Ludwig Schnorr von Carolsfeld—names of dim history today, but these were the first to be dubbed *Heldentenor.* The new operas of Wagner created the need for this dramatic voice. Winkelmann became the first Tristan, Tichatschek the first Tannhäuser, Unger the first Siegfried.

G. B. Shaw had some interesting observations about Wagnerian singing in *The Perfect Wagnerite,* 1898: "With the single exception of Handel, no composer has written music so well calculated to make its singers vocal athletes as Wagner. Instead of specializing his vocal parts after the manner of Verdi and Gounod for high sopranos, screaming tenors and high baritones, and for contraltos with chest registers forced all over their compass in the manner of music-hall singers, he employs the entire range of the human voice freely, demanding from everybody very nearly two effective octaves, so that the voice is well exercised all over." Of the dramatic demands, Hanslick was to note in 1883, after the first Vienna *Tristan* with Winkelmann: "Wagner, by imposing increasingly difficult task upon his singers for the past thirty years, has strongly developed and strengthened their memories—just as continuous gymnastics achieve strengthening of muscles."

This *Heldentenor* classification, emerging from Wagner's maturing operatic style, was not always met, however, in terms of freedom, heroicism and the requisite *bel canto* style Wagner himself wanted. Tichatschek was praised for a brilliant voice, damned for his lack of subtlety—and he failed as Tannhäuser.

Ander (the first Vienna Lohengrin) found Tristan impossible, despite his vocal ability. Niemann, the first Bayreuth Siegmund and first Paris Tannhäuser, was called a crude artist led only by his basic instincts. About Unger, one critic wrote: "He was the earliest of a class of *Heldentenors* that has since been numerous in Germany, by whom pure singing and the preservation of the voice seem to be systematically avoided." The ideal seemed to be embodied in von Carolsfeld—the first Tristan—who seemed the only man able to combine the vocal stamina and poetic insight Wagner had been seeking. The composer said of him that the way he "could pierce the soul can be compared with nothing but magic."

By common consent, present operatic circles have been bereft of such supermen as these, a situation made even more vivid by the fact that the last of these powerhouses was the phenomenal Lauritz Melchior. The need has grown in epic proportions in every leading opera house, including the citadel itself, Bayreuth. And Jess Thomas—developing along an intelligent, shrewdly plotted way beginning with his debut at the Baden State Theater in Karlsruhe in 1958 and moving on to Munich, Bayreuth, Vienna, Berlin, Salzburg, San Francisco, London and the Met—has come face to face with Wagner's heroes. How has it happened?

"For the past years," he admits, "the question has always been *when* to make the jump into the heavy repertoire. My teacher said only *if* first—the *when* will come when you feel you can sing a Tamino the next day. Then this might be the time. In San Francisco, after the *Tristan* premiere (you don't sleep much after such a performance!) I woke up early and ran to the piano and sang the 'Bildnis' aria—and it worked." The magnet, too, has been his continuing work since 1961 at Bayreuth with the late Wieland Wagner. As early as 1961, he was after Thomas for a new production of *Tristan und Isolde*. "Oh, dear God," was all the tenor could respond, and Wagner's grandchild even offered to make the necessary cuts as a further inducement—but to no avail.

"Later," Thomas says, "Wieland and I discussed how to make the jump. He said Siegfried, then Tristan and, finally, Tannhäuser, since the latter is the most difficult vocally. But I did just the opposite, feeling that Tannhäuser was better for me. I was not a really heavy type *Heldentenor,* more a *jugend-lich Heldentenor* with a passable top—and the things in the role were better for me. The top of Tannhäuser is worse than any other tenor role in the repertoire, with more high As in the first act alone than in all of any other opera." Ironically, it was with Wieland Wagner that he sang his first *Helden* role at Bayreuth in 1966, and it was the last role the late director worked with anyone.

"I've gone out on a long limb, I admit. The vogue today is to be a Renaissance man, and I want to be just that in my private life—but not in my professional life any more. I've committed myself almost exclusively to the Wagnerian repertoire, except for Strauss and Beethoven, lieder and eventually *Otello,* when the right constellation of house, conductor and director comes along. After Tristan [which he sang for the first time with the San Francisco Opera in the fall of 1967], nothing seems difficult. Then in Vienna, we did the third act complete with no cuts, something which only Bayreuth had regularly done—and this was a challenge. I will do my first *Siegfried* this spring in Salzburg and next August at Bayreuth I'll do my first *Götterdämmerung* Siegfried. Then I will have come full circle in my Wagnerian heroes. So now I limit myself to Wagner. In Vienna, my home, I have given back Mario in *Tosca* and other roles. It's just not possible to keep up all the repertoire. I want a commitment to the Wagnerian school!"

For one who began his singing career as Fenton in *Falstaff* (Stanford University) and proceeded to build his reputation with the diversity of Tamino in *Die Zauberflöte* and Radames in *Aida,* the route has been one of steady vocal development, as well as the psychological preparation to tackle these monumental parts. And Thomas specifies very definite conditions about becoming a Wagnerian: "I have no intention of becoming the loudest *Heldentenor* that ever sang. I want to give new facets—quality, voice and complete involvement in the role. And I don't make excuses because my voice is not large enough! This is no rationalization, because it is more important to *sing* every one of the roles, to sing and phrase in both the lyric and dramatic moments. This was the intent of Wagner, but over the years singers have gotten off the track. When

it is done in the right way, it all jells. When I did my first
Parsifal at Bayreuth with Knappertsbusch, I learned the greatness of his interpretation, of the classic, old school. Even in
Tristan, the most dramatically written role, in the great moment of the third act at his outbreak, '*Verfluchter Tag mit
deinem Schein!'*—at this great outbreak, Wagner wrote in the
score, 'Don't ever leave a sung tone': in other words, do not
shout, do not leave the singing line and the *vocal* interpretation. Yet we all can forget this and fall into the pit of trying
for a dramatic moment."

The most obvious point of comparison any *Heldentenor*
faces today is that of the inevitable Melchior, and this Thomas
feels strongly about, too. "The only comparison that can be
made is that we sang the same roles. Otherwise, it is completely wrong and irrelevant, like comparing Melba and
Sutherland. I wish that there were a better understood word
for *Heldentenor.* The word is outgrown today—we need a
new name, like we have for our modern heroes and cham-
pions and astronauts. Martin Bernheimer in the *Los Angeles
Times* came up with 'heir apparent to the heavy, dramatic
Wagnerian roles,' avoiding mention of that word *Helden,* a
word that has both good and bad connotations."

Has Karajan's controversial approach to the *Ring* had any
influence on his decision to enter the Wagnerian ranks? "Of
course, this way is not without voice. Karajan in *Time* last
fall said, in essence, that since the great voices are no more,
we must shut off the orchestra, adjust the orchestra to the
voices of today. This was Wieland Wagner's idea always, too.
People have mistaken the music over the years by emphasizing
the *forte* climax when, in fact, the music should be stressed at
the *piano* climaxes. Wagner is one composer who made known
what he wanted, since he built a place expressly for what he
desired. He wanted a covered orchestra, and at Bayreuth the
orchestra can blare and you still hear the voices. Conductors
should keep this in mind in other theaters."

The very structure of Wagner's operas, or music-dramas,
has demanded that the dramatic aspects of a part be on an
equal plane with the vocal, and it is this dramatic involvement,
this character identification—to bring these characters alive
—that has eluded many who had all the notes in the throat.

Irene Dalis—with whom Thomas has sung often at Bayreuth and with whom he sang his first Tristan to her first Isolde—has said that he was "one of a handful of singers who become so involved you forget that you are actually performing." A clue to his method is his background in clinical psychology before he ever considered a musical career. He has a deep psychological fascination with every character, giving scientific impetus to his interpretations.

"There are so many levels for each character. My interest in Wagner has grown because of the levels of understanding and probing. He was so full of genius in so many ways. It goes without saying that there is the sensuality of the music on the surface. Then you go deeper to understand the periods of when the music was written, of the people of the time and their interactions. And then deeper to the eternal problems of human beings throughout time.

"The symbolism, too, is interesting—and this comes from long work with Wieland Wagner—particularly the *constant* in every opera of Richard Wagner, as expressed in words by the Landgraf in *Tannhäuser* in the second act when he says: 'Tell me the purest essence of love.' Wieland's idea was that his grandfather was trying to project this very thing in every single opera. Both Siegfried and Parsifal, for instance, face the confrontation with Purpose and Woman. Parsifal's meeting with Kundry brings him to the moment of decision and he rejects all sensuality, taking the course of purity and the Grail. With Siegfried, Brünnhilde is the first woman he sees, and she awakens him so that he goes to the human direction. The two men develop in two opposite ways. I see both facing the Moment of Truth—maybe it's the Presbyterian background in me. Their moment of decision seals their doom. I don't think you can call Parsifal's end a satisfying or warm human experience, and the agonies of Siegfried's death are not a happy end either."

Siegfried, Thomas admits, is a difficult role to come to terms with. "But I think that if the wound of Hagen's sword in *Götterdämmerung* were not fatal, then Siegfried and his period of development would be at the same place as Tristan at the beginning of Act I. Tristan lives ahead of Siegfried, so that if Siegfreid had gone on, he would be Tristan.

"Tristan is far more developed. He is noble, with a set of values that are hard to understand today. But in Act III alone is revealed the central part of his character. He is on a trip—like the one world youth is on today—of drugs, despair, discovery, doubt, one of critical self-analysis of where one is from and where he is going, of existence itself. Wagner produces in musical form the raw fiber of existence as I've never heard before. *Tristan* is the peak of his genius—it speaks strongly today, amazing for an opera one hundred years old. I tell students to sit and hear the sound, and it will be a psychedelic experience for them. Music, we know, produces a chemical change in the body, in mentality. If things are presented today, we must make them live for today."

About a really ideal production of *Tristan* the tenor says he can imagine it any number of ways—he'd even be willing to play Act Two in the nude, given the right director, circumstances and, no doubt, the right Isolde. He imagines it in modern dress too, because of the relevance of the story. "The opera is so apropos today because it is a search for identity, for the shadowy side of our identities which leads to the productive or destructive sides of our personality. Their love is selfish and destructive—the solution is death. It is a brutal story, it's a complete denial of all values either one has set up.

"Their union at the end—is it two atoms at the end of an explosion . . . is it two individuals who become one . . . is it two selfish people who become selfless? Even after much discussion, no one knows what the answer is . . . but there is resolution in the music, the two are transfigured. Wagner's directions are that she falls lifeless on his body—and in 1865 that was pretty exciting stuff."

Of all the roles, Thomas finds Tannhäuser the most uplifting, and he was praised in Bayreuth for his thoroughly modern, Freudian interpretation when he sang it for the first time in 1966—a far cry from the customary "heroic" portrayal of the role. "He is a manic-depressive who cannot tolerate anything that is not hot or cold. He knows no middle ground or compromise: it must either be religious ecstasy or sensual passion. Despite this passion and madness, he does all he does knowing the consequence of damnation. He dies knowing he has destroyed himself and Elisabeth—but, at the moment when the staff turns green, he is forgiven. The question for me in performance is *when* to die. Wieland and I talked and agreed that Tannhäuser should feel the staff turn with his eyes open—at this symbolic moment, he should show a final sign of life.

"As a serious-minded artist," he argues, "I've got to find what is *in* these roles. And I don't think this decision is put on the wrong horse—it is all there in the operas! The purpose is deep in Wagner. In most Italian librettos, there is not much in the characters to discover or develop. Even Erik in *Die fliegende Holländer* is one Wagnerian role I will never do. It is beautiful to sing, but the character says nothing to me. It's the same with Alfredo in *Traviata,* which I tried over fifty times early in my career—but he always came out a milksop."

It was Kirsten Flagstad who said that when singing Wagner "One should build a voice from the low notes to the high ones—the low notes are always important." Thomas, in the manner of many other famous *Heldentenors,* began as a baritone. "I really wasn't a baritone," he confesses, "but I sang in this range first. However, I am basically more tenor. My doctor said that no man on earth could tell by my vocal cords if I am a tenor or baritone. The tenor sound is an unnatural one —the thrilling point of the voice, the last four or five notes, are not natural but are 'made-and-paid-for' notes. If the top is stressed in Wagner, the richness is missing in the low and middle voice. You have the choice of two things: there is never perfection. For me, I do not open the middle and bottom for a broad sound there, I keep it tenor all the way through the voice for the lyric moments, for the high soft passages. There is nothing in Wagner's vocal writing that is against the voice or wrongly emphasized, even though he stretches it to the limits. Can you imagine any tenor or soprano singing an *Aida* as long as *Tristan?"*

He stresses that "in Wagner, as in the love act or a good book, the climax cannot be consistent. You must build up and stretch out the beautiful lyric moments, so that the climax becomes more important. Psychologically, it is important to have nuances. So I hope we get to the place when something doesn't have to be the biggest in the world to be good.

"We have to have more than the voice. Birgit Nilsson is not

successful strictly because she has a fabulous voice. As Wieland once said, she became great after she became famous. She refines her art, works constantly and doesn't just strut out on stage to say 'I have the biggest voice.' She does something with it." At the same time he feels his voice is growing too. Singing, he states, is like a strenuous athletic feat—the muscles grow and stretch. "I'm in my final development at this age (a few years over 40), when the tendons harden and the whole structure is harder. It's the peak of my development . . . from now on it's downhill," he smiles slightly uneasily. To keep the voice from turning hard, there must be technique and flexibility—so Thomas trains from a purely physical point of view in what he terms "a Renaissance approach. I'm stuck in hotels, so I have an expander for my arms and yoga exercises for breathing and flexibility—I still have a full lotus. I also do diaphragm exercises to relax the gut . . . and I hike, swim and ride."

Jess Thomas derived great artistic reward from his work with Wieland Wagner, and the composer's grandson profoundly influenced his thinking as an operatic actor. At that time Thomas began designing productions and discussing them with Wieland, who referred to him as "Herr Kolleg." "I asked him what he thought and he said that before I do anything elsewhere to come to him—but that he needed me on stage now. I feel cheated, because I could have been his apprentice if he had lived. I've had several offers to produce opera and am very interested. But it's still a question of when, why and how. I came close this past year, but I don't want to mix metaphors yet—I can't do both now!"

Now that he has run the course, slowly and wisely seeking his grail of all the great *Heldentenor* roles and winning acclaim for them, what happens inside when he notes another new Tristan in this opera house or a new Siegfried in that one? "There is no competition," he frankly states, "because in Wagner there are not enough singers to go around. If I see any new young ones, I say 'God bless them,' because we need them. I need relief all over, because sometimes I feel I'm on a team where I play eleven positions. There's room for everyone . . . the top is so uncrowded. If I see that Jon Vickers, for instance, is doing Tristan, I know he can do it differently

. . . if and when he does it. No one can operate metaphysically to express what I can, the way I do it. It's as simple as that. The only competition I set up for myself is my own standard. 'Christ, I know I can do better,' I'll say to myself. But if you begin competing with someone else, you create a totally unrealistic standard—one day it's this one, the next day that one.

"It's hard for me to be objective about my own performances. I don't like the sound of my own voice, because I hear it differently than others do. I don't know how it sounds, except in my head and throat. The basic thing is that when a human being meets a challenge (for me it's the notes of the great Wagner) it elicits a will to do the best he can—and I consume myself in this. Someone may say that singers are overpaid or underpaid, but no one could really pay me for the physical and mental exertion of a Tristan. So it has to be something more than money, some kind of flame that burns inside you. Someone recently gave me a gift, an old card with a Breton fisherman's prayer that is so implicit, so simple: 'Dear God, be good to me. The sea is so wide and my boat so small.' That's the way I feel when I stand up there. Even with a singer's enormous egotism, humility is required."

★ *Michael Tilson Thomas* ★

The fall of 1970 was an important time for young conductor Michael Tilson Thomas, for it was just a year after he had made headlines by jumping in for the ailing William Steinberg, later being appointed Associate Conductor of the Boston Symphony. Since then he has gone on to the conductorship of the Buffalo Philarmonic (with his innovative series of "Spectrum" concerts), directorship of the New York Philharmonic's Young People's Concerts (televised nationally by CBS-TV) and an

exclusive contract with Columbia Records where he is explor-
ing all sorts of offbeat music.

Still in his mid-twenties, Michael Tilson Thomas is very much
his own man. His kind of intensity, penetrating analysis, intellectual curiosity and highly original musicianship have already made him a special spirit in the musical arena. Not too
many people knew just who Michael Tilson Thomas was
until October of 1969, when immediately after becoming Assistant Conductor with the Boston Symphony he was called
on to replace the ailing William Steinberg midway through a
Philharmonic Hall concert. A few days later at Carnegie Hall
he conducted the same program with which he had made his
Boston Symphony debut in Symphony Hall some weeks earlier.
During the 1969-70 season, after conducting more than thirty
concerts with the Orchestra, he was appointed Associate Conductor. Now, of course, the dam has burst. There are engagements in Europe and with the New York Philharmonic, and
recordings for DGG with the Boston Symphony.

One of his most compelling qualities stems from his own
statement: "What's interesting about a lot of the young conductors—I mean anybody between the cradle and about 50
or so, or 40 anyway . . . 40 is the traditional period, I
guess, between being a young conductor and a distinguished
conductor—what's interesting is that the young conductors I
know who are close to my own age don't have quite so much
the sense of one model. Like, I know a lot of people in their
thirties who model themselves after a specific older conductor
whom they admire. But whether it's because of more exposure
to more different kinds of music, because of TV or because of
records or just because of the sudden burgeoning of all kinds
of music that we all grew up hearing, I feel there have been a
lot of polar influences in my musical development—but I don't
feel that I could say that I am really a disciple of or I am part
of this. There are just too many conflicting things, which is
very exciting."

The result, he feels, is that he doesn't have to search around
for music that would be interesting for its own sake, or for
something new or for something exciting. "It is just automatically there—it comes to mind because it's part of the way I

think about music. Like last night, the concert we did in Boston was really a crazy concert, but it proved something to me. We did the Bach Suite No. 4, then Lou Harrison's *Canticle No. 2* for Percussion, Guitar and Ocarina, *La Valse,* intermission, and then the Piston Second Symphony. It was really a crazy concert! But it was a *huge* success. In the Bach, you know, you start off with a small orchestra with trumpets and strings—and then suddenly you have an ensemble of only seven on stage for the Harrison. When I came out for it, the audience was really confused, because they thought we were still setting up and the orchestra wasn't there yet—and suddenly there was the conductor! But they went wild after the Harrison because it makes such a glorious racket—it's such a lovely piece. Then suddenly to have *La Valse* come on stage is like the whole world or something arrives—because the stage has nobody on it and suddenly it's mobbed with people. This is the kind of thing that I think does make programming and music-making exciting. It's not doing everything in a predictable way."

What he says follows Pierre Boulez' statement that he sees nothing wrong with regarding the orchestra as a great museum with all different kinds of wares on display—but that today the orchestras aren't good museums because they only do a very restricted part of their repertory without breaking up the orchestra into small ensembles for earlier works. Thomas' repertory with the Boston Symphony this season, however, encompasses a piece of 15th-century organum and the Harrison of 1968. "I am incorporating these pieces and I am doing them, again, in orders which I feel sound well. I'm not concerned too much with the way it looks on paper. As a matter of fact, last night the composer David Del Tredici said to me, 'You know, this program looks absolutely impossible on paper—but when you hear it, it's marvelous.' And I really have to kind of put myself into the situation. What would it be like to finish this piece, and what would this piece sound like afterwards? It's a matter of contrast and also I'm a great fan of retrogression. I don't believe in historical order, because I find that going from Messiaen to Schütz or Gabrieli creates such a powerful shock with this very triadic music coming afterwards—it's really much more interesting to me this way. On another program I am putting a Baroque work with Stockhausen's *Punkte* and Schumann's Third Symphony —and on another I'm doing a piece first by Harrison Birtwhistle for only ten players (a 20th-century piece and very strident) followed by a Haydn *Salomon* Symphony, which puts the whole idea of a Haydn symphony in a very different light."

From a purely pragmatic point of view, this kind of programming has generally been a problem in terms of unions and rehearsal regulations and employment of the full regiment of musicians. But Thomas says it can be done: "You have to plan rehearsals very carefully and it very often means that I don't get any break in the rehearsal. When I was an orchestral musician playing the oboe, the thing that I absolutely despised and that all players despise is waiting while another instrument works out a difficult passage. So what I generally do is plan ahead to accomplish what I want. I think in my mind that there are a lot of sections in the piece which require balancing or whatever, and I split the rehearsal so that I give the winds a break, then the strings—so that during these two twenty-minute periods I can accomplish the work that has to be done with them, while the other people have their break; then I reverse the situation. Then everyone comes back and we play together. This means I get no break, but that's not important. It's much better for the orchestra not to have to waste its time."

Michael Tilson Thomas, as he admits, is part of the new guard of conductors, a new generation which does not bridge the gap with the older disciples of the late 19th century, a tradition or school that produced a Szell, a Reiner and a Klemperer. Thomas always comes back to the term "polar personalities" as far as his education is concerned. There were days in Los Angeles, he relates, when he would work with cellist Gregor Piatigorsky in the morning and Pierre Boulez in the afternoon. "And the teachers I worked with at the University were also obstinate types; the work I was doing in contemporary music and improvisation, etc., was very different from the kind of work I was doing in chamber music class. But it was all building a kind of total picture rather than the feeling that I was committed to *one* particular idea. This is why I really feel that there have to be these polar kinds of situations, because if you study only with one person, you develop a proprietary interest in the ideas of that particular teacher. Some of the most distinguished conservatories are classic examples of this. And that's such a pity because there are very different and fascinating people in the same place, so that students could have contact with lots of them and learn a great deal. But they feel that they must allow themselves but one teacher, and the teacher insists upon this, and it becomes very restrictive. That's one very good thing about the West Coast, because this wasn't that way at all. Everyone is very open . . . at least I experienced it so."

Then he qualifies: "That's not bad; in other words, one expects that as a student you are going to be very much under the spell of a teacher for a while. That's a very good thing, because that's how you learn—but hopefully there always comes that day when you realize that, despite your respect for the teacher, you must do it your own way—you just feel it must be this other way, and you do it. Or, what's really more likely is that you think it should be a certain way and your teacher tells you, 'No, it should be done this way,' and so you do it your teacher's way. Then, after the performance and after you've done it that way, you say, 'No, next time I do it my way.' I know exactly when it happened with me, the piece and everything. It was Mozart's Symphony No. 34, it was about the second movement and my super-beloved, super-respected, great teacher Ingolf Dahl thought he wanted me to do it in four and I felt it should be in two. In the performance I did it in four and I was very dissatisfied —and ever since that time I have done it in two."

Thomas says he knew he wanted to be a conductor when he came to the Berkshire Music Center at Tanglewood during 1968—only two and a half years ago!—even though at that point he still played the piano and was composing and involved in scholarship in various ways. But at the end of Tanglewood, after having conducted the premiere of Stanley Silverman's *Elephant Steps* and winning the Koussevitzky Prize in conducting, his mind was made up. Six years earlier he had enrolled at the University of Southern California with advanced standing (because he had attended the University simultaneously with his last two years at high school). His father's family, the Thomashefskys, had been connected with the theater for several generations. His father had come to Los Angeles to work for Paul Muni, to write and revise material for him. "But I really should say something about my mother's family. She is a teacher, but before she was head of the research department at Columbia Pictures. Now she is very much involved in changing ideas of education concepts, concept-oriented education, in the L.A. city schools. I think I've said so much about all the things I've gotten from my father, but I think that from my mother there are these immense areas in which she was acquainted. It was a home in which literature and art and music and science and philosophy and psychiatry and everything were always being discussed. I was an only child, and most of the people I saw up to the time I was 10 or 11 or 12 were thirty or forty years older than I. There were lots of books always and trips to museums and things like that. And I never minded being by myself, working by myself."

Musically he began his formal musical studies at 10, but he played by ear. "I couldn't pass the piano, so my parents tell me, without touching it. They always knew when I was coming and going, because our house had a large living room and the piano was at one end of it, right next to the door that went into a hall where the bedrooms were—and they could tell exactly where I was because every time I would go back and forth between the living room and another part of the house I would have to go by the piano and have to play it. Lots of pieces I heard on records. It's interesting, the pieces I liked. A friend had a large record collection and the ones I liked most and that I played right through when I was like four or five were the Brahms Haydn Variations, the Bach B-minor Piano Concerto. Prokofiev's G-minor Violin Concerto and *The Rite of Spring* . . . and the Mozart G-minor." Not exactly an unsophisticated beginning. For four years he was conductor of the Young Musicians Foundation Debut Orchestra at the Music Center. At the Monday Evening Concerts he was conductor and piano soloist in many premieres of Stravinsky, Boulez, Stockhausen, Foss and Dahl. He also played for the

Piatigorsky classes and prepared the orchestra for the Heifetz-Piatigorsky concerts.

Then in 1966 he went abroad to the Bayreuth Festival, where he became assistant to Boulez on the production of *Parsifal.* "Actually, that was the first time somebody got sick and I stepped in," he smiles. "I learned a great deal there because I really went there in a rather antagonistic frame of mind. I went because Larry Foster—who had been my predecessor in conducting the Musicians Foundation Orchestra —whom I respected enormously and still do, said, 'It's a very good thing and you should go.' But I had been through a Wagner phase before and thought I was really kind of out of that, and well . . . you know. But then I thought it's an interesting place and I'll go . . . I'm sure I'll learn something. At least if I decide to dismiss this music, I'll be able to dismiss it from a standpoint of great familiarity.

"So I went and this position suddenly became available, I got it and I was just clobbered by Wagner—I just got completely converted! I really just worshipped that music. In that atmosphere you get the balances of the orchestra and the stage, the focus upon the stage with no distraction. It's very sad that people criticize Wagner and condemn the *Ring* and so on without really knowing it, or the one opera they do know is *Walküre,* which is probably the weakest, I think . . . except, well, the first act is great. But people criticize the *Ring* without even knowing *Götterdämmerung* at all, which is just . . . well, I can't imagine even a quarter-note being deleted from it. It's so solidly inspired, absolutely brilliant. The terror, the psychological intensity of those pieces! There are no successors! I used to play rehearsals, stage rehearsals—and even when I had been through it and I knew how it moved, how it worked and everything else, my hands would shake—not from cold but from terror, because of what is embodied in that music. And, of course, the whole message of the *Ring:* that all the people who lust after power are destroyed."

Perhaps this image of lusting after power has made the young conductor a unique podium figure in rehearsal, someone who has been quoted as saying: "The musicians and I are completely honest with each other. If I find that something is not going well, if my directions are not getting through, then I have no hesitation about going to the musicians to ask them how I can be more effective." Yes, he feels the day of the autocratic conductor is finished in terms of high-handed treatment. "I always found that I very often performed or worked according to what I felt the expectations were. And I generally found that if you put your faith in a player or a group of players and show that you really want a certain kind of sensitivity and a certain kind of giving on their part— generally you get it. They're very happy to give it and get into that sort of relationship, which is a wonderfully exciting thing. Look, I mean it's a very easy thing to be an arrogant son-of-a-bitch conductor! Because you are out there and you're nasty and harsh—and you probably get a good result, maybe, if you can scare them into it. And if you don't get a good result, well, then you've already adopted the position of, 'Well, these awful people . . .' and so you're protected.

"On the other hand, if you go out and what you really want is collaboration with the orchestra—this mutual understanding, this thing that you build together—there will be times, you must realize, when it won't work, when you aren't going to get what you think should happen, or the magic doesn't happen. And when that happens, then you are in a much more vulnerable position. I mean, you have been rejected. You have placed yourself in all good faith on the line, you stood there with your hands open and have asked for something and given something—and it didn't happen. So that's much more difficult psychologically to deal with."

Behind this attitude lies an even deeper significance, because Thomas believes that if a difficult conductor puts the orchestra on its mettle, he is saying, "O.K., there is a performance which is already *there* in the orchestra which maybe is descended from Maestro X and so and so. It's already there, and if you are difficult enough you can get them to play that performance."—"That's exactly what is wrong with music at the moment," Thomas insists, "because we cannot go on playing *that* performance. The whole point is that one must each time *re*create the piece. The excitement of doing a piece in one place and then in another place with different people is that you have different people, there are different factors. There are different acoustics involved . . . everything is different. Then you make this performance for this place for these people under these conditions, with everybody giving. But just to repeat the same performance always, that's death!"

As for the future of concerts and the symphony orchestra, he does not wax enthusiastically over combining rock and symphonic music—"It does a terrible disservice to both musics"—or mixed media—"Most mixed media, it seems to me, disguise or attempt to disguise the fact that some particular level of the work is not very good, whether it's the music or the visual or the text. I'm only interested if it works on every level, but generally it requires much more work than what people generally want to put into it." As for what is going on in new music today, he hedges at first: "I have my own very strong preferences for what I like, what I'm interested in hearing. There's music interesting to hear and certain music that's not interesting to hear." Pause. "Well, I do not like very much collage pieces and I think they're not very effective because they operate generally on a principle of a continuous 'something' happening. And there's not enough figure-ground relationship there. As a matter of fact, I would say that that's one of the great problems of a lot of new music. And it's very interesting that two of the composers who very much kicked the ball in this direction have totally retreated from it—the problem being that above a certain number of parts, above a certain density of activity, it's meaningless. One can't hear it and it becomes simply a texture and a texture which can be recreated by another means. So then you say, O.K., you have like the Polish school of music where it is all texture and you just sort of generally try to play the part and it comes out. And then I say, 'Well, that's very fine, except I find texture rather boring.'

"I want ideas, perceivable, beautiful, musical ideas which are dealt with in an interesting way. It's interesting to see the enormous simplicity in Boulez' and Stockhausen's recent music, composers whose music at one time had great density. Actually, they aren't the ultimate sinners. I think American music incorporates certain excesses of activities going on— specific parts going on—so many that it's beyond perceptual ability, at least at this time." At the same time he is interested

in aleatory or chance music or improvisation when it is interesting and not cliché ridden. "I think what I'm really *for* are
decisions. I mean, after all, composing is a process of choosing
things. And what's interesting about a piece is to see what has
been chosen and what has been left out. When the piece is
such that either everything is there . . . or the choices are
so anonymous . . . or so much based on something completely impersonal like total serialization that one has no
impression of what is there and what has been left out, then
that's not so interesting. That's why I'm so interested to hear
this performance of *Hymnen,* which the Philharmonic is doing,
because the electronic piece itself is a masterwork. I love it
simply because the choice is made and the kinds of develop-
mental processes that go on are *so* personal and *so* powerful.
And the same with Boulez' new piece, *Domaines*—it's very
personal, with very powerful decisions. But, of course, those
two always did make very personal and powerful decisions."

He admires what he calls a kind of "enormous boldness"
about the best of American composers, "a boldness either in
the kind of sweeping grandness or power of the gesture, or
else just the reverse of that, the completely minimal kind of
thing that happens. And in between those I think that sometimes where American composers get in trouble is in their
pursuit of what they consider to be intellectually respectable.
This whole movement of intellectual respectability really
started off in Europe in the Fifties and unfortunately seems
to have swept over everything. You can see why this happened, because, after all, the two great composers of the 20th
century, Stravinsky and Schoenberg, both started out writing
music based on just what they chose and neither of them could
sustain it. Neither could go on choosing within the framework
of just what the next note would be. So they both developed
kinds of systems and styles, really systems, which allowed more
possibility for the system itself to determine a good deal—
like a total system. But, again, you know, it's that *choice,* that
specific choice that is the most interesting thing musically. A
piece has to have limitations, because things have to be left
out. But the limitations have to grow *out* of the piece. When
you start off with a limitation and then write the piece based
on a limit, that's not so satisfactory."

Thomas himself composes, and in a variety of styles—he calls it a good way of learning about music. "Yes, I choose every note. It is so hard, this business of choosing. It's an enormous strain but, by God, some of the best music is written just that way, and it's *hard*. I think that most of the systems that have been evolved for escaping have not worked out so successfully—except in the cases of Schoenberg, Berg, Webern and Stravinsky, who were all people who first knew how to choose consummately. And then they could make any system lose the classic example of how you can write whatever music you want using serial music. If you have a powerful way of making choices and what you're after is clear enough in your mind, then you can get all those variation tunes out of *Lulu,* and it all works out."

From looking at his programs it is obvious that Thomas is drawn to the neo-classic period in 20th-century music—and he does, in fact, feel that it's time for another look at the music which ten years ago was obliterated by the whole new wave of total serialism and electronics. "But now, in this time when the clichés of the 1950's and 1960's are with us, one listens to the music of the Forties and early Fifties and can sort out which is the best. Clichés are sort of modish at the moment in avant-garde music. It's very funny that I should be saying this because I'm really very much involved with performing this music, but I try to be very honest about what I think. Because if I hear one more piece in which there's sort of disjunct activity which gradually—it's very sparse at first—builds up to an enormous *crescendo* and there's a whole wall of sound which then all at once cuts out, leaving six cellos playing harmonics *pianississimo*—if I hear that one more time I'm going to incinerate that piece, no matter who has written it!"

Just at the time he was entering college in California he was trying to choose between music and a career in science or, more precisely, in crystallography. "But I think my musical thinking is very much influenced by my studies of crystallography and the special integrity of those fields—particularly in terms of my sense of formal balance. When I study a piece or when I rehearse it, what I try to do is first to work vigorously on just the bones—I mean knowing how it's put together, how it works, how it happens, what's there, what's exactly on the page and what's happening in the orchestra. And in the same way in the rehearsal . . . getting things together and getting it right! And knowing what's on the page; and if I do it right, that means that during the performance I can forget everything. I can just allow my whole non-rational faculty to take over and to work that way. And that's the most exciting thing: to have found that freedom of letting yourself open up and just fusing completely with the music. There's nothing like that feeling of complete freedom . . . if the rehearsal work has been done right.

"Generally, when I study a piece, I study it completely according to what is on that page—and what I know about sources and stylistic practices of that period. And I might say that here's a big difference between the generations in conductors. I went to a university and had three or four years or whatever of classes in performance practices of many periods —Middle Ages, Renaissance, Baroque and so on—with notation transcription and all that. And even though I wouldn't classify myself as an authority on these subjects, I know enough about them and the sources that I possess and how to collate them, so that I'm not limited to just what is on the page before me. I can look at it and, in addition, say 'Ah, ha! This particular transcription is not really accurate notationally . . . and the barring probably should go like this.' And I can go to an original manuscript and get some idea of what that's about. And that's an enormous difference right away, because it opens up the large area in terms of repertoire. But even in the 19th century there are whole areas in terms of size of orchestra and numbers of people who play at any one time that remain to be explored and liven up the institution of just having a group of people on stage who always play. And this Bach Suite I've been doing with the BSO: I mean the numbers of examples of not only *soli* and *tutti* but also instrumental choirs alternating rhythmically, double-dotting and ornamentation and ornamented repeated schemes and such—it takes a long time to work these things out, but they come off very effectively."

A great musician he defines as a person who knows all the things that are *not* printed in the score. He knows everything that's there and understands it and understands the way a piece is built, etc. But at the same time he knows exactly what has to be done and all the things that aren't printed. "The kind of performance I'm really interested in is not a correct performance. I'm interested in a *revelatory* performance. I go to a performance even if it's a piece that I conduct—but I don't want to hear it the way that I do it. I'm not one of those people who sits there and shakes his head and says, 'No, no, no, this is wrong.' And I hate that kind of provincial attitude. No, I want to hear somebody else's performance, just as if I were an actor I would want to hear someone else perform his Hamlet or Lear or whatever—to see another perspective. And I want it to be a revelation. I want to see things in that piece that I never knew were there. Even if it infuriates me. I don't care, as long as I feel that there's some real original perspective operating, some original interpretive perspective. Records have done a disservice to us all in this respect. People judge things by a fixed model.

"Piatigorsky tells this wonderful story which affected me greatly: When he first did *Don Quixote* for Strauss, the composer told him he shouldn't sing the part, he should speak it. And to me this idea of speaking through music is enormously important. That's where the interpreter is great and that's when the music projects. It should not just be an anonymous series of recreations that with this gesture and that fill a specifications chart—that's not so interesting. What's much more interesting is that you *feel* both the presence of the composer *and* the presence of the interpreter who is a flesh-and-blood person living and breathing in the year 1970. And that this person *speaks* to you through the medium of the piece. That's the proper kind of collaboration between composer and performer, I think." With Michael Tilson Thomas—a flesh-and-blood person living and breathing in the year 1971—all one can say is, "Stay tuned, listen and watch."

★ Jennie Tourel ★

The late Jennie Tourel gave her later years to teaching, cen-
tered around her activities with the Juilliard School. At the
time of this interview in 1970, she was involved with a series
of master classes as well as her first concert in the new Alice
Tully Hall with the then-emerging James Levine at the piano.
Her death in November 1973 came too soon, and her loss to
the New York and national musical scene will be felt for years
to come—for she lent it a magnificent presence.

"It is difficult to be simple on stage. Young people think they
have to do something—but if they don't do something, it means
much more." Jennie Tourel was on stage at Carnegie Recital
Hall with a handful of students during one of her annual winter
Masterclasses. The evening was being devoted to Thomas'
Mignon, and Mme Tourel, striking in a long black gown and
shocking pink and white polka-dot blouse, was explaining:
"You know, I did Mignon in Paris for the first time. I won an
audition and made my debut at the Comique in *Carmen*. I
had to make it good. I had the idea of being on the stage, and
I hoped for the best. After the performance, the executive director called me in and told me it was beautiful—and gave
me a two-year contract. 'You started at the top. What would
you like to sing next?' And I answered Mignon." Since that
fabled era of Paris in the Thirties, Mme Tourel has covered the
vast expanse of musical territory both abroad and in this country, where she has been based since her exodus from France
in 1941. Currently she is combining a career as a concert artist
with that of teacher at the Juilliard School.

The words "simplicity" and "dedication" emerge as the key-
notes of Jennie Tourel's art and teaching. During her Master-

class—where her students learn how to work in front of other
people—there flowed forth a stream of ideas any singer, sea-
soned or in the rough, would do well to imbibe. "The most
difficult thing on stage is *not* to act. Acting is a mental thing,
a reflex of a thought, not a lot of gestures. We singers can act
with the voice much more. . . . When we have two hands on
the stage, we think we have 200. Sing without your hands, forget you have them. . . . I beg all young singers with me to
learn the whole opera, not only their parts—to understand
their character in relation to the others. Then you can round
out your character if you mentally understand it, not just to
start acting it. . . . All young singers have to be in love with
their work—it must come from inside."

One of her treasured bits of advice comes from Feodor
Chaliapin's *Autobiography* and to an extent sums up her own
philosophy: "No labor can prove fruitful unless it is based on
an *ideal*. My work had as its *leitmotif* the struggle against the
sham glitter which eclipses the inner light, the complexities
which kill simplicity, the vulgar externals which diminish true
grandeur. There can be no two truths, and from this I recognized that there is only one road that leads to the attainment of
beauty. That road is truth . . . *Nel vero e il bello.*"

She insists her students know the meaning of "simplicity"
because, as she states: "I never learned how to act. I talk, I
don't act, and it has always been this way. Since I started I
never liked the superficial. I have to act only as I feel, because
that's me. In a song I don't do something just to make an effect,
but as you see, my imagination is very far-fetched. When I
sing and I have to recreate the music and the words of two
people, I feel what they want to say and then add my own feeling for them, still respecting their value of words and notes.
The most difficult thing in life," she believes, "is to be simple—
simplicity means much more in communicating. I think it is
a matter of age and experience—so a performer should not be
afraid to grow up, for there are so many good things that come
with it.

"I matured as an artist, but I did not stop my enthusiasm
to be involved in everything I do. You must be excited always
in all you do—excited in the best sense of the word. You must
burn inside yourself to give and share. When I first began sing-

ing songs, I understood I had to give my best, which comes from the heart. The audience has a heart; if what I say goes straight to its heart, then we have communication. I am so lucky, because now I sing for a completely new audience, a new generation which discovers me near the end of my career."

This unique blend of performing and teaching careers began in 1957 when Jennie Tourel was invited by Norman Singer to teach during the course of the annual Aspen Festival. In fact, he insisted that she start teaching so she could pass on her exceptional background and experience to young artists. She was intrigued, for this was a new adventure, strange waters. "When I began to be in contact with the young people, I understood how marvelous it was to give something to them, for they are so eager. The more I teach, the more I get involved with my students." Since 1963 she has been associated with the Juilliard School, and currently she is teaching six days a week, including a full Saturday of private pupils. "I don't even have time for the hairdresser, whom I must beg to see me in the evening!" she sighs. "All this teaching doesn't help me to perform, so before each concert I must stop for a few days to bring myself into shape. Since I am now at Juilliard I don't have extensive tours. My conscience will not allow it with my students— I can't neglect my obligation. But I had a career for many years," she reflects, "and I enjoyed it."

She is particularly eager to make her teaching interesting for the students. "I teach each one individually, yes, but there also must be a basic approach to them. Everyone in a voice studio has some mystic words—to control the vocal chords, to rest the voice on the breath, to use a bow over the chords when you sing—all these are essentials of singing. But voice production is so intangible, each student is different, for when we learn to sing it is all connected to the individual nervous system. Students say that it seems so simple for me to sing freely and easily today. But how long has it taken so that it can be so easy?— 25 or 30 years of learning! So I try to make it interesting. I don't bore them with exact technique, which is something that cannot be taught quickly but comes with years of study. When I find a student with that special gift or talent or *feu sacré* inside, then it becomes tremendously interesting for me to mold this person. I have some beginners; actually, it's easier if they come not knowing anything than if they come with the wrong things learned."

Today, nearly thirty years after coming to the United States, following an enviable career in Paris, Mme Tourel tries to maintain a delicate balance between her own singing and her teaching. Her remarkable vocal condition she attributes to "a right way of singing and being true to oneself. I never wanted to do more than I could and I never went beyond my capability. Even when I was much younger at the opera, they asked for Azucena or Amneris, but I knew these weren't for me. I was a lyric mezzo, and I knew it very well. 'Don't force the voice' should be the motto for everyone. Some feel they must have a bombastic voice, but I am for a singing instrument. We are our own instruments that live inside ourselves. If we come out of our own context, we can injure ourselves."

With this healthy attitude she strongly expresses a desire to pass on all the dedication she has given to her singing. "Since I was sixteen I realized that all I wanted to do was sing and perform on the stage. Even though people do not associate me with the opera here [a claim rather wrongly taken, since the singer had over a half-dozen seasons at the Metropolitan as Rosina in *The Barber of Seville,* Carmen, Mignon and Adalgisa in *Norma,* as well as some fascinating concert performances in Rossini's *Otello* and Offenbach's *Grande Duchesse de Gérolstein,* among others], I started as an opera singer in Paris. Then after I started to sing recitals, I had the same dedication, the same fire for programs of songs *and* opera. Many feel that an opera singer cannot do songs, but if you know that songs are intimate, then it is possible. Of course, songs are more accessible to people who have achieved a certain maturity."

As a young student in Paris, Jennie Tourel heard Chaliapin and it was one of the greatest experiences of her life. The other was the presence of Conchita Supervia, whom she heard in recitals, in the Rossini operas, as Carmen and as Lehár's Frasquita—all of which the younger singer was later to inherit from the great Spanish mezzo at the Comique. "I never wanted to meet her, but I went to all her performances and recitals. In fact, she gave me the idea of recitals, for she was an exciting performer and a fantastic experience for me." In 1937 Tourel gave her first recital in Paris, influenced not only by Supervia but also by Madeleine Grey ("especially in the Canteloube *Chants d'Auvergne*") and Marian Anderson. "I heard her at her first concert at the Salle Gaveau and afterwards I wondered whether it could ever happen that I would be able to come out on the stage and share something as she did with an audience.

"Then I was engaged at the Comique, and I always toyed with the idea of giving a recital, for then I would not be just one personality in a night—not just Carmen or Mignon or Charlotte—but many different ones. Maria Freund, whom I met in Paris, was a very famous interpreter of *Pierrot Lunaire* and contemporary music of Milhaud, Poulenc and so on. It was fascinating to be in her presence and feel her different insights into music—we had very similar temperaments. I studied songs with her, and she gave me an enormous enthusiasm for this literature. She gave classes at the Salle Debussy for the interpretation of songs. She had sung with Mahler and knew the lied very well—I'll never forget her singing of Mozart's 'Das Veilchen,' for she made an intimate opera out of one song. She had a fantastic mind to clarify a song and a style. I realized that you have to sing with feeling and imagination. It is not the grandiose performance of opera but still. . . . What is interpretation?—to bring life into a song. There were many beautiful moments with her, and I owe the beginning of my concert singing to her."

What she calls "heartbreaking" is the simple fact that throughout the country the demand for the solo recitalist appears to be in serious decline. "After I started my recitals here, I had tremendous tours with eighty cities year after year. And I feel I paved the way for others with unusual songs and programs. [Her unhackneyed concerts included Hindemith's *Marienleben,* Poulenc's *Fiançailles pour rire,* Stravinsky's *Cantata on Anonymous Elizabethan Songs,* Bernstein's *I Hate Music* and *La Bonne Cuisine,* Rossini's *Sins of Old Age,* and songs of Tchaikovsky, Rachmaninoff and Chopin.] I sang in seven languages—I made it my business to do this, because I felt it was important for the culture of the country. Audiences were grateful to me for bringing them this unique music, and I thought it necessary for an audience to hear everything, sung with a desire to communicate.

"Now, somehow, this field of singing and interesting programs has fallen off, and I don't know what is the reason. Did managements send out something that blocked off solo recitals? Today, they are not very interesting . . . unless, of course, there is a very great personality or star, and there are very few of these. But the fire of singers must be kindled to perform intimate recitals—they are the core of musical culture, the language of communication and of emotion. Songs tell stories of hate and love, jealousy and tenderness. People love to be in contact with emotions, or maybe it's my Russian blood that believes and loves this—but I have never been disappointed in projecting my emotions."

The phenomenon she finds most helpless is that "this is a time of terrible hurrying. Singing has to take time and patience. In the period of Garcia or Marchesi, they never allowed singers to appear right away. Now a career is like instant coffee. But a voice has to be cultivated, and this needs time. You have to know how to save and conserve the voice, even if it is natural and beautiful." She is dismayed at the number of frauds among voice teachers—"what is happening is that they all feel they are good and doing the right thing." But she stresses that it takes enormous patience on the part of the teacher and the student to come to a good result. Her pupils are fortunate because she can demonstrate anything for them. But she is careful not to let them imitate her color or vocal timbre. "But I want them to see *how* I mold a phrase. Rhythm is the backbone of singing—organized rhythm is our own pulsation. If we do not know rhythm, we can't form the voice . . . and this is what is so difficult in singing.

"When an instrumentalist begins his instrument," she reasons, "he knows he is young and has lots of time, and he is prepared to work ten or twelve years before he moves out into the professional world. Singing is different—the real start is at sixteen. But now at sixteen, young people are already formed personalities, and by eighteen they want to perform. I tell them to look into the situation of singing: no good performer on the stage is very much below thirty. Then you reach the prime of your possibilities. Before this it is important to develop the voice, the sound, the musicianship, everything. Also until you reach sixteen, you should know an instrument—then it is easier to cope with the vocal instrument. I played the piano, others the violin. It doesn't mean that we are now great pianists or violinists, but we have a certain musical sense. I was sixteen when I began to sing—I knew I had a voice and that I wanted to be an actress on the stage."

Her career in this country she calls "a great experience—it was great for a singer who had the hopes of working with the greatest men. I feel I was repaid for my dedication to art in having the chance to work with Toscanini (who opened the horizon of my career here), Koussevitzky, Stokowski—and then, of course, Bernstein, whose First and Third Symphonies I created. I have total recall of the first moment I met him. In 1943 Koussevitzky called me to sing a recital in Lenox, Massachusetts, at the time Tanglewood was closed. It was to be a program of French and Russian music. He said he would like to send a gifted student of his to play for me. Leonard Bernstein. So he called the next day and said Dr. Koussevitzky had told him he would play for my recital on August 25—'That's my birthday,' he offered. 'I'll be 25.' I told him that I remembered him from the summer before when he had conducted a student orchestra, and he exclaimed, 'How marvelous!—I'm already famous.' So, I continued, 'if you play and conduct, do you compose?' and he answered yes. When I told him that if he would write something I would sing it for his birthday, he admitted he had some songs but that I couldn't do them, since I had a bad accent in English. . . .

"The next day I was struck by the personality who entered my room. The first song we did was 'La Vie antérieure' of Duparc—'Gee, you are really good,' he said. 'You're not bad yourself,' I replied—and that was the start of our musical friendship. He brought with him the songs he then called *American Kid Songs* and was surprised that I could really sing them. So I learned them and did them as an encore for his birthday. In November, at my first New York recital, I introduced them as *I Hate Music*." The next day's Virgil Thomson was to write: "One had the impression of being present at the takeoff of some new and powerful airplane for a round-the-world flight. . . . Miss Tourel is, I believe, unequaled among living singers for the concentration in one artist of vocal skill, sound musicianship and stylistic flexibility."

As her Masterclass proceeded twenty-seven years later, there were moments of pure magic, as Mme Tourel launched into a radiantly expressive "Connais tu, le pays?" . . . and when she quietly told her student Anita Terzian, "See the whole country of trees and oranges and the sky—and there I want to die . . . feel you are there already." Or when, again, as she built the vocal inflections of Mignon, "You are not Mignon, you are *thinking* of Mignon. Remember that her life is terrible, it's nothing. Then you *are* Mignon." She was obviously delighted with Miss Terzian's progress during the evening, but later confessed, "You know, there are not many born performers. You have to be completely dedicated—to put blinders on your eyes and go to your chosen goal. Everything else is not important. The road to perfection is as intangible as the road to the stars . . . the stars are always far away, no matter how high you reach."

★ Jon Vickers ★

The Canadian tenor Jon Vickers has been electrifying opera audiences for nearly two decades, but as an interviewee he is as elusive as they come. OPERA NEWS *photographer Erika Davidson was finally able to corner him with a tape recorder in the 1973–74 season (just after his first Met Aeneas in* Les Troyens), *and together we set down some of his most strongly felt ideas and views.*

As Jon Vickers stalks lionlike across the stage as Otello or thrusts his arms to the heavens as the imprisoned Florestan, there is a nobility of bearing that must have marked the great

nineteenth-century actors Kemble, Kean, Booth, Salvini—
something bigger than life but relating to life. A Vickers performance is as wrenching an emotional experience as it is a
musical and vocal tour de force. He stands among opera's
chosen few. During the 1973–74 season the Metropolitan has
seen and heard three of his greatest roles: Wagner's Tristan,
Verdi's Otello and Berlioz' Aeneas. Together with Britten's
Peter Grimes, he considers these the most difficult in his
repertory.

"But each one is difficult in a totally different way," he
was saying not long ago. He finds Otello the most physically
exhausting, because of the character's introverted nature—
a volcano of a man, always struggling to contain his passions.
"This is more difficult than Tristan, who is a complete extrovert.
He agonizes, but he pours it out, never controlling himself
except for that short while in the first act with Isolde when he
is trying to conceal his emotions. Of course, Tristan is about
four times longer than Otello in terms of sheer singing, so you
need staying power.

"For Aeneas, Berlioz thought of a tenor as just a tenor,
without any classification. In his first entrance Aeneas is a
pure spinto, a real *Trovatore* type. Then he is almost a lyric
baritone, suddenly snapping back into a spinto again. The
next scene is pure dramatic, and in the garden scene you need
almost a Gigli voice. Then his big final scene is pure dramatic
again. So the danger and difficulty of Aeneas is that you need
to be four kinds of tenor. Then you must be a big, heroic
character, the son of a god, the successor to Hector, the center
around which everything revolves.

"As for Peter Grimes, no other work I have sung requires
such absolute technical ability. You are always exposed as a
dramatic tenor, as in the pub soliloquy where he says 'Now the
Great Bear and Pleiades' all on E natural, *mezza voce,* at an
incredibly slow speed, with crescendos and diminuendos, right
in the *passaggio* of the voice. Then in the hut scene you have
this very pliant sort of coloratura on E, F, G, A and even B-
natural, a high tessitura that is extremely controlled. But you
know," he continues, "I made my career on the basis of refusing to be classified. I have fought that tooth and claw. I find
it amusing when people say, 'Oh, Siegmund is absolutely for

you.' Then they turn around and say, 'Peter Grimes is just built for you.' This is nonsense. Siegmund is the other end of the spectrum from Grimes. So when people say these parts were built for me, it is not true. I have made myself conquer these parts."

The fierce will to scale the heights of a part, the craggy absorption and strength one feels as the Canadian-born tenor wraps himself in it, is a Vickers trademark. "My father said the responsibility of a human being was to take whatever talent he has—whether to be a gardener or a president—and do that job to the utmost of his ability. That is the fundamental philosophy of my life. My father was of Methodist-Presbyterian background, and the Christian influence in my life has been very strong. My father was a lay minister who did a great deal of preaching, quoting Scripture to us. Over and over again he would say, 'You will do with your might what your hands find to do. You will do it to the best of your ability.' He pounded that into our heads; no matter what we did in this pursuit of excellence, we did it for the glory of God. I have never lost that. I don't know how well I have succeeded, because I am just as human as the next guy, but that is what I try to do."

Musically, a towering influence has been Herbert von Karajan, for whom the young tenor auditioned in 1957. "At that time," he recalls, "Karajan was artistic director of Salzburg, general manager of the Vienna State Opera, one of the music directors of La Scala, resident conductor of the Berlin Philharmonic and the Vienna Philharmonic, all simultaneously. Although there were all kinds of jokes about it—even a corny parody on 'Largo al factotum' about 'Karajan here, Karajan there'—his genius elevated the standard of every one of those institutions. I went to sing for him, and after less than half of the 'Lamento di Federico' from Cilèa's *Arlesiana* he called me offstage into the auditorium. He was working on a production, and there he was in his jeans, a sweater thrown over his shoulders, and he said, 'Let's do *Tristan und Isolde* next year.' And I said, 'You are crazy!' He was serious, but I said no, because I was much too young. Then he wanted me to make my debut with him in Vienna that September—this was August!—in *Carmen*. He slapped me on the knee and said, 'One day you will be my Tristan.' And today I am.

"I have been through many, many experiences with Karajan and found him incredibly loyal. He has supported me in very difficult situations. The Berlin Philharmonic responds to him and loves him and works for him. When you record with him, you are not singing with a conductor and an orchestra but you feel you are part of a total cooperation between conductor, singer and every member of the orchestra individually, from the timpanist to the last piccolo player, all trying to do the ultimate, each in his own way contributing to a total unity. Karajan has taught me, has led me to higher musical and dramatic standards because his standards are a lot higher than mine, because his vision was greater. Being older, he saw that I also was striving for a standard, and I was striving for it in the way he wanted. That is why, I believe—we never discussed it, but I am convinced—I had his support."

Vickers also mentions the late Sir David Webster of the Royal Opera House, Covent Garden, who "convinced me not to quit singing. In the very early years of my career, a time of difficulty, he gave me tremendous support. I was young and starting out on the international scene. In three years and two months I made my debut in London, Vienna, Bayreuth, San Francisco, Buenos Aires, the Metropolitan and La Scala. Caught up in the whirl and having to make so many decisions, I leaned heavily on Sir David, picking his brains, asking his advice." Vickers remembers reaching a point of deciding to quit singing, a decision made as a result of the same philosophy "that if I do the best I can, and if the door does not open, I don't believe in forcing it. But Sir David's faith in me represented an open door that I should walk through."

Of a vast list of new productions and working experiences he has had with conductors and directors, the tenor says that a production of Britten's *Rape of Lucretia* which he sang at the Stratford Festival early in his career stands out in his memory. "Then I recall the production of *Pagliacci* I did in Vienna back in my first season there, a *Parsifal* in London with Rudolf Kempe conducting and the Tristan I did for the first time in Buenos Aires. What gives me satisfaction in productions like these is that the conductor, the director, the designer work in total cooperation. The Met's *Peter Grimes* is one of the great things I have been part of: we had a great director, a very great conductor, a designer, an entire cast all there just to serve the work. Not only the work but what it is trying to get across, what it means."

What is wrong with opera, Vickers says, is "the enormous emphasis put on lavish sets and costumes, like the Met's *Otello*, which are beautiful to see but an absolute tragedy in which to work. They are physically impossible; you have no conception of how Otello, with armor and long capes, gets tied up in ropes and wires and cables in his first entrance. I have been in many great productions of this opera, ones just as spectacular, like Karajan's in Salzburg, but there the whole production serves Iago and Desdemona and Otello and Verdi, not vice versa. When I was singing *Pagliacci* in Zeffirelli's production in London, he expressed straight across the boards, 'In my productions the principals are of the least importance.' If that kind of directing continues in opera it will kill it, because what Verdi and Shakespeare and Boito are, what they stand for, is so much bigger than any silly ass who thinks his singing or conducting or production or designing is more important than what the work is trying to say."

Talking about creating real characters onstage—such as Aeneas, a man torn between his personal desires and his responsibility to destiny—Vickers says that every opera hero is to a certain extent both a symbol and flesh-and-blood. "If an artist cannot formulate in his mind a clear concept of both, he cannot play the role. That is the absolute fundamental basis of an interpretation. There is never a role I play where I *consciously* make him timeless, placeless and so much a symbol as when I play Grimes. He is the absolute embodiment of all feelings of rejection. That is one of the great tragedies of our time: everybody feels rejected, because we are caught in a system where we may have become mere numbers. But the fundamental interpretation of a role is based on that very thing of symbol and reality. The characteristics of a human being onstage are displayed so that the person observing can see and relate to an extension of his own emotions, even if they represent aspects of his own personality which he may not like. They are magnified up there, they stand out in a blazing way, so the public can experience their own feelings. Then the audience, both observing and experiencing these emotions in retrospect, should be forced into an analysis of themselves, hopefully for self-improvement."

As for Otello, Vickers insists, "Anyone who does not play him as a great regal personality is insulting every intelligent black man. All you have to do is see the great city of Venice to realize that Otello was a kind of Julius Caesar of the Venetian empire, not a hysterical fool. If Otello is not an aristocratic, noble creature there is no tragedy, and Desdemona is a fool to have married a savage. Otello is a frustrating part in many ways," he concludes, "because your interpretation—and I insist on *my* interpretation, not a carbon copy of Martinelli or Vinay or Del Monaco or McCracken—is so terribly affected by Iago. If you don't have a strong, subtle Iago, it is very hard not to look like a fool as Otello."

The longest learning period in his career was for Tristan, on which he worked for three months. "I was sort of flirting with it here and there for different periods of my life, picking out some of the most difficult moments, seeing if I could sing them and then putting it away for a while. I said no to Tristan for fourteen years. What has happened over the *Tristan* here was very sad. I wanted to sing many Tristans with Birgit Nilsson, and now it looks as though I have sung my first and last one ever with her in this house. I think that is a tragedy, and I'll even be arrogant enough to say it is a tragedy for this theater." More Wagner? He is considering *Tannhäuser* and *Götterdämmerung*. "The *Götterdämmerung* Siegfried is a very interesting personality; however, I refused to sing the young Siegfried, because I think he is a bore. I always call him a Wagnerian L'il Abner. The only section I find really beautiful is the Awakening of Brünnhilde; then it's great. I may be exposing my own ignorance, but if I do a role that hellishly difficult, I want more of a challenge than the simple one of just getting through it physically. I want a role that says something all the way through." Along this line he mentions d'Albert's *Tiefland,* Pfitzner's *Palestrina,* Smetana's *Dalibor* and Stravinsky's *Oedipus Rex.*

"I don't think there has ever been a period in my career when I have been so frustrated as I am today," the tenor confesses. "The real, basic problem now—and it is reflected right to the financial aspect—is that all the theaters have been deceived, or deceive themselves, as to what opera and theater are. They have lost sight and are confused as to whether opera is an art form or an entertainment. The day of the ad man has taken over. A man who sings is judged not by his artistic ability but by his ability to get himself in the right newspaper with the right quotes. Contrary to what anybody thinks, I never had any burning ambition to be a singer. I never drove and forced myself into a career. And I have never paid for a line of publicity. If I had been that intent on having a career, I would certainly have tried to capitalize on everything I have done. But I don't have a publicity agent, and I am violently opposed to them. I think they are corrupting our art form.

"Whether I was raising cattle or driving a truck or managing a Woolworth store, I have always felt I must do this to the best of my ability. I like to feel that people appreciate what I have done, but the main thing for me is to strive after a higher standard. Maybe it isn't good enough—then I can only say don't hire me anymore. I just believed in doing my best, so my career has grown. I never tried to embellish it, make it bigger than it was. When I had sung in the major western houses, people tried to get me involved in this publicity thing. One of the sicknesses of our society is the credibility gap created by the projection of inflated images—a tragedy compounded by the fact that even when something truly great is seen or read, we unconsciously make an automatic adjustment in our thinking.

"The whole American Dream is tied up with trying to be bigger than we are. One of these image-builders tried to persuade me to hire him. When I tried to explain why I thought it was not true to an art form, he said the difference between a great and mediocre performance is only a hairline, and angrily said there is no singer who is an artist. What an attitude for a man who takes thousands of dollars from my colleagues to inflate the image of what great artists they are! To quote the Chinese, if one holds a yen close enough to the eyeball, one can blot out the universe. We are guilty in our society of demanding that one person be the greatest. Publicity tries to say Miss X is Miss A-B-C-D and E all rolled into one. An artist who allows that kind of thing is in great danger as far as his own mental equilibrium is concerned. I want to know that when I am hired it is because of my ability, not because of an inflated image. That keeps me sane. I can go onstage without being hysterically nervous, because I am not trying to live up to something that has been projected about me."

★ *André Watts* ★

Setting some kind of record, André Watts has appeared on every "Great Performers at Philharmonic Hall" series since 1967, all to sold-out, cheering audiences. His second such recital in the fall of 1968, as part of his 21st birthday celebration that also included a State Department world tour, was the reason for our visit. He has since completed his studies at Peabody and has gone on to take his important place in American musical life.

It wasn't too long ago that Harold C. Schonberg wrote in *The Great Pianists:* "Just as most Russian pianists take kindly to Romantic works, very few Americans do. Where the Russians revel in Chopin, Schumann and Liszt, sporting happily and naturally in those waters, Americans seem to be either inhibited or embarrassed by it all. The best of the Americans have been impeccably trained and are far more sophisticated musically than their Russian counterparts. Their musical culture, thanks to the free exchange of ideas, is extremely wide. But they do not have the direct Romantic tradition to fall back on. It seems to be a tradition alien to contemporary American feeling, and only a very few American pianists have allied themselves with the Romantic literature."

It is always thorny, at best, to set down hard and fast rules, and a current exception to this particular one is a Romantic figure by the name of André Watts, who has rocketed ahead to the forefront of today's young American pianists.

In the few short years since the winter of 1963—when the career of the slight, unknown sixteen-year-old was ignited off the launching pad and set into orbit by an emergency appearance with Leonard Bernstein and the New York Philharmonic —André Watts has been identified as an interpreter of Liszt, Chopin, Beethoven, Brahms and Rachmaninoff. Yet, when you try early one afternoon to pin him down, he will retort quizzically: "What does it mean, Romantic school? May I say this, even though it may be an unpopular thing? I am in a fortunate position, because things have gone very well and I've had limited critical abuse so far. I can gripe and state things as a fact in terms of my repertory and what people say I can play. Many say that the American pianist has no heart— that is the cry. But this is the situation: if he plays a lot of Chopin and Rachmaninoff (and he likes to play it), then the claim is that he can play only flashy music, and what about his Beethoven Opus 111? And if you play the Beethoven 111, there will be those who will say that this is only old men's music, but what about such and so?

"I believe that you should play what you want. I am called a Liszt player because of my debut with the Philharmonic in the E-flat Concerto. But up until a year or so ago, I played the Liszt only about eight times in public. Mostly, I had played the Saint-Saëns G-minor and the Chopin Second when I was in my late teens. When someone is known for his Liszt, people want to book him for this—then you play Liszt and the public thinks that maybe you can't play anything else. But to justify my range, there is Mozart, Beethoven and Haydn. It doesn't include a lot of Bach, but I think there is a whole world in the Haydn sonatas—he's a very underrated composer. There is also Schubert, Brahms, Chopin and Liszt."

Despite this disclaimer and his eagerness not to be associated only with the music of Liszt, the 19th-century maestro of his mother's homeland, Watts is deeply involved with it, delving into the later aspects of Liszt, the twilight of his creativity, which Watts attests, "look ahead musically. The first twelve-tone row was written in the *Faust Symphony*—the first *honest* row, since others stop short of the full twelve tones. And his *Les Jeux d'eaux à la Villa d'Este* is very revolutionary as Impressionistic music, looking toward Debussy and Ravel."

He has also played all-Liszt recitals. "The repertory is very interesting and comes as a shock for those in the audience waiting for the *Hungarian Rhapsody* No. 2. His Nocturne, *En rêve,* is like Debussy, misty and impressionistic, with no bravura at all. The *Schlaflos, Frage und Antwort* is a realistic piece about sleeplessness and restlessness. And I end the first half with the *Hungarian Rhapsody* No. 3. After intermission I've programmed the Sonata and the second and third movements of the *Faust Symphony.* Although Liszt reduced the whole Symphony for two pianos, he only did the second movement for solo piano. August Stradal did a reduction of the whole thing, and I've used his third movement with my own alterations. I looked at Liszt's other transcriptions to see how he did it, then changed and added where Stradal dropped certain phrases."

As far as Liszt's famous, but today neglected, operatic transcriptions are concerned, Watts claims not to understand the mentality that has banned these transcriptions from fashion. "Even though everyone now knows these operas, we still could hear Liszt's versions. Of course, too often when we hear these transcriptions, we hear only the bad ones." He, however, is eager about "the insane *Prophète* 'Skater's Waltz' transcription, which is a marvelous reworking, like ten hands going all at once. The Godowsky things are great, too. He made real compositions with strange harmonies, like the three Strauss waltzes being played all at the same time."

Repertory, Watts offers matter-of-factly, "is really a matter of what we choose to play—as long as it is not junk. I've played the Rimsky-Korsakov Concerto with the Philharmonic. It is not great, but it is good, and I want to play it again if the circumstances are right. It's not like Beethoven at his peak, but everything can't be—thank God! There are also some interesting works of Hummel and Weber. Hummel has Chopin in some of his writing, and I'm sure Brahms lifted things from Hummel's Piano Quintet. Artur Schnabel, in an article prefacing his collection of the Beethoven sonatas, says that the public, *per se,* never really decides the repertory of the artist. Once the performer decided that his program no longer would be interspersed with arias, it happened. He decided how it would be, and so it was."

The major obstacle to all these various curiosities that beckon to André Watts is the matter of time. Not only does he now pursue a world-wide concert career, but he is at work on his Bachelor of Music at Peabody Conservatory as well. "I guess I am old-fashioned and pedantic, but I feel I need a thorough knowledge of the standards first. I've wanted to handle the standard recital of Haydn and Mozart and Beethoven and the Impressionists successfully. From here I will move into other things, like this all-Liszt program."

He has been studying at Peabody in Baltimore for the past two years and took summer courses there this past term for the first time. At the Conservatory he has been working with Leon Fleisher, with whom he studied for the past three years. "Maintaining school and concerts during the season is a problem," he admits. "I've tried to study on planes and in hotel rooms, but I like to concentrate on one thing at a time and cannot do both. So I've worked out my schedule so that I do five dates and come back to school work. I have days of cramming between concert dates. The school has arranged that I have flexible class schedules, as long as I can do the work and keep up my grades."

Studies with Fleisher have meant an important link with the past, since Watts can draw on the experience of his teacher's ten years with the great Artur Schnabel, who, in turn, was a pupil of the famed pedagogue Leschetizky. Going beyond his teacher's Romantic impulse, Schnabel was to become known as the epitome of the modern pianist of intellectual strength and an analytical objectivity. But he also drew from Leschetizky an attitude of treating each pupil individually according to the nature of his talent. "I'm not here to turn out little Fleishers," he told Watts. A teacher, out of his own experience, can show the possibilities for playing something— yet this doesn't mean there still can't be yet another possibility.

Of his work with Fleisher, Watts agrees that he, too, has followed in this logical and sensitive approach to music. "He has not influenced my way of playing, but rather the way of thinking about music. The biggest tribute to him—and the most beautiful thing—is that when I first came to him, he told me what the position of a teacher is. He told me to bring him a piece of music and, with it, several possibilities and ideas for the music. 'The ideal way,' he said, 'is that you have your own ideas and then I give you mine. Then you can see them all in front of you and finally evolve your own way and your own manner in the end.'

"I don't study piano technique with Fleisher, except in the sense of getting a new tone color for certain passages. It is more a refined kind of thing. He also has unique ideas on physical or muscular distribution in difficult passages. You can often sit six hours working on such a difficult spot and eventually figure it out physically. But I can save five hours of sweat if I can think through what is hanging me up. So, I think this is a good collaboration—we get along well. Mainly, the thinking process is used, and with it I arrive at new formulations in my music."

Going back, André Watts was introduced to the piano by his mother, Maria Alexandra Watts, a Hungarian by birth, who married an American career soldier in Germany. André was born in Nuremberg and spent his early years around U.S. Army camps in Germany. His first musical instrument was not the piano, but a miniature violin, which he began playing at the age of six. At seven, he began receiving piano lessons from his mother, who did not introduce music into her son's life for career purposes. "She just wanted me to learn music for my own enjoyment. It was to be a part of my education and a part of my life as it had been a part of hers." When the family moved to Philadelphia, he was enrolled at the Musical Academy and his teachers have included Doris Bawden, Genia Robinor and Clement Petrillo.

Watts describes his musical beginnings as "unorthodox. I started playing Chopin études, Liszt and some Schubert pieces —not a lot of Bach. When I came to the U.S. and my mother thought there was some talent to develop, I began working for more discipline with Czerny and then the Haydn D-major Piano Concerto, which I played at nine. So, when people ask me about basic foundations of playing the piano, it is difficult for me to say. The basic mechanism is the same: music is music—but it's just that different areas are exploited in different repertories. I agree with Arrau's idea that if you can play Beethoven, you can play everything—I go along with this because it is tough and makes many demands. But then there are some who play Beethoven and can't perform Chopin."

After Watts had mastered the Haydn Concerto, he won out over 40 young pianists in a contest of the Philadelphia Orchestra Children's Concerts. A year later, he performed the Mendelssohn G-minor Concerto at the Robin Hood Dell, and at fourteen was again soloist with the Philadelphia Orchestra in the Franck *Symphonic Variations.* Two years later he auditioned for an appearance on one of the New York Philharmonic's nationally televised "Young People's Concerts." He was engaged by Leonard Bernstein to play the first movement of the Brahms Second and, twenty days later, when Glenn Gould fell ill for two of the regular subscription concerts, Watts was called in as his replacement in the Liszt First Concerto.

From then on, his path headed upward, though slowly and carefully held in rein by both his mother and manager, who have had the wisdom not to allow him to be exploited. "After Bernstein convinced my mother that I needed a manager, I went to Bill Judd at Columbia. He felt that the major consideration was to use the great thing that had happened to my advantage in such a way that it would last. It was important to be careful and not to try to do too much. I was concerned in my own way, of course, but then I was only sixteen and it was great to go out and play—much greater than to practice. But, after a while, it dawns on you that if you don't practice, you can't play. And the great problem is that you find yourself suddenly having a career, and, at the same time, while maintaining this career, you find that you have to grow and develop as an artist.

"Bill felt I should do only twelve concerts for the first season —my mother said four, and I did six. Next year it was twelve, and it went like that. Now I have about 25 or 30 concerts and recitals each season." He has proved that he has made that crucial crossing between prodigy and manhood.

His growth to maturity and his careful work with Leon Fleisher have brought about a definite approach to his music. He says with typical self-assurance and naturalness: "I have no hang-up about the concern between textual fidelity and personal emotion. I don't really understand it. Recently, I was reading Berlioz, where he tells of Liszt playing the *Hammer-klavier* Sonata—and note-perfect. On other occasions, Liszt was known to change many notes. This is to say, he was not in any bind about this, one way or the other. For instance, after the introduction to the Beethoven Opus 111, leading to the main body and meat of the first movement, the crescendo can be made immense or threatening or understated—it is all up to the individual for the fine variation within a piece.

"There is no problem for me. I look at a piece and if I am unhappy about the markings indicated, the instinct can question and you can check definitely if these are the composer's own markings or the editor's. But, if you can't play it his way with conviction, then don't play the piece at all. I draw the line here, because you lay your life on the line with everything you play. But there are also the certain things you learn only in performance. Sometimes, I will play a piece that I feel I should play and even want to play—then, in front of an audience, I can feel it is not right and I will take it out of the repertory for a while. It may just be me, but I can't overcome it."

As he is about to return to the afternoon half of his daily six practice hours, he points with pride to a bust of Beethoven on the piano, and with amusement to a print of Franz Liszt over the piano. "That's called 'Rhapsody' or some other grade-B movie title like that. Liszt is at the piano with figures of his imagination—one is a fiddler in Hungarian folklore that combines Robin Hood with Paganini," he smiles. Does he see any rigid divisions between schools of playing? "No, I think of individuals and different styles, not one defined group like this or that. As for me, I just play the piano."

★ *Alexis Weissenberg* ★

*The controversial Alexis Weissenberg vanished completely
from the American musical scene for a decade, returning in
1967 with the New York Philharmonic to replace an ailing
Michelangeli. Now he annually tours America, has a brilliant
career and records extensively in Europe. I saw him in the fall
of 1971 before a recital on the S. Hurok series.*

There he sat, tensely at ease, much less formidable than his
stage manner or album covers lead you to believe. His manner
is friendly, frank and altogether disarming, via a rapid-fire
staccato patter in nearly immaculate English. Alexis Weissenberg admits, yes, he is a man of today. His attire is boutique
chic—brown suede pants with tight black knit shirt. Though
it is only a few short years since his reappearance from European self-exile, he is equipped with all the accoutrements of
someone who has arrived: the Hurok banner, recordings with
two major companies, prime engagements and the inevitable
critical camps—some thrusting him into the Horowitzian
heights, others who call him cool, detached and IBM-like.

As to his position in the pianistic echelon, he says, "After
you are 40, you suddenly realize you are a certain kind of
pianist. You cannot be every kind of pianist, you cannot be
everybody's like or dislike. I think the greatest thing that can
happen to an artist is to be controversial—not because he's
eccentric, but because he's original. If he's original, obviously
certain people will like him. But you always find those who
prefer Doris Day to Greta Garbo, and that's something that
cannot be changed. Garbo will basically be an intelligent, cool
interpreter, and Doris Day the very opposite. What each has
done differently is to identify with certain characters that fit

her own personality better than anything else. And I think this is what one suddenly realizes—what direction to go. A man decides it even in his own physical and mental life: what kind of literature he likes, what kind of people he can find to love or admire—and what kind of music he is best fit to make. And *there* one becomes, whether people want it or not, an authority. You *have* to be in order to perform. And this same conviction that makes you an authority makes people feel that you are sometimes aggressive—and they dislike you for it, or they admire you for it. But that is how it should be."

Alexis Weissenberg has always followed his instincts for originality, and it more than partially explains his disappearance from the American musical scene (and most of the world's as well) between 1957 and 1967. The great piano authority, Jan Holcman, visiting with Weissenberg in 1960 for *Saturday Review*, began his piece by declaring, "Once in a while there appears a talent capable of interpreting work in unexpected yet simple idioms, which seem to have entirely bypassed other imaginations by the merest fraction." He told of Weissenberg's "triumph *and* tribulation" and his decision to disappear from the stage. Intrigues, disappointment with his management, personal tangles all created an unhealthy artistic climate. He claimed that his bookings were mainly in the provinces, without major exposure. Playing the same standard program for community concerts left little time to study new repertoire. When he issued an ultimatum to his manager, he was told he could leave.

Today his explanation takes a few detours—as does much talk *à la* Weissenberg—but it does explain the kind of crisis he felt as a performer. He sees the need to perform at an early age, to be exposed to an audience early, "because this contact is important for a performing artist who must have this quintessence of communicating which one calls magnetism and personality. There is something called projection which is definitely palpable—and you should know exactly how to deal with it; it's a fever you create. But there is also that time when a performer is exposed early because of contests [he won the Leventritt in 1948] or other encouragements, "and you become an active artist much *too* early—that is, long before you have developed your real repertoire, long before you know all about yourself. Then comes the moment when you have to continue developing, when you have to make the transition between a young artist and the mature man you will become. A new juxtaposition has to be made between what you have assimilated and learned, and the personality that will be definite in you. And that osmosis can only happen privately. It should not be exposed in public because either the public will be cheated or you will go through such a crisis yourself that you will not be able to stand both external exposure and this sort of inner 'kitchen' that is taking place in you. And rather than risking this I decided to keep away from the stage for some years and eliminate many bad habits which a young artist always has."

"The habits," he explains, "come because the artist finds himself up against unnatural things, such as learning new pieces very quickly because an orchestra insists on it—he is eager to play with a major orchestra and eager to learn new works. But then, ten years later, things that have been learned quickly and have a varnish of interpretive qualities on them, can (because of repetitiousness) become a caricature of yourself. So I decided it would be the right moment to disappear, all as part of this inner development." It was a difficult decision because he could not then set an exact time for coming back. "The career is like a wheel. If you don't perform for several years anywhere, people forget you and managers are not interested anymore and the fee doesn't exist anymore, and there are a lot of things you have to sacrifice. I decided it was worth it in my case, but you need an enormous amount of strength. And it's important to do it at a time when you're successful so that you don't work on a negative psychological background. It's not easy to come back so many years later. But once you feel you are ready, then you wait for the right occasion."

So he waited, stylishly enough, in Paris and the right occasion finally presented itself. Herbert von Karajan saw a TV film the pianist had made of *Petrouchka* in Sweden and asked him to film the Tchaikovsky First Concerto with him. He then played with the conductor in Berlin, and an American manager asked him about coming back to New York. "I said yes, because I knew that I would have definite friends in certain conductors who had worked with me before, among whom

William Steinberg was the most important. He said he would bring me to the Philharmonic; then Michelangeli cancelled, and I was called in." Looking back on certain dissatisfactions, he comments: "It was just that there is no prefabricated mold that can apply to an artist who is original. And the moment you are original, as opposed to being eccentric, you cannot be put into a special mold. It would never fit." He stresses the difference between being original and eccentric, in effect establishing his own raison d'être. "If somebody is original by birth and his entire outlook on music is new, even if it is completely misinterpreted or misunderstood, he cannot be otherwise. Originality is something an artist has or doesn't have." It was this kind of originality—mixed with a dash of youthful eccentricity—which alienated certain segments of the public and press at the beginning of his career.

Born in Sofia, Bulgaria, he studied with Pantcho Vladigerov. He recalls that while some children are impressed by colors or objects, he was impressed by sound. "It has been something that has obsessed me from my earliest years. I sang a lot as a child, referring to melodic comparisons in my own mind. Everything was sound, and it had all sorts of effects on me: it made me sad or happy or nervous or impatient or comfortable. And today, whenever I walk in the street or go to sleep, sound is part of my inner thinking." He also remembers falling in love with the dog on the recording labels and dreaming of becoming a pianist and seeing his name connected with the dog on His Master's Voice. German and Russian occupation of Bulgaria during World War II sent him to Israel, where he also studied, and then to America, where he worked with Olga Samaroff and Wanda Landowska. The influences were many and strong. In Bulgaria he had been drawn to the Russian pianists. "This kind of pianism became a goal, but it also sounded logical to me, not because it is an effective kind of playing but because I was emotionally much closer to it. There is nothing you can do about temperament. If you're a Slav, you remain a Slav. And you are much more logically connected (in the best sense of the word) with Chopin, Rachmaninoff, Tchaikovsky and Prokofiev—because of your inner system of rhythm, melody and harmonies."

He calls the influence of Samaroff "gigantic," because she

had a great knowledge of pianism in general. He went through a strenuous period under the potent spell of Vladimir Horowitz, but claims "I don't know of a single pianist who did not. If a pianist is in love with the instrument, he cannot ignore Horowitz's existence—he marked all the pianists not only of his generation but the ones that followed. Even today a Horowitz recital remains something absolutely unique. He goes so much farther beyond the instrument—and that is what makes it exciting. One may agree or disagree, but that is of minor importance. What he does with the instrument is what Landowska did with the harpsichord, which she made into something else." Working with Landowska was still another, more classical force in his life. "She helped me to understand how one should not only interpret Bach but also how to go about the ornamentation of Bach—and that one can create the same emotional intensity and structure in a work of Bach as one would in any Romantic piece. Her playing had a marvelous, improvisational quality."

His talk about playing is colored by such terms as "possessing" and "mastering." The more you know a piece, he believes, "the better you possess it. It is the same as knowing a human being: the closer you are, the more you can detach yourself from that person and remain an individual man yourself. And in music we are expected to be, finally, absolutely objective—a recreator. In order to reach this when you perform on stage, you first have to have been involved with the piece many years—and then you have to get away from this involvement. The umbilical cord which ties the artist to a piece has to be cut by the time he reaches the stage, so that he can intelligently recreate this new child independently from his own being, completely detached from the possessive quality that can make an artist negative. You should be completely involved *cosmically* with a piece, just as you have an inner cosmic knowledge of your entire work. By the time you reach the age of 40, you have spent your early years being a promising young pianist, gifted and admired for the wrong reasons— facility, talent, charm, memory, stamina. Then you eliminate many things—and you can only do this when you know the things you cannot do. You have to know your utmost limitations, and then you're within a frame that is finally so clear in your mind that from that moment on you're a free man. *So,* when you have worked and lived and slept with a piece, and you know exactly how you want to project it, from that moment on each time you perform it you make reference to this cosmic knowledge that you have inside you—and then you're satisfied or not, in terms of this understanding and feeling for the piece."

He admits there have been pieces that he has rejected just because he could not come to terms with them, but he believes it's wrong when people feel that one should come to certain composers only later in life. "That's nonsense. I adored Bach all my life. Some feel they have to be 50 to like Bach, or that they come closer to Beethoven later. What is important is to identify; and after a certain age you suddenly realize the music that you can identify with temperamentally, emotionally and physically. And it's not so much composers as *pieces*. There is not one great pianist who plays *all* Schumann wonderfully." He believes he is made for music that is of large size in time and strength. "But when I say strength sometimes people misunderstand and feel it's a matter of brutality, I think we live in a violent world. I identify so perfectly with the people of today. I am a 20th-century man and therefore cannot be a 19th-century man and therefore cannot be a 19th-century pianist. Everything that excites me personally belongs to this era; and I look forward to the next years. The means of communication are more naked today—writers, poets and painters are working in an idiom that goes along with what is developing in the psychological society today. But musicians, somehow, have remained backwards. It's partly the audience, partly certain critics and partly certain kinds of recordings. Music has always been last to develop—especially in interpretation, which is the last to take the new trend and the new emotional development. After all, the great mistake is to forget that music is a language that is living—it cannot be kept in a museum. In recreating we direct music to an audience that is alive today, the same people who take the subway, see movies, buy books. They must be moved and shaken emotionally in the same way as they are in their own lives. You cannot bring them back into a museum of the last century and make them feel the way people used to. Man has always had the same emotions, *but* the elements that make him excited have changed constantly. And if we are now in an age when things are completely naked, when man does not want mystery around the body or feelings anymore, music has to be given in that blunt a way—which does not make it *less* exciting and certainly not *less* emotionally involved. People don't write a letter to insult someone today—they smack his face. You don't tell somebody in a million different ways that you love him—you say it directly. People sleep together immediately. And that has to happen with the contact you have with the audience. But the same people who go to a Magritte exhibit or the most recent Picasso show or whatever is happening now in books and movies, those same people go to a Chopin recital and expect it to be played as it was 60 years ago. That's unforgivable! Music is meant to look forward—it's a moving art."

As an anti-traditionalist, he stresses that "tradition is basically wrong because what one calls tradition (and wrongly) is often simply imitation of particular artists who are so important in their own personality that they create a school of followers. One must always take a completely new look at compositions; and once you have felt and created it your way, you should not forget that you are addressing it to an audience that you want to partake in this feeling with a set of emotions of today." For the same reason, he feels tempo is wrongly criticized, because the listener makes comparisons. "It will obviously be too fast or too slow, but it can only be this in rapport with its *own* context—how it builds to its own climax —and once you have heard the whole piece, *then* you can decide for yourself whether in this context it was too fast or too slow. These things are in constant evolution." He points out that Horowitz always spoke the language of the new people that were hearing him and therefore drew young people to his concerts. Callas, too, established a new outlook on singing. "She did to opera what Brigitte Bardot did in the movies— after her you couldn't stand to see Martine Carol with corsets and trying to be half-naked. I try to speak the modern language and address myself to the people of today."

Although Alexis Weissenberg is less known in America for his Bach than for his spectacular concertos and Russian war horses, Bach is a composer to whom he feels especially close. "But that is one of the big problems in any career. In some places where I first appeared with the *Goldberg* Variations or the Partitas, they are horrified if next time the orchestra wants me to do the Tchaikovsky Concerto. It's almost as if I want to open a bordello in the middle of the city! If I play Rachmaninoff or Tchaikovsky first and *then* try to give a Bach recital, the reaction is the same. I always accept the fact that people will not like something I do, but I do not agree with this preliminary idea that somebody does only one thing—it's ridiculous in any art." At the other end of the stick, he is closely shouldered with the music of Rachmaninoff, whose concertos, sonatas and preludes he has recorded. "So then for a long time I will probably be condemned for it, but I love the music."

Music, he believes, should be a matter of pleasure and joy. "When I go to a Horowitz recital I enjoy the transcription he plays at the end as much as the first Bach or Mozart. Why shouldn't you let yourself go in a concert? Music is not to be evangelized as it is by some who feel that if it is Schubert, even if it is dreadfully played by some completely unimportant musician, it is great. Or any Beethoven immediately looks profound, and there is a sort of frown on the face and spitting on the keyboard once in a while because of the bad, unpianistic jumps. And this brings up the question of pianism in general. Beethoven, as much as Mozart and Schubert, needs very great pianism. Mozart and Bach were fabulous instrumentalists, and everything they conceived is pianistic. So only a great pianist who has absolute control over the piano can perform them. Unfortunately, Mozart has usually been given the crowning and acceptance for certain pianists who play the most irregular piano I've heard in my life. They can't play a normal scale properly—and Mozart is based on scales and trills, clarity and beauty of sound, all matters of technique. What your feelings are behind a piece mean nothing if you can't produce it. Eloquence is essential in piano playing, as it is when you speak. I don't want to go to hear a Beethoven or Mozart sonata badly executed because the musicianship behind it is marvelous. There are enough great ones who are also very great musicians—I don't separate the two."

In this category fall Horowitz and Glenn Gould. "The mind behind what Gould does is phenomenal, the pianist and the musician are extraordinary. Pianistically, it's perfect." The mind and the pianism are co-partners, he emphasizes, and projection is only possible because that kind of artist can be objective and because he's thought extensively away from the piano. "It's what you do in thinking about the work away from the instrument that does the trick. I think of fingerings when I'm on a plane or when I'm in the street—suddenly it dawns on me that a certain fingering would give my playing more evenness or more clarity or would take away an accent that shouldn't exist." He says he learns a work first by heart before going to the piano. "I must read the score and learn it completely and feel my way about it. Then I go about assimilating it this way and think about it. From that moment on it becomes part of me and I come closer to it—then one day it's not a stranger to me anymore. From then on I know that I can work on it on my own terms, physically, mentally and psychologically. And then I apply mechanical work at the piano, trying to find the resources of fingerings and so forth." He practices relatively little, about two hours a day. "But that means nothing. It's partly a question of concentration and *thinking* of a piece."

What are the ingredients of a great pianist? Weissenberg says they are the same in any great artist. "He must have, along with his talent, an artistic sense. It's what I expect from a music critic and an audience as well. It is a sense for the artistic, it's beyond the text and the Urtext and the correct notes and the style and the performing attitude. There must be something *inventive* about the performance, and this is inborn. That man would always live artistically; his concept of life would have something original in it. That's the first thing I expect of an artist—and that's what I hear when I go to hear Horowitz or Michelangeli or Gould. I am only afterwards interested to know what they're performing, because I've reached the stage of admiration that I think even if they played their own mother's concerto I would still go, because there would be something so artistic about the attitude that the music is secondary." He pauses. "I want to be bowled over. I want to forget *my* ideas about the music."

He admits to being a tense performer: "I'm exhilarated by the stage, however, and the larger the hall the better I feel. The main reason I became a public musician is because I like to communicate with people. It's a need. And there are two ways of performing—either because you have a theatrical love for it or because it is the only means for you to communicate and share something with others. I do it in an aggressive, active way. I expect to possess an audience, and I expect an audience to come to me. Others go out to the audience, such as Rubinstein, who has an extraordinary generosity of sound, and as a man. Others such as Horowitz and Michelangeli enter their own skin and play from within. It goes out, God knows, but the audience has to make the effort and go towards them—because they draw the audience. To me that is the more exciting way of performing, but you don't choose it. You are made one way or the other. With those that draw, it takes more effort on the part of the audience to understand them. My major interest is to want to share—so then I had to make this career. And if you have to make it, then it's necessary to go out and make it as best you can—with everything that goes with it and enhances it: publicity and public relations, everything. I'm not a believer in success, because I have seen that success has been attributed to people I don't trust artistically. I've also been successful many times when I have not been in good shape—as opposed to times when I felt that I'd given an important performance and nobody noticed it. I've seen too many nonimportant artists hailed and loved and cheered; and others who have played a gigantic slow movement and have not had the success they deserved. But I think being accepted as successful is essential so that one should finally come to the top—and this does not mean being considered one of the greatest pianists in the world— so that you can at last play with the great orchestras, perform with the great conductors and make music in the best 'cream' sense of the word. To be famous and important means absolutely nothing except that it allows you to have the sufficient energy to stand the life that goes with performing. The joy of performing and playing and sharing with other people is so overpowering that hotels and traveling and airports and *mostly* being alone can be tolerated."

So, what Alexis Weissenberg dreamed about in the Fifties has come true in the Seventies. He has his career on his terms. He plays with whom he wants, he records prodigiously, he is among the upper strata of pianists. Yet there is that restlessness, that nervousness that persists. No, there has been no single performance that has fully satisfied or thrilled him. "If that were true, then I would stop playing. I think then you should never want to play again. I believe that if an artist feels he has reached the top, he should throw himself out of the window. Basically, this is the marvelous thing: that you become 40 and you know the personality you have and you have a cosmic knowledge of yourself and you know your limitations completely—from that moment on you continue developing. You keep searching for the absolute truth in what you want to say, towards yourself. And the work you know already at the age of 40 will be much greater in scope than the possibility of your life. You will die long before you've not only said the last word but even found the last solution. That's why music is such an exciting element, because there is no end in finding out how much you can say."

★ *Ljuba Welitsch* ★

In the winter of 1972 the legendary Ljuba Welitsch returned to New York after nearly two decades' absence for the brief speaking role of the Duchess of Krakentorp in Donizetti's Fille du Régiment *at the Metropolitan Opera. My fascination to meet this colorful, once-great Salome led to this visit and a piece written purely on speculation. It has never been published—until now.*

If the Esplanade Hotel didn't already exist on New York's West End Avenue, Tennessee Williams would have had to

invent it. Like much of the area, it has seen better days—and
the general seediness is populated by an indefinable cross
section of New York. Last spring, a flame-haired dynamo
defied the fact that the surroundings weren't quite what they
used to be when she was the toast of New York in the early
Fifties. The filmy curtains of her room were fluttering before
an open window to usher in the spring air, while the Castro
Convertible-style furniture was crowned with heady bouquets
of roses and lush azaleas. "Hallo!" comes the greeting at the
door. "What would you like to drink? Cognac or champagne?"
Ljuba Welitsch, the former great Salome and Donna Anna and
Tosca, rushes back with a chilled fifth of Moët and three juice
glasses. "They're not champagne glasses . . . but I am not
in my own home," she apologizes. The third glass is for a
mustachioed Bulgarian gentleman in his late 60's who once
sang operetta and studied with his companion long ago in
Sofia—and more than occasionally interrupts with the fact
that Mme Welitsch is the pride of Bulgaria.

In her all-too-brief singing career, Ljuba Welitsch was more
than that: she was the pride of Vienna, London, New York.
Today, sitting attentively in a gleaming turquoise and gold
lamé suit, jewelled belt and gold shoes, fingers covered in
antique diamond rings, she is busier than ever—as a stage and
screen actress throughout Germany and Austria. "Horuk!"
comes the still vibrant voice of the singer, urging her guests to
drink up so she can refill the glasses. "Do you smoke?" she
asks. Laughing heartily at the negative reply, she jibes half
jokingly, half suggestively, "Oh, you are good?" No, she never
smoked while she sang, but "now with TV and movies I do
because of all that waiting in dressing rooms and between
takes." Since the mid-Fifties she's been making films in Hamburg, Berlin and Munich, and she starred in *The Killing of
Sister George* in Berlin, directed by Hildegard Knef's husband.
"I did it for four months every night! Do you know what that
means, my dear?" She's also been doing character roles in
such operettas as *Czardasfürstin, Bettelstudent, Zigeunerliebe*
and *Opernball,* and at the mention of the latter she launches
full voice into "Gehen wir in's chambre séparée" with that
extraordinary high voice still full of that fruity, bright, womanly
sound. "And now I have to be back in Vienna for *Opernball*

at the Volksoper and a new production of *Fille du Régiment*
there with Reri Grist and Irmgard Seefried." The reason Ljuba
Welitsch was back in New York was her return to the Met to
do the spoken role of the Duchess of Krakentorp in the new
staging of *Fille du Régiment* with Joan Sutherland, Regina
Resnik and Luciano Pavarotti. "It's an important role, yes?"
she asks in a way that demands but one answer. "You must
be a personality!" she answers herself. "There are no bad
roles, only bad singers. Mr. Bing asked me to do it. It was his
idea, and he wrote, 'I started my career in New York with you
in *Fledermaus* and so on, and so I wish to make my farewell
with you too.' So I came."

She hadn't been back to New York since the last time she
sang and eagerly confesses, "I haven't had a holiday in 16
years! When people are swimming, I am on stage or behind a
camera. I am working winter and summer." Pause. "S-U-M-
M-E-R-T-I-M-E" and the voice unfurls in Gershwin's song,
before exclaiming over her current career: "I'll earn money
until I'm 80—and you can't sing until then. My dear God
is good to me. The voice was not going as I wished it and I
went to the Director of the Vienna State Opera to tell him I
couldn't take responsibility for my work, because the middle
voice was not right—and I needed that for my singing. I asked
to be pensioned and retired, and he said that was an historic
moment because singers only come to ask for more money
and more roles. At the time I had the chance to go to the
movies to do Shaw's *Arms and the Man,* and it was a break for
me. It was a success, and now I've made over seventy movies
and thirty-five TV plays as an actress. There are many titles
you don't know here. But I am very happy and it makes me
younger. I am healthy and I can work. I make a good living
and live well—not rich, not poor, not Onassis. But the most
important thing is to be healthy . . . and then to work . . .
to have the *chance* to work. If you have enough money and
stay in bed and eat and drink, that's not enough. It's important
to share with the public. It's a gift to share, and for me a great
satisfaction . . . even though the artist life is not easy." She
has never been unhappy since the end of her singing career.
"It's a wonderful thing that God gives a gift for one to enjoy
for a time and then takes it away to give to another. That's

why I enjoy going to hear others now." Did she find it hard to perform in front of the camera after all those bigger-than-life portrayals on stage? "Yes, I come from the big stage, but I made my movements small, and I know where the camera is. It's not hard . . . and I'm supposed to be an intelligent girl, eh!" Pause. "Horuk," and the champagne flows on.

In her years at Vienna, the Met, Covent Garden and other houses, Ljuba Welitsch had one of the most extraordinary careers of this century, based on the philosophy that "you must give everything—and then people don't forget. I gave feeling and heart and singing. I didn't save the voice—I *never* did!" Asked if she could describe her own voice to someone who never heard it, she shrugs, "Is possible? It's not only voice, but the whole personality. Even the records are only one-tenth of what happened on stage." In Vienna once, though, one leading critic wrote she was a woman with a voice which changed for each part—for Tatiana in *Eugene Onegin* it was light and virginal, for Salome it unleashed tremendous top tones and for Aida it concentrated on richness and beauty. Each role brought forth a vocal character to suit it.

No one could contest that it was the sexually frank, red-haired, white-skinned, fleshy and vocally dazzling Salome that put her in the operatic history books—although today she won't say it was her favorite: "It was always the one I was doing that evening, even yesterday in *Fille*. In *Salome* you have to have everything—presence, the voice of a woman and the clear, soft voice of a girl. It takes years to get the ripeness and just to learn the score, because you must do it by *heart,* not by the conductor or whatever. You must jump and sing and act *and* be beautiful. I worked with Strauss in 1944 for his birthday—this was my first one, under his control. That was Vienna during the war. Then in 1946, Vienna again." Strauss had heard her Composer in *Ariadne auf Naxos* in Munich and asked her to sing Salome for his 80th birthday, telling her it was a Mozart role—and ultimately, "I never knew my score would be sung so well." She also did Chrysothemis with Sir Thomas Beecham in London, and Strauss was there to coach the cast that included Schlüter as Elektra and Schoeffler as Oreste.

One historic production of *Salome* was the one designed by

Salvador Dali at Covent Garden after the war. "It was a little crazy, but the singing and conducting were beautiful—and that's enough!" Before that she had created a sensation in the role and as Donna Anna in 1947 with the visiting Vienna State Opera. To demonstrate her great range to London, she also sang Aida, Musetta and Mimi in *Bohème* and Lisa in *Pique Dame,* as well as a Verdi *Requiem* with Barbirolli, the Beethoven Ninth with Furtwängler—and Amelia in *Ballo in Maschera* and Donna Anna in *Don Giovanni* at Edinburgh and Glyndebourne (where she first met Rudolf Bing, who was director there in the late Forties). She came to the Met in February of 1949 as an unknown to sing ten Salomes with Fritz Reiner, whom she recalls being "a little fast in spots—but there was a give and take with us." During a dress rehearsal in the Bing régime, John Gutman recalls that the soprano's costume did not fit too well and the management didn't know what to do. They went to Reiner and he, with typical sardonic wit, said to tell her, "Vesti la giubba."

As to singing both roles in *La Bohème,* she nods, "I sang Mimi very beautifully, but people thought my Musetta very beautiful. And conductors make the mistake of casting a light voice for that role. It must be dramatic—both Krauss and Karajan told me this." There was also Janácek's *Jenufa* (1948) in Vienna and Tosca—and Karajan wanted her to sing the Marschallin. "But I did not believe in it because of the Viennese dialect." Later in her career she also added a little Wagner: Helmwige in *Die Walküre* with Karajan, the First Rhinemaiden in *Rheingold* and the Forest Bird in *Siegfried* which, she insists, "must be sung in a strong, clear voice with flexibility." Bing wanted her to do Senta in *The Flying Dutchman*—"I learned it for eight months and I am severe with myself. I couldn't find the right way for my voice to do it, so I decided not to. But the one role I wanted to do and never did was Isolde. I love it, but mine was not the voice for it. It was a dream role. It's for the other world . . . or when I come back again in a hundred years to sing," which she promptly does by launching into the opening of the "Liebesnacht."

"I have been on the stage now for 37 years," she declares proudly, after the glasses have been filled to the top once again.

"And I'm the only singer who admits her age—59. I was born in 1913. I'm not ashamed, because they have been so beautiful." She was born in Barisovo, Bulgaria (near Varna on the Black Sea), as Velichkova and went to Sofia with no money to attend the Conservatory. "I went to the Opera House at the beginning of the season and asked the manager for a job. 'Can you sing?' he asked. I sang, he engaged me and I spent one year doing small roles. Then I found my voice and *theaterblut*—the theater blood that I have." She went to Vienna and the State Akademie to study music and style, working with Prof. Lierhamer (the teacher of Maria Reining and Erich Kunz). Her first engagements came in Graz (1933), where she mastered Mozart by singing Cherubino, Barbarina, Susanna *and* the Countess in *The Marriage of Figaro,* as well as Fiordiligi and a variety of Puccini, Verdi and Strauss. Then it was Hamburg for two years, Dresden, Munich (where she first met Clemens Krauss) and finally Vienna, which became her home. "Austria is where I learned my style, where I learned to be a musician. The air is singing there. My home and successes are there. In Vienna people listen and know about style—in America they listen with their heart." She is a Kammersängerin and Member of Honor of the Vienna State Opera, and is proud that only a dozen singers have the latter award, including Jeritza, Lehmann, Schumann, Slezak and Schoeffler. Every time she has gone to hear Salome in Vienna, she sits in a box and the audience turns towards her, applauding in tribute. And they say that when Inge Borkh first sang the role there, after Welitsch, she put a cast of her predecessor's head on the silver tray for the final scene.

Ljuba Welitsch keeps an active interest in opera and singers, going to the Staatsoper for all premieres and debuts. Here in New York she was spotted at the revival of *Salome* with Leonie Rysanek, a Corelli-Crespin *Werther* and the Albanese-Di Stefano concert at Carnegie Hall. Asked whom she admires, she names Sutherland and Price, but adds, "I don't know. There are emotional things. . . . You need to change the sound for different characters. Chaliapin understood that." She likes Nilsson as Isolde and Turandot, but hedges about her Salome. She admires Rysanek's line and beautiful vocalism, especially as the Empress in *Die Frau ohne Schatten,* and was looking forward to seeing how she would fare as Salome. "I love Seefried and Schwarzkopf. They were my dreams. We were on stage together a long time and sang Mozart like you will never hear in the world again. After the war," and she brings her fingers together to blow a kiss, as a great chef would over his quenelles, "it was the Golden Age of the Vienna Staatsoper with Schwarzkopf, Schoeffler and so on. It was a great style—and you won't find it anymore." She shakes her finger. "Schwarzkopf was fantastic—and what is Dorothy Kirsten doing? She always reminded me of her. And what about Risë Stevens?" She is pleased to learn that the former is in her 26th year at the Met and that the latter is rich and retired. Noting she is not a jealous colleague, she declares, "I am *artiste,* not a businessman," and talks of Schoeffler, Lorenz, Hotter, Höngen, among others. What did these singers have that many don't have today? "Learning and studying and learning again. Now the young go on the stage with no style, no breath, no control. They have two or three years in the theater and then what? Finish! I believe in the German saying, 'The exercise makes the master.' "

Today, between films and theater and operetta, she lives in Vienna near the Opera and has a house in Klosterneuberg. Now divorced, she was married to a policeman for fourteen years. "For three or four years I was happy. But I sacrificed my private life for my art. I travel here and there, and he found another girl—not so beautiful as me, but. . . . It didn't work out and I am lonely in my private life. Yes, I have many admirers, but I don't love anyone. And this is heartbreaking. It's just my poodles and birds. I am a nature and animal lover, and I have 1,000 roses in my garden." As the champagne is again refreshed, she produces a photo of her two poodles, Bobby and Scheherazade. "Why did I give her that name? Because when they lie together in bed, Bobby lies like this and Scheherazade tells him fairy tales with her mouth to his ear."

Ljuba Welitsch was obviously delighted to be back. "It's a fantastic country, so warmhearted. They don't forget. And what happened to Walter Winchell?" she asks at the door. "You know, he once wrote that 'She is sexy and sings like a . . . *lerche* . . . lark.' I'll never forget that." And with a mad flurry of blown kisses and good-byes, the door is closed, latches are bolted into place, cries of "Horuk!" go up, and the clink of juice glasses resounds down the hall.